CONSTANTINE ISSIGHOS

PRISONERS
OF
OUR IDEALS

NORTHWATER

Books by Constantine Issighos

My Six-Sided Log Home

The Magic World of In-Laid Pictorial Tapestry

Constantine Issighos: a Fibre Artist

For God, Country and Drug Prohibition

Prisoners of Our Ideals

Copyright 2010 @ Constantine Issighos. Printed and bound in Canada. No part of this book may be reproduced or transmitted in any form or by any means, electronic or mechanical, including photocopying, recording, and/or by any information storage and retrieval system except by a reviewer who may quote brief passages in a review to be printed in a magazine, newspaper, or on the Web without written permission in writing from the publisher. For information, please contact: Awaqkuna Books Inc.

Northwater is an imprint of Awaqkuna Books Inc.

www.awaqkunabooks.com

PRISONERS OF OUR IDEALS

Library and Archives Canada

ISBN 978-0-978-2018-8-3

Library and Archives Canada Cataloguing in Publication

This book was designed by the author.

ATTENTION UNIVERSITIES, COLLEGES, LIBRARIES, HUMANISTS AND ATHEIST ASSOCIATIONS: Quantity discounts are available on bulk purchases of this book for educational or membership purposes. Book excerpts can also be created to fit special needs.

IN MEMORIAM

ROBERT GEORGE ISSIGHOS
(1968–1999)

"A human being is part of a whole, called by us the Universe, a part limited in time and space. He experiences himself, his thoughts and feelings, as something separated from the rest of a kind of optical delusion of his consciousness. This delusion is a kind of **prison** for us, restricting us to our personal desires and affection…Our task must be to free ourselves from this prison by widening our circles…to embrace all living creatures and the whole of nature in its beauty."

Albert Einstein

CONTENTS

BOOK I: CONSEQUENCES OF DESTRUCTIVE IDEALS

MEANING OF WORDS 3

INTRODUCTION 7

1 IDEALIST SYSTEM OF THOUGHT 13

2 NAÏVE AND DESTRUCTIVE IDEALISM 39

3 CONSEQUENCES OF DESTRUCTIVE IDEALISM 63
    Destructive-Idealism & the Human Social Environment 71
    Religious Bigotry and Female Sexuality 77
    The Prophet's Own Words 88
    Religious Laws: Sharia 94

4 IDEALISM IS A MENTAL ILLNESS 99
    Idealist Mental Illness in Children's Education 113

5 FOR THE LOVE OF SUFFERING 127

6 RELIGION AND SLAVERY 147
    Slavery in Islam 152
    Contemporary Islamic Paedophilia, Slavery, Bestiality 166

7 THE ART OF RELIGIOUS TRICKERY 173
    Heron's Mechanical Devices 192
    The Shroud of Turin 193
    Weeping Virgin Mary's Statue 194

8   Idealism in Advertising   195

Book II: Quest for Cognitive Knowledge

9   Language Use in Idealism and materialism   217

10   The Literal Brain and its Metaphorical "Mind"   241

11   Metaphoric Nature of Cultural Memes   261

12   Mimesis: as Source of Knowledge   283

Book III: Elegance of Reality

13   Objective Reality of the Material World   307

14   Scientific Materialism   331

15   Humanist Art of Loving   373

     Men and Women as Complementary Natural Opposites   393

16   A Dialectically Secular Society   399

Reference

17   You Are Not Alone   419

18   Bibliography   427

19   Index   431

BOOK I

CONSEQUENCES OF DESTRUCTIVE IDEALS

MEANING OF WORDS

Belief: a mental process that is accepted as true or as certain to happen, without proof. Beliefs have the gravitational primacy of ideals-in-the-mind over reality. The word "belief" is a non-investigative term that forms a bridge-link between reality and the ideal, in order to give legitimacy to the latter.

Brain: a part of the certain nervous system that contains and controls the mental processes and the physical actions of a human being.

Bridge-link: it is a mental method of connecting the real (matter) with the delusional (ideal) to legitimize the latter: Jesus (physical body) resurrects (delusion) presented as a fact or I pray (physical act) for a miracle (delusional-belief) or *mind over matter*.

Delusional beliefs: religious or secular thoughts which cause us to believe that beliefs can change the laws of nature, reality or social conditions, including terms such as, a miracle, super-human, super-natural, divine-mind, virgin-birth, the Nazi's "Jewish-problem" etc. Delusional beliefs, when used as a "bridge-link" of the real world with a delusion, which causes distortion in the interpretation of reality with tragically outcome i.e., *mind over matter*.

Dialectics: stands for the Greek word for dispute and debate. It is a science of the general laws governing the development of nature, science, society and the unity of the balance of natural opposites i.e., matter over spirit. It considers all natural phenomena and social relationships to be in movement and to a perpetually changing.

Dialectical materialism: dialectics of materialist essence are meaningfully related to the material world (nature) and to social conditions as these are related and bound by reality. It recognizes that matter (physical world) is in continuous motion, and that the laws of nature exist independent of ideals, and that matter existed long before humans appeared on earth i.e., *matter over human thoughts.*

Dialectical material conditions: the social conditions that are immersed in reciprocal relationships, always developing and changing (matter in motion) whether we know of them by cognitive knowledge or by trial and error. Also, consisting of physical objects and reality-induced ideas which are related to material-reality, its movements and changes i.e., *matter over mind.*

Deceptive Advertising: Idealism is used to distort the reality and usefulness of a product or a service, by "selling" the idea of the product and its imagined qualities or benefits.

Gravitational primacy of ideas: is the foundation of religious or secular idealism which places thoughts, beliefs, mysticism, and esoteric-mental processes as being primary. Thus, social reality and the natural world, its events etc., is regarded as being secondary. Mind over Matter, as such, is primary over objective reality.

Idealism: it separates ideas from the material world and conditions. Ideas exist independently of the natural world. Ideal or mental processes are primary and objective reality is secondary: "mind over matter" or "If you don't think about it, it does not exist", or "I think, therefore I am." As a system of thought, idealism views things as isolated and unchanging, and is primary in religious thoughts and secular spiritual ideals. Religious beliefs are fundamentally regarded as idealist-thoughts. (See also Secular Idealism).

Imitating: imitating behaviour or when a given culture imitates ideas, beliefs and acts of another, such as Islam imitating ideals from Judaism and Christianity in worshipping Moses, Abraham and the Prophets. Cultural imitation exists when a culture imitates social/cultural acts in arts, architecture, sports, music etc.

Memes: cultural information, an idea, a popular belief, value, pattern of behaviour, catchphrase, concept, speech, gesture that is spread from one person to the next, from one family to another, by non-genetic means–as by imitation or mimesis. Memes are hosted by a willing recipient or a group of recipients. Memes are counterparts of genes.

Mind: refers to the thought process of the intellect, memory, imagination, reasoning to love or hate, fear and joy, and a myriad of mental functions that are carried on "inside our heads." The term "Mind" is metaphorical because its functions are the functions of the literal "brain." The term "mind" simply identifies the sum total functions of the brain. The mind and its multi-functions do not exist independently of the brain, for those functions are of the brain itself.

Mimesis: (Greek for imitation) is the transmission of cultural habits, ideas, beliefs, social customs and activities, musical tones. Mimesis is passed on to a host-mind from person to person, from one group to another, from one generation to the next and from one society to another. Mimesis carries singular or multiple ranges of meaning i.e., imitation, representation, mimicry, similarity, resembling, and reproduction. (see also Memes)

Mimicry: occurs when a group of biological or cultural organisms mimics and evolves a common characteristic of another group i.e., mimics a lifestyle in dressing, sharing communal property etc.

Reality: the natural world or the state of things as they actually exist, as opposed to an idealist or irrational idea of them. Matter in the physical world or material activities—as the object of perception has real existence and is neither reducible to universal mind or spirit nor dependent upon man's perception.

Religion: originates in an attempt to represent an order of beliefs, feelings, and imaginings in something spiritual which is based on awe, sense of mystery, sense of guilt, fear, rituals, adoration and communication with an invisible entity through prayer.

Representation: Linguistically naming and identifying objects, reality and indications in order to make sense, like, resemble, represent, to stand for or to take the place of.

Reproduction: as in reproducing a work of art in painting—using identical technique, colour and material.

Root-source: of idealism is its distortion of reality as a means and an end unto itself. The **End-gain** is the perpetuation of the institutional benefits of religion, and its organizational structure and its members.

Resemblance: as "you have a resemblance of your father."

Secular Humanism: emphasizes a person's capacity for self-actualization through dialectical reasoning, ethics and justice, and rejects religion and the existence of the supernatural and mysticism.

Secular Idealism: is closely related to religious idealism in that it is also separates ideas from their direct relationship to material reality. It substitutes the God-spirit for another form of spirituality that also distorts reality.

Similarity: is some degree of resemblance between two or more objects or finding partial similarities between two or more objects that are relatively distinct from one another.

Spirituality: maintains that the ultimate nature of matter is not material, but it is based on the mind (virtual reality), ideas, and the altogether spiritual character of reality i.e., reality is what you believe it to be—be it mental or spiritual.

INTRODUCTION

"A confusion of what is **real** and what is **ideal** never goes unpunished."

Johan Wolfgang von Goethe (1749-1832)

"When a man forgets his ideals he may hope for happiness, but not until then."

Pearl Mary Teresa Craigie (1867-1906)

My core purpose for writing this book is to offer a clear defence of the real world of biological materialism against several reproaches made by the "world" of idealism. From the ancient Greek philosophers of whom European philosophers are but a continuation, contemporary social thinkers have had to contest with the question: How does the reality known as materialism and the delusion known as religious idealism affect our decision making process in daily life?

For most of human civilization, philosophers have debated issues regarding life, the cosmos, morality, realism, idealism, materialism, religion and systems of thinking. Most of their writings have been responses to others' points of view. All but a few, even today, have forgotten to direct their attention outside their own "world" of academia. Informing the public has become the task of the interpreters and re-interpreters of these philosophical works.

Radical philosophers, such as Karl Marx, Frederic Engels, Lenin, Mao and others, were unable to reach more than their core followers. This was because their aim was to transform their societies during their lifetimes. Much later, their works became historically more popular as the distribution of their books became wider spread. Their philosophical concept of dialectical materialism served as a political tool against various political opponents, whether other materialists or idealists.

This is understandable because the historical conditions in which these radical philosophers lived were in turmoil. Poverty, sickness and human misery were paramount. Social solutions needed to be found in the 18th and 19th centuries to ease human suffering. At this time of political and apolitical unrest, "re-inventions" of old philosophical concepts were proposed in an effort to better human conditions. The materialist propagators wanted to solve social problems by looking outside the human character. They were politicizing the redistribution of wealth into an egalitarian mode.

Equally, the religious and secular idealist propagators were concentrating their attentions on solving the "short-comings" of human nature or on promoting personal beliefs of religious devotion as solutions to social problems. In my book *For God, Country and Drug Prohibition*, I include the Temperance Movement of the 19th century and current anti-drug prohibitions, as examples.

Others, for example the Christian-Socialists of the 18th and 19th centuries, were dualists that emphasized external social solutions in relation to personal, religious and moral convictions. In psychological terms, the materialists were the extroverts, the idealists were the introverts and the dualists tried to find a common bridge between the two opposite schools of thought.

The dominance of idealism in the Western world, in the forms of religion, mysticism, superstition and man's genuine wonderings about the workings of the natural world, began in early human civilization. Everyone who was anyone had his or her own favoured theory of where or when mysticism and the superstition of religion originated. Lack of genuine scientific knowledge of the biological world led to various explanations to answer the question of why we existed. This fundamental question was finally answered by the Darwinian theory of natural selection. The idealists' "answer" would be that we were "created" by God.

This is the fundamental division between the biological materialist's world of natural selection and the idealist's belief in the creation of the world. The dialectics of nature gained prominence against the impulse of religion by demonstrating that human beings were an integral part of the biological and botanical life on earth. It scientifically showed that living matter was in constant motion throughout the world, and that every bit of variation, even the slightest, went through a change, preserving or adding all that was necessary for the survival of the living matter. This constant motion of matter, wherever and whenever, had one sole goal: the improvement of every living organism against rival organisms that did not survive in order to reproduce. In short, nature was not a poetic or metaphorical concept!

Across the entire world, human culture has integrated within it some sort of deep and destructive idealism in the form of witchcraft, tormented fear of magic, clutter of personal beliefs, hostile rituals, wasteful time-consuming "spiritual" practices such as kneeling, fasting and praying, monotonous and repetitive nods towards a wall, crusades against "others" and so on. These repulsive practices tended to consume valuable and irreplaceable time, endanger human life and in extreme cases, terminate it. Religious and secular idealists live in a constant stress-related environment, with a destructive obsession of self-doubt and with a tormented fear of the future.

At times, the opposite is true! An idealist may be happy or content with his or her religious or secular beliefs. This fact, however, does not speak to the beneficial effects or true humanist value of religion. The notable Bernard Shaw said, "The fact that a believer is happier than a skeptic is no more to the point than the fact that a drunken man is happier than a sober one." Religious idealism is similar to homoeopathy, in the sense that both provide ideals to reduce personal anxiety, but their remedies are ineffective.

My aim in writing this book is to inform the educated layman on the effects that both scientific materialism and religious/secular idealism have on our daily lives. Both subjects are vastly too broad to be analyzed in this book. I, therefore, have taken the liberty to briefly analyze some of the most important areas we all encounter in our daily lives. My basic aim is to rationally show that idealism whether religious or secular, is about the deliberate distortion of external reality. My sincere hope is to help the reader escape from religion and destructive idealism.

In dealing with the concept of idealism, the reader should always keep in mind that its premise is mind over matter. It is a premise that regards ideas, feelings, emotions, abstractions and beliefs as a primary directional force, and external conditions and reality as secondary. For idealism, apart from our immediate perception and awareness of the world, there is no such thing as an outside objective world. The world takes places entirely within the cranial confines of the mind. Outside of that, nothing exists! These arguments are no longer mere philosophical concepts, for they are affecting our daily decision-making processes, our economic activities, our social practices, love relationships, education, religion and sentiments. I will try to briefly show various examples where the delusion of mind over matter becomes destructive in a very real and personal way.

Scientific materialism covers the relationship between Matter over Mind and the basic proposition from biological science that living matter existed before mankind, that the mind did not appear until the organic matter of the brain was organized with the complexity for it to think. Without the brain's highly intricate form, the mind does not exist. In terms of the natural world, biological and botanical matter existed before the appearance of a thinking human being on the earth's surface. In short, the human mind is a metaphorical by-product of the brain's special matter.

The term "brain" is literal; the term "mind" is metaphorical. This is the dialectical materialist's proposition that puts in primary place organic or non-organic matter, material conditions, external reality, scientific evidence, experimentation, space and social and cultural circumstances. All promote the modes of existence of matter in motion. Thus, matter is a primary directional force and mind is secondary.

These aforementioned premises are divided into two major schools of thought, centered on what is considered to be humanity's directional force. These opposing forces contradict each other hourly, daily, in social, personal, and cultural relations, and in every minor or major decision we undertake, whether we are aware of it or not. It includes areas of the environment, mental health, home economics, illusions, delusions, spiritualism and religion, morality, language, cultural memes and the humanist outlook of our future. All of the above, and more, are to offer the reader, in plain language, an intellectually rational tool to deal with and recognise the elegance of external reality.

For the sake of clarity, I have divided this book into three sections: the first deals with various aspects of idealism (religious and secular), the second deals with analyzing and identifying various social and cultural factors, materialist energy, external reality and the pedagogy of dialectical thinking as *matter over mind*, and the third section deals with the scientific materialist approach to human relationships, including love, morality and ethics.

Idealism has worldwide influence, but its power lies most notably in the United States where the religious right has an unprecedented political and cultural influence. However, we are also in an age of unprecedented humanist and atheist growth.

Admittedly, there are people who are humanist because their religion has let them down, and others call themselves atheist because they are superficially religious. There is the cautious approach expressed by people who are agnostics. There is also a notable gap in which people are looking for a replacement for the idea of God with another idealized form of "spiritualism." I sincerely hope that agnostics may wish to replace the idea-God, not with another delusion, but with the rational thought of Geo-Philae, the Love of Earth. The latter is not a mere idea-in-the-mind, which can be replaced at will, but refers to the infinite of reality and complexity of our human and natural world.

1

IDEALIST SYSTEM OF THOUGHT

"Idealism increases in direct proportion to one's distance from the problem."

John Galsworthy

"Don't use the foreign word "ideal". We have that excellent native word "lies."

Henrik Ibsen

Idealism can be defined as the distortion of reality by means of thinking or advocating the "ideal" as being reality. This is such that the terms "materialism" and "idealism" bear no moral connotation. In this sense, the term "materialism" refers to the actual reality of the external world. "Idealism" refers to the idea of the mind's perception of reality. With these simple statements we can analyze issues of idealism.

Most of us go about our daily lives thinking, acting, and making decisions on issues of family and social affairs in relation to the rest of the world. Most people are not even aware of the system of thought they are acting upon. They might live under the illusion that their own ideas, feelings and inclinations are of their own original creation. Because they are individuals, they believe that their opinions, perceptions, and beliefs are products of their own thought. Furthermore, they might believe that it is mere coincidence that their own individual ideas are similar to those of the majority of society. This fundamental consensus is held by most people as a proof for the correctness of their individual ideas. This also satisfies the notion that there still are minor differences among the general beliefs of others. Any need for differentiation or individualism is expressed through style rather than in essence.

Knowledge about human social relations with the natural world is not at all a monolithic field. There are numerous systems of thought and dialogue, each with its own characteristics and idiosyncrasies. Such systems (or schools) of thought can inform people on how to answer questions about life, how and what to learn, and how to conduct their social relationships. Idealism refers to a system of thought that propagates the primacy of ideas. The real world and its reality are somehow dependent upon the individual's mind rather than independent of it. Thus, idealism places a gravitational primacy on mental processes (i.e., ideas) over the external relations of material reality. Mental processes would include religious ideas or beliefs of another world that "exists" in the mind of the believer (i.e., within the functions of the brain. Some examples include: heaven, hell, miracles, ghosts, spirits, etc.). To lend some validity to the mental images (or ideas), idealism acquired the "existence" of a virtual reality. This is a mental process that includes an idea, a feeling, and a real or delusional sensory perception that a person believes exists. Reality, therefore, becomes synonymous with one's own perception of it. This is exemplified in the thought process that includes: "my reality," "your reality," "our reality," "God's reality," and finally "my-reality-is-different-than-your-reality," or vice versa. This is an idealist system of thought that is not exclusively directed to religious, cultist, or spiritual followers. A delusional sense of guilt, prejudice or bias, righteousness, and dogmatism are idealist products of irrational fears that believers tend to hide.

Idealism is the formation of a belief system of thought that pleases one's imaginary impulses instead of appealing to cognitive knowledge. The relationship between belief and cognitive knowledge is very subtle or superficial. Idealists might argue that what they believe is true regardless of whether those beliefs lack evidence or they are being delusional. In the western world, those religious beliefs held by idealists are regarded by some psychologists as being "genuine beliefs" and therefore, their thoughts can be validated.

As a belief system, idealism would include alternate beliefs or motifs that could be termed "spiritual," "super-cosmic energy," "the force," "burning bush," "out-of-body-experience," or "crossover spirits," by believers who do not follow the prescribed dogmas of organized religion. Still, such believers prefer a sort of fixation of ideas in their own minds over the state of the natural world. The consequences for fixed ideas are inevitable. In the case of some uncertainty, an idealist might make a decision that is either "for or against" certain choices. This essentially amounts to a polarized view of the world.

An idealist bolsters a personal belief in which he is emotionally involved while always attempting to resolve objective social problems without experiencing contradictions. Religious idealists often believe merely what their religion entices them to believe as being true. They fortify their beliefs without regard to whether those beliefs diametrically oppose circumstances in their external lives. Religious and secular delusion cannot be verified and scientifically reconciled to the external world. In fact, objective reality is either non-existent or is miniaturized because a person's beliefs are "facts" and the object of those beliefs is to act upon them.

An idealist imitative spread is contentious to others who also think that a belief is equal to cognitive knowledge. Secular idealists, who have "studied" the workings of the human mind, use the term "belief" to refer to a system of thought. Roughly, whatever a person believes is to be regarded as true. To believe something, in this sense, a person need not actively rationalize it (at least for the vast number of daily things he or she comes across). For example, I can state that "I believe this is the twenty-first century," or, "my car is red," or "my office is located on the second floor." If this is the twenty-first century, does this fact depend on being true or false simply because I believe it is? Or, is it true regardless of whether I believe it to be or not? If my car is red or my office is located on the second floor, does my belief of these facts determine their veracity? Does my belief (or my consciousness) determine my physical surroundings, or is it the other way around?

The formations of beliefs are thus irrelevant to reality. The concept of belief does not play any crucial role in the above facts. A potential state of belief is simply an idealistic attitude about a potential state of affairs and not an actual external state of affairs. A potential state of affairs—as a mental proposition—does not justify or qualify as cognitive knowledge. This is because a set of beliefs may be based on doubts, hopes, fears, desires, intentions or wishful thinking examples of idealism, not realism.

Idealism has demonstrated a preference for the term "belief" which conveys instant certainty over an unverifiable process. This is true even if this certainty of "beliefs" is unverifiable. Both religious and secular idealists provide a basis to draw automatic conclusions that forces them to make either "for or against" polarized choices. Secular and religious idealists often "believe" merely what they wish to be the truth, and fortify this "ideal belief" in their mind. They place the primacy of the ideal over the reality of verifiable evidence. One of the most influential idealists was George Berkeley (1685-1753) who, in my opinion, is the founder of western idealism. In his *Treatise Concerning the Principals of Human Knowledge*, Part 1, paragraph 6, he wrote:

*"Some truths there are so near and obvious to the mind that a man needs only to open his eyes to see them. Such I take this important one to be, to wit, that all the choir of heaven and [objects]... of the earth, in a word all those bodies which compose the mighty frame of the world, **have not any subsistence without a mind**, that their being is to be perceived or known, that consequently so long as they are not actually perceived by me, or do not exist in the mind or that of any other created spirit, they must either have **no** existence at all, or else, subsist in the mind of some eternal spirit [God]."*

Idealism as a system of thought maintains that the existence of the external world is dependent upon whether we have it fixed in our mind. This gravitational primacy of ideas in the mind over external material circumstances is adopted by both religious and secular idealists. The religiosity is evident in the claim that God implants ideas in our mind in an orderly manner. Or, that in God's mind, all things exist always. I sometimes wonder how Bishop Berkeley had access to God's mind to accurately know its inner workings. By placing doubt in the existence of the world without the human mind, Berkeley's eternal spirit of God's mind sustained the necessary source of all worldly things.

However, Berkeley still faced the dilemma of how to think about the physical sciences. These sciences purported to establish proofs about the physical world which Berkeley declared to be non-existent "without the mind." This view pronounces that sciences are useful theories rather than factual accounts. In short, Berkeley placed "ideas-in-the-mind" as primary, and the existence of the natural world as secondary.

The term "belief" is a core component of religious-idealism which was mimetically transmitted to and was hosted by secular idealists without its religiosity. In religious circles we have the terms "I believe God created the world in six days," "I believe in God's Bible," "I believe that God created all men equally," "I believe Jesus died for me." In secular idealism, we have terms such as "I believe men and women were created equally," "I believe things will get worse, before they get better," "I believe in me," "I believe in you," "I believe in the American Dream," "My personal belief is...," "Do you believe that..." Such a term as "belief" is also used metaphorically to convey larger or more general ideas as in "I believe in God, the Son and the Holy Spirit," which implies that Christianity is a polytheistic religion (i.e. three Gods) which contrasts with the monotheistic Muslim religion of Allah.

What people believe to be true is that which has been integrated into their system of thought. They place the primacy of their idea-belief over verifying those beliefs what already exist. A belief of something with no verifiable physical evidence of truth is potentially flawed and irrelevant. For example, if I say that "I believe John's weight is 200 pounds" how is that really relevant to John's actual weight? How is John's weight relevant to my "belief"? How is this random "belief" related to a real condition or situation? How does the true weight relevant to whether I believe it to be the case or not? Even if my belief appeared to be formed based on a logical idea, an idea-belief often relies on a mental construct that blinds us to the external reality. What we believe may create today's perception of an existing reality. This may have been consistent with a prior belief, but it could change or be modified with no relation to the reality of John's physical weight.

Religious or secular idealists who have poorly developed cognitive analytical skills and whose beliefs are subjective and moralized have little energy for dealing with analytical verification of a real situation. This reinforces his or her illusory beliefs which would affect how he or she performs (i.e., thinks and acts) in everyday life. The negative effect of the term "belief" as used by a secular idealist is of concern if we are to develop a cultural society that is capable of identifying an objective reality based on an objective analytic thinking process.

Secular idealism is an idealist system of thought without the religiosity of God, heaven or hell. It has found a home in the western world, and although no one believes that the natural world does not exist, this system of thought has been embedded in every aspect of our daily lives. It is integrated into our educational system, in commerce, in our philosophy of life, in advertising, in our ideological consumerism, and in our daily thinking as the mimesis-delusion of "Mind over Matter" that still persists as a belief system.

The implications of such a belief system are felt in the manner in which we exploit our environment, where our wishful thinking is primary and the reality of material consequences is secondary. The roots of such a delusional wish are based on God's biblical command for humans to "be fruitful and multiply" which had an impact on (and continues to affect) millions of religious families with over breeding. Secular idealists take the same root but without using religiosity as a distractive directive against the environment. Instead, secular idealists are following their wish that "We can have it all" which places belief as a primary directional force. This is regardless of the negative effects that such beliefs promote on the environment.

Religious institutions like Hinduism, Christian Science and others promote subjective idealism which teaches that all that really exists is God and God's ideas. They perceive the world through the human senses (e.g., seeing, hearing, tasting) and the underlying spiritual ideas are underlined as those senses act or react. Any distortion of "spirituality" is corrected by a reorientation of feelings and thoughts. Such a system of reorientation teaches "miraculous healing" which is directed towards the mental perceptions of the followers and adjusts them more closely to the underlying idealism. This is a core tenet in subjective idealism, which denies the existence of the world independently of the human senses, and that there is no material reality. Subjective idealism also teaches that, since we humans can only "see," "feel," or "hear" the so-called "world" through our senses, there is no way that we can bypass those senses to prove that the world really exists. All is Spirit and His Creation.

Teaching their followers that since there is no material reality independent of the Spirit (and since the Spirit is powerful and divine), only God and His Creation (which is Spirit) exists. It has nothing to do with the world. Religious idealism regards the existence of the whole natural universe as an illusion and thus non-existent because we view it as a dream. The illusion of the existence of the natural world arises from the projection of the dreamer (i.e., the mind). The reader can recognize the idealist's gravitational primacy on ideas in the mind (spirit, beliefs, dreams, etc.) over objective reality, because this is the core foundation for their claim of the existence of God. It includes the claim that ideas have some crucial role in the making of the world the way it is—that thought and spirit and the physical world are inseparable from one another, or that they create one another. More accurately, religious and secular idealism are based on the root terms "beliefs," "perfect," or "ideal," whose meanings form a make believe system of thought.

Idealism is a philosophy and not a science. Its roots lie with Platonism, the oldest form of idealism. One might say that the Greek philosopher Plato himself is the forefather of idealism. Plato's transcendental idealism had a decisive influence on the morals and aesthetics of the Greeks. He maintained the conviction that the first and highest invisible of all things is God of the invisible world, and the lowest principle is the physical world. By means of this philosophical speculation, idealism maintains that God is distinct from the material world.

Philosophical principles form an integral part of the term "idealism." Its meaning encapsulates the word forms: *idealism, idealized, ideal* (adjective), *ideal* (noun), *idea, image, belief, figure, likeness, copy, type, model,* and *pattern.* The term *"the ideal"* is of the mind. That is, when a person is said to *"idealize" a* subject or an object to an ideal level of perfection, then it is in material reality. Idealism in life, therefore, is the characteristic of people who regard their ideas in their minds as standards and directive forces, a subjective truth, and a philosophy of nature.

On the basis of Platonic philosophy and widespread public teaching in various ancient Mediterranean societies, idealism became the definition of the dogma in which the Christian ideology found a foot hold and has since retained. That is, a divine intelligence is permanent but incommunicable, and it has patterned the things of the physical world. With this divine intelligence only the human soul can fix its gaze with the faculty of the mind and reason. That is, as ideals in the mind, they subsist in the divine mind—before things are created into existence; they exist as products of our thinking. So it happened that the term "ideal" in various Mediterranean languages increasingly took on the meaning of "divine design," "appearance," "object of thought," "phenomenalism," "mental image," "spiritualism," "God," "underworld," "heaven," "miracle," and so on.

The illusion of Idealism, however, does not provide the means to realistically ensure religious believers that the "ideal" can become rooted in reality. They dangerously need to reconfirm their constantly doubted pursuit to "realize" the inconceivable (the ideal). This is best expressed in the words of a philosopher:

I affirm without hesitation that the assertion, "the existence of the world consists merely in our thinking," is for me the result of a hypertrophy of the passion for knowledge. To this conclusion I have been lead chiefly by the torture I endure in getting over "idealism." Whoever attempts to take this theory in downright earnest, to force his way clean through it and identify himself with it, will certainly feel that something is about to snap in his brain. (Jerusalem, "Die Urtheilsfunktion," Vienna, 1887, p. 262).

"Any man who carries his theoretical doubts or denial of the external world so far that even in his everyday experience he is forever reminding himself of the purely subjective character of his perceptions....will simply fined himself flung out of the natural course confronted with the danger of losing his mind completely." (J. Volkelt, Erfahrung und denken, Hamburg, 1888, p. 520)

The basic message in both statements is that the "ideal" is nothing else than the material world reflected by the human mind and translated into forms of thought—realistic or delusional.

For the Christian dogma of the existence of the "soul" and its future life separated from the human body, this was and still is one of the most fundamental doctrines. The religious belief in the existence of the soul and its ability to maintain its life after bodily death goes beyond the "importance" of the relationship between the human body and its soul. If idealists believe that the soul and spirit are independent of the body, then the spiritual entities of God, saints, life after death, the spiritual world, good and bad spirits, and even new or recycled "spirituality" would be well within the aspirations of church institutions.

Humanity's idealism makes religion, but religion does not make the human being. Idealism is a form of internal conflict within a person who has either not yet found himself or has already lost himself. Prison inmates, persons in mental distress, and abusers who feel guilty are a few examples. However, a human is not an abstract or spiritual being encamped in the supernatural world. A human being is of the material world of human beings, part of his social organization, and of his society. His society, both ancient and contemporary, produced religion, which is an introverted worldview, because it was propagated by introverted minds. It is magical thinking about the human essence, because human essence has no true material reality. Simply put, the delusional world of idealism is the spiritual perfume of the religious believers who need the opium of the spirit in a spiritless world.

Idealism, then, suitably stands opposed to scientific materialism. One may say that generally, spiritualism, religion, and idealism deny the existence of any real material being outside of the mind, or, at the very least defend the "reality" of a spiritual being. It may claim that there exists a single universal mind (i.e., God's), from which all finite minds (i.e., man's) are infused with experiences that *create the belief* in the existence of an external material world.

Modern idealists have frequently fallen prey to their own delusional belief systems. Their criticisms of scientific materialism and their desperate attempts to prove the reality of a supernatural spiritual being always seem to contain forms of linguistic trickery. Their line of formal logic against materialism has not been met with any real creed to hold on to, and has landed them in hopeless absurdities. They claim that matter cannot arrange itself, yet there is arrangement in the material universe, and this is attributed to God's divine design of the highest intelligence. Yet, scientific evidence shows that matter in motion in the natural universe is the forceful outcome of previous physical conditions.

The most common characteristic of an idealist is that he or she passionately believes that something magical was "felt," recognized as "obvious," or that he or she has been "touched" by the spirit of a dead ancestor. Across different cultures, theistic and non-theistic idealists have enforced the "ideal" of the everlasting immaterial life of the spirit or soul. That is, those rituals can change the physical world, and that an ancestor's spirit is looking down on you in order to protect you from illnesses and misfortunes that are caused by other "evil" spirits. They also believe that "good" spirits like saints, tooth fairies, angels, gods or goddesses are protecting you from the "bad" spirits of demons, devils, or djinns. The underlying point is that idealism is not a single issue or topic.

Who then is an idealist? A simple answer is that idealists take some mental comfort in the notion that so long as they are in control of their minds; they are also in control of the world around them. Of course an idealist does not realize that the more psychologically insecure a person is, the more control he or she seeks in order to "feel" secure against nature's and society's constant change and movement. Thus, by believing that real power lies in their minds, thoughts, or consciousness, they are in control of the operative part of their material and social surroundings. By enforcing the "ideal" that the mind has a real distinct energy—independent of matter but capable of interfering with it underlies the subliminal message that mental spirits influence the movement of matter, like the spirit of an artist in the "creation" of art, literature, or science. Or, they believe that consciousness has modified the movement of matter throughout the history of the human race. Further to this, the natural universe is mindless and only God's intelligence makes the world go around, or that a "good" relationship between two people is fundamentally based on a "meeting of the minds."

What the followers of idealism do not know is that historically speaking, religions, cults, non-theistic idealism, pop-psychology, and pop-philosophy often serve the interests of the people whose ideas they spread far and wide. For example, food taboos keep members of the Jewish and Muslim communities from becoming socially intimate with outsiders. Pop-psychologists of the self-help industry sell their books and charge hefty fees to join their "self-realization" groups. Secular idealism is heavily peddled in consumerist advertisement and the mass media, through promises of improved self-image, feeling good, of fear of not buying this or that product, or imaginary privileges of social status for anyone who wants the benefits of membership in a social club. In societies of the Mediterranean, witches, priestesses, and temple priests peddled prophesies, as do today's tarot card readers, tea readers, numerologists and astrologists.

Idealism is a very profitable image-related business. In fact, contemporary idealists, writers, self-help gurus, women's and men's publications, television psychologists, and talk-shows advocate an extreme form of idealism: believing equals reality. A mind's beliefs are more intimately known and easily manipulated by political ideologists, advocates of extreme individualism, religious fanatics, and a public education geared to serve the latest business expectations. The combined effort here is to serve as an advocate for the market economy as a belief system.

Let's focus on the truly distinctive part of the idealism-of-belief. I maintain that the common thread of idealism's practice in our western culture is that believing is a "technique" for success. Its root lies within the idealist advocacy that states "anything is possible, if you put your mind to it." What kind of mind would do something as useless and utterly irrational as inventing the belief that it alone can bring a valid material or social change "if you put your mind to it?" How does that fit into the scientific and biological natural selection explanation of how the world works? It does not! But for the propagators of idealism, this delusion (and a score of others) fits rather well.

For example, we know that most believers in idealism are neither delusional nor psychotic (i.e., incapable of distinguishing fantasy from reality). To fantasize that I can fly in the air like Superman, that I can imagine to be in Africa in one instant and in Asia the next, or that I can be like the Wizard of Oz, is as normal as having a ham and cheese sandwich for lunch. However, to believe that "if I can put my mind into it" I can make the laws of the Universe be nullified in order to cure my sickness, or pray to a spirit for my recovery from illness, for success in business and love, for winning the Super Lotto, for surviving on the battlefields of Iraq or Afghanistan, or for having fine weather–this sort of "believing" would be deemed utterly irrational.

A belief in the power of the mind's ideas is a desperate attempt that idealists resort to when the stakes are high, when they wish for successes, and when they have either exhausted their dialectical reasoning and techniques for the causation of social and personal successes, or if they are ignorant of them (i.e., advanced medicine, dialectical strategies, courtship in love, etc.). The point is that everyday laypersons know that the natural world and societies are governed either by the laws of nature or by the laws of social contract. But they find that the absurdity of positive thinking, praying, and seeking magic in the spirit of idealism is what fascinates them; it is also because idealism violates their common personal intuition about the natural world that draws them towards it.

Religious idealists and secular spiritualists think of and imagine a spirit, an object, a person or animal, a talisman, a god, Satan, or an angel, and "idealize" it by adding or crossing out a vital part of another's natural substance. For example, a horse or an elephant will be granted another animal's standard-issue body parts or traits—wings or horns—to become a unicorn or a flying elephant. But otherwise, both animals are still expected to behave as nature intended. A man with imaginary wings becomes an angel who is granted additional power to fly and serve as a messenger and killer of another imaginary entity, be it God or Allah. They are all imaginary by the simple dialectical fact that they are all exempt from one or more of the laws of biology (birth, decay and death), the laws of physics (matter-in-motion and visibility) and the tenets of human psychology (ideas, thoughts, desires, feelings, imagination and delusions, that can only be known through bodily or external behaviour).

For the idealists, however, fantastic ideas in the mind are "externalized" in the form of spirits and take on the anthropomorphic shape of a person or animal. For the tribal animist elders of North America, and around the world, the spirit of a bear or salmon, wolf or an eagle can see and hear, or can cause punishment or issue threats. When the elders propagate those religious beliefs, do they also believe that their spiritualism is essentially different from the delusional beliefs spread by the Catholic Church?

This question has a twofold answer: first, the religious leaders don't seem to bother answering such pedestrian questions. Furthermore, religious leaders don't have to. This is because their experience from their extensive knowledge of human psychology has told them that the minds of their believers will avoid working out how nature and ordinary things work. Idealism is a difficult mental default to overcome. It is also extremely monotonous and boring when compared with the mind-bending of scientific materialism. Science and biology are mind-stimulating and socially beneficial for both the scientific community and the recipients of scientific discoveries. Religious beliefs are without a doubt noted for their lack of innovative imagination. The standard traits of religious beliefs are fixed, in that heaven and hell are somewhere, angels are man-spirits, fear and obedience are paths to salvation, and God or Allah is vindictive and selective.

These are points of immediate interest—they are a compressed but a wholly accurate description of what has been happening to our ordinary ways of understanding real human concepts. Idealist and religious advocates have stressed the "ultimate power of ideas" as a governing force (i.e., mind over matter). This statement deliberately excludes the far greater power and authority of material reality and circumstances. Material reality and the circumstances of generations of believers demanding miracles as quick fixes for personal crises have created a market for power and wealth that would-be priests, cultists of all sorts, and self-help pop-psychologists compete in. They have succeeded by exploiting people's weaknesses and dependence on "experts." Divorced from this material power, their ideas would amount to nothing. Reinforced by such material circumstances, their idealist beliefs have become inescapable for millions and millions of believers over many centuries. This is because human concepts have been exploited by the few who make them, appear wondrous to our dialectical way of knowing.

This question still remains: why do reasonable and rational people waste time in speculative ideas and religious rituals that they know are inane and possibly dangerous? Why don't they accept that idealism has led humanity to commit religious wars or mass crimes, maintain ignorance and superstition, and produce books on how to rape people, commit acts of genocide, incite slavery, promote incest, engage in polygamy, and so forth? Why don't they conserve their thoughts for those domains of humanity in which they could do some good?

Throughout my many years of travelling and investigating religious practices and their propagators, I have come to understand two possible reasons: domination over others and the accumulation of wealth. Secular and religious propagators know that humans are social beings, that they place their trust in others whom they regard as trustworthy, and that they seek love and attachment for their comfort and survival.

For example, consider the scenario of having the unpleasant experience of visiting a dentist or going for day surgery. We trust that the dentist and surgeon both know what they are doing. However, we do not often seek to verify their skills before they begin their task. Corporations and other such entities today have institutionalized such basic trust to form part of their financial transactions with their clients. They essentially have direct access to their clients' bank accounts. For many centuries the same human sense of social trust would have been given to priests, witches, magicians, medical charlatans, and political and religious leaders. Most of their remedies, predictions of events, and stern warnings of punishment from invisible gods or spirits were designed to maintain their positions of power and wealth.

Through part of this social enterprise and entrapment, most believers were given a sense of individuality, but others were not. As believers, they were exposed to social and religious doctrines which upheld the false righteousness that an individual's mind and ideas possessed ultimate power. Yet, these individuals saw that their communities, churches, corporations, and governments promoted idealism and exercised extensive socio-political power. As believers and consumers, they were expected to behave as subordinates. In time, a triumph of indifference and apathy was ingrained in the populace, which simply preferred "herd-mentality" obedience rather than learning how their social and natural world worked. The "divine" trust and beliefs about spirits are true or false human concepts, but their public demand created an exploitative economic market where ancient temple-priests, the Catholic Church, idealist philosophers, our contemporary market-economy belief system, pop-psychologists, and peripheral idealist groups have succeeded by creating a culture of experts and a pathological public dependency on them.

As I said before, idealism is not a single subject, but its main historical propagator is religion. Religious institutions of the world have used the artistic talents of painters, architects, poets, literary artists, philosophers, music composers, lawyers, etc., and have propagated alternative rituals and customs that have survived to this day. One can see that religious rituals and customs appear intense, meaningful and, in the case of symbolism, organize metaphorical images and visions of the world. For example, a painter's religious affiliations are not merely reflected in his paintings and murals in churches, but condition the metaphorical vocabulary and understanding of the viewer-believer. For many centuries, the Christian church provided such doctrinal visions of the world. These visions enticed the human race to abandon the dignity of its material reality and become degenerate and depraved creatures under God's heaven (a tragic outcome resulting from defective understanding and dialectical reasoning).

The spread of religious and secular idealism was possible because most believers, as children, were indoctrinated by their parents and communities. But there comes a time in many lives when *material reality* becomes *apparent,* and people discover the natural world and the reality of their personal relationship to that natural world. It may have been previously hidden by the delusions of idealism. The mystical rituals, awe-inspiring music, awe-inspiring architectural ecclesiastical structures, occult experiences, all of these things form an integral part of the delusion of "God's divinity." The recipients of such awe-inspiring acts or visions may be conscious of nothing, or regard men as failures. They feel that sin, suffering, evil and guilt become meaningful in ritual acts of prayer and help enforce the adherence to taboos within the framework of the entire idealistic system of religious ritual symbols. However, to be meaningful is not equivalent to dialectical reasoning.

Idealism, which includes dreams, images, fantasies, and religious beliefs, is primarily symbolic and metaphorical. Religion provides a narrative expressed in metaphors, interiorizes the logic of elusive perspectives, uses semantic metaphors that have dual meanings, prefaced with "as if." Spiritual, enigmatic, and mythological (metaphorically speaking) experiences are the "eyes of the soul." And so we humans have long ago been conditioned to "living" in a simulated world that, most of us anyway, don't realize is, in fact, simulated.

Such cultural conditioning has resulted in an auto-delusion: "the metaphorical mind." For example, let's take the term "went" which simply means that someone or something moved from place A to place B or vice versa. The term "went'" therefore indicates a bodily movement as, "the ball *went* straight into the net." But if I say that "the light *went* from yellow to green" or "I *went* out of my mind from anticipation" or "the meeting *went* fast today," things stay rather put: they don't move at all. They are actually stationary. In other words, the traffic lights are set in a fixed place and don't travel, the meeting cannot even be considered a thing that could travel, nor could I physically go somewhere and leave my mind behind. One can see that we are using space and motion as a metaphor to further support highly abstract ideas.

Furthermore, we must be careful here and not blame idealism for the entire cause of all human delusions. Human ignorance of how the unrestricted use of metaphors affects our minds can also be held responsible for tragedies against our own species and environment. For example, the metaphors of virtual reality not only co-opt words, but there is the danger of misleading us into believing in things that do not exist. A metaphor's reference to God or angels (as persons), and heaven or hell (as places), are extremes of delusion.

The same problem arises when we take the virtual reality of a metaphor literally—wherein the human mind converts *abstract* concepts into *concrete* terms. The problem is not only when a single word is borrowed for a metaphor but when an entire grammatical construction or narrative is propagated in the name of another metaphor such as God or something holy. Narratives constructed in their entirety by a mix of metaphors are an integral part of Christianity, Judaism, and Islam. For example, the metaphor "holy" in the act of war creates the abstract concept of a holy war. Yet, war is not about abstraction, for war is about the killing of men, the slaughter and dismemberment of men, the destruction of families, and the devastation of communities. The metaphor "holy" is an abstraction that is attached to the concrete term war referring to a physical event or activity.

Evidently, many of us speak in metaphors. Slang terms are a set of metaphors that we use whether we realize it or not. Conditioned by centuries of idealistic systems of thought, humans can claim that we live by metaphors. True enough, metaphors make our expressions vivid and interesting–one can see examples in poetry, philosophy, or art. However, when metaphors structure our life's perceptions and understanding, this may lead us to a distorted set of expectations. For example, one must recognize how profoundly metaphors not only shape our view of life in the present but may also set up delusional expectations of what life will be for us in the future. Remember that metaphors are ideas in the mind, expressed as linguistic devices of imagination, rhetorical flourish, and tools of the intellect. Thus, if we take the metaphor of the "American Dream," that we all must live "Bigger and Better," the financial crush of 2008 (credit card overspending, housing and banking speculation, etc.) took place because our wages (i.e., material reality) could not support the metaphorical fantasy of the widespread consumerism of the "American Dream."

As idealists, we regard our ideas in our mind as standard and directive forces and place them ahead of the dialectical material conditions that are external and real. Another example: one of the most enduring metaphors is the word "crusade" which first appeared in Latin in the twelfth and thirteenth centuries. The metaphoric idea of "crusade" refers to a religion-backed military campaign, "pilgrimage," or a "holy war" to recapture the "holy land." Today, the metaphor "crusade for" or "crusade against" is used by idealist, zealous religious persons to advance the "moral good" and to oppose "evil's immorality" as perceived by Christian theology against abortion, gay rights, etc. These idealistic metaphors of the ideas of "good," "evil" and "crusade"—when placed as a directive force and acted upon—result in the dominance and control of living, breathing, actual human beings.

Scientists, who are 95% scientific materialists and atheists, use metaphors as well. They would probably agree with me that metaphors are rampant in science. Astrophysicists have described the distribution of mass in the universe as *"foam-like."* However, using the simile "foam-like" does not change the essence of the scientific materialist investigation into the distribution of mass in the universe nor does it place the idea of "foam-like" as a directional force to explain the material laws that govern universal bodies. The simile "foam-like" is a *link-bridge* to comprehend material conditions in space that are still mysterious to the average layperson. Nuclear scientists tend to describe atoms as if electrons were planetary bodies spinning around our nuclear sun. Biologists and environmentalists describe our natural world as a living organism when explaining concepts of cells and global warming. The difficulty begins when people use a *metaphoric* term not to suggest similarities between non-identical things or objects but as a method of directional thinking to legitimize a delusional act, a non-extant thing or an event (such as "holy" war, "time" is money, the more you "spend" the more you "save").

While a metaphor is a linguistic tool, symbolism is a visual metaphorical indicator of something external and concrete. A symbol signifies or stands for something concrete, but its message is metaphorical: "a picture is worth a thousand words." The Greek word "symbol" means "that which is brought together." A symbol unifies and links our subjective intuition with our conscious immediate awareness. The value of symbolism was understood and practiced by many ancient and contemporary cultures on all the Earth's continents. The symbolism of life's opposites Yin-Yang (represented by pictorial works) stands for when the natural forces turn into each other. As a particular form of unity, it is used as a basis for contemplation. Several kinds of visual symbolic messages were the old English Shoppe sign hanging above the entrance of a bakery, a blacksmith's foundry, a carpenter's workshop, etc., depicting only a symbol of an item or a service that was promoted, such as a loaf of bread, a horseshoe, and a saw and hammer.

Religious symbolism is very effective with believers because of its underlying simplicity, and more especially through the metaphorical expression of religious rituals that appeal to followers. In the particular cases of the Old and New Testaments, these writings are full of symbolism that are used as manipulative instruments to direct believers to particular religious worship. A combination of symbolic images (icons, paintings, murals, statues of saints), and metaphors (creation, miracles, holy water, etc.) are sufficient to propagate their mysticism. However, the problem with religious symbolism and metaphors is that they remain fixed and real space and time eventually pervades them.

For example, when one reads a chapter from Genesis of how "God created man in his own image," the early religious believers hardly doubt of the reality of this metaphorical claim. Space and Time however shows that this claim cannot hold true against the weight of contemporary biological and scientific evidence. This pervades the original religious claims and now these stories are essentially interpreted as "moral lessons" rather than the reporting of material facts. Nowadays, religious advocates maintain that such claims concentrate the author's moral attention. In other words, the scientific refutation couples with the symbolic reinvention and with the reinterpretation of the origins of "creation." For the religious believers, the idea in the mind of "God's creation" is a directive force that compels them to follow this or other delusional religious or idealist claims contrary to scientific evidence.

At the core of religious and secular idealism lies the concept of belief. The term belief is a non-investigative term. A belief is an abstract idea or a set of abstract ideas about whatever a person is willing, or has been culturally conditioned to accept, without the support of evidence. This results in a conviction which is taken as a basis for acting or non-acting. Former President George W. Bush is the epitome of a believer:

"I know what I believe, I will continue to articulate what I believe–I believe what I believe is right." (Rome, 2001)

For religious and secular idealists, a belief is set of ideas that are the driving force of one's behaviour instead of basing ideas on an external reality. Often a belief is not based on experience and so it does not reach the true dimension of material human existence. The very essence of belief makes it impossible to include the necessity of material evidence, and it dispenses with the evidence of material experience. It may also go much further and deny the evidence of material experience.

This is a belief's directive force and therein lays the delusion of belief. A belief is a mental image of a distorted version of reality. I also want to underline that this is not a case of believing vs. not believing. The real issue is belief vs. dialectical learning, or believing vs. material investigating. An unexamined belief is simply not worth holding. One may conclude that an examined belief is also not worth holding onto. This holds true for many religious beliefs, since once examined, they may prove to be worthless, and only serve to confer no more than a sense of belonging.

Human beings are social creatures living within social structures where social interaction takes place. This social interaction consists of a shared knowledge of language and communication, and groupings which represent an array of secular idealist and religious beliefs. These are all based on people's social status and values. A related problem with values based on the idealist process of belief formation is the tendency to disregard all evidence which is contrary to a desired belief. In other words, the wishful desire to maintain a certain belief for idealist reasons, rather than as an actual necessity, can be so strong as to override a person's rational evidence.

On the other hand, if a person "belongs" to a particular social or economic group he or she may be forced or persuaded to obey a set of beliefs that go against his or her best social values. For example, a belief that is imposed from one's familial, cultural and or religious group and is accepted as a task, obligation or role assigned to the believer, rather than chosen on a voluntary basis, and can contain contradictory and opposing elements that confuse the believer.

This may compel the believer into hostile behaviour towards others, which relates to a way of believing and to a prescribed code of conduct. This may result in uncompromising or fanatical behaviour often associated with violence, if not directly used as a justification for violence. A case in point is the fanatical belief system of anti-abortionists, racists, anti-Semitics, anti-gays, etc. Their ideas and beliefs are regarded by them as primary and human reality as secondary. Thus, in a standard idealist methodology, their ideas are held as the directive forces of their beliefs, imposed upon external material reality. Believers host delusions from an idealist religious tradition, which be altered or questioned; believers are functioning in an ideological mode. That is, in abstractions held and enacted. In short, it's "all or nothing" thinking. The irony is that our western societies are to a large extent tolerant of religious beliefs which are in turn so intrinsically intolerant. Here are some related comments on the subject:

"A man's ethical behaviour should be based effectively on sympathy, education, and social ties; no religion is necessary." (Albert Einstein)

"If the obstacles of bigotry and priest craft can be surmounted, we may hope that common sense will suffice to do everything else. I have...been examining all the known superstitions of the world, and do not find in our particular superstition of [Christianity] one redeeming feature. They are all alike, founded on fables and mythology." (Thomas Jefferson)

"One is often told that it is a very wrong thing to attack religion, because religion makes men virtuous. So I am told; I have not noticed it. You find this curious fact, that the more intense has been the religion of any period and the more profound has been the dogmatic belief, the greater has been the cruelty and the worse has been the state of affairs." (Bertrand Russell)

"The so-called Christian Nations are the most enlightened and progressive—but in spite of their religion, not because of it. The Church has opposed every innovation and discovery from the day of Galileo down to our own time, when the use of anaesthetic in childbirth was regarded as a sin because it avoided the biblical curse [of painful birth] pronounced against Eve. And every step in astronomy and geology ever taken has been opposed by bigotry and superstition." (Mark Twain)

One major problem in the western world today, and this applies especially to "educated" laypersons, is that they are not very perceptive. As a result, most people suffer from an inability to look at and see their surroundings dialectically, as it really is. Among the many reasons for this is that the layperson is most familiar with the ideas and notions of the secular idealism of the times. Having been "educated" with a system of cultural blinders prevents a person from understanding anything outside of the current "thinking-box." It is a framework in which the layperson has been indoctrinated to prevent him or her from being able to view and understand anything outside the often limited framework of secular and religious beliefs and attitudes.

But our "thinking-box" of formal logic is not a scientific materialist law which governs nature, society, and the universe. It is also not a set of rules which governs human behaviour. This can be seen from the fact that we all have conflicting logical goals. A logical belief is an idea that is held based on some support, even if that logical support is the result of prior fabrication by someone else that needs you to believe as he wants you to believe. Believing in something is not the same as knowing something. On the other hand, if something is objectively true, is it true because you believe it is, or is it true independently of whether you believe it or not? After all, a belief is just a belief, not an objective truth.

2

NAÏVE AND DESTRUCTIVE IDEALISM

"…it is the Christian tradition that is the most fundamental element in Western culture. It lies at the base not only of Western religion, but also of Western morals and Western social idealism."

Christopher Dawson

"Every form of addiction is bad, no matter whether the narcotic be alcohol or morphine or idealism."

Carl Jung

Secular idealism is a system of thought that does not include religious beliefs or practices. It concentrates on the individual's emotions, wishful thinking, imagination and sensations as its sole primary focus. The only bond that connects religious idealism and secular idealism is that both place a gravitational primacy on mental process (ideals) over the external reality that exists independent of the mind. The motto of secular idealism is **"Mind over Matter."**

Secular idealism is a pervasive belief system of thought that has penetrated every facet of our society. It is evident in our concept of love, self-esteem, consumerism, commercial advertising, ethnocentrism, political ideologies, children's make-believe stories, self-help, "alternative realities" out-of-body experiences, "cosmic energy," the "world within," paranormal beliefs, horoscopes, palm reading, tarot card reading, pop psychology and all sorts of "spiritual realities." The basic human lifeline of mutuality between two individual secular idealists is a "meeting of minds." All of the above are interpreted and propagated in terms of metaphorical thinking and language.

In the past few centuries, religious beliefs of what constituted the Natural World were dictated and influenced by the believer's interpretation of it. God's creation of the natural world, with all its manifestations, was also shared by believers of most religious cults. How Christianity regarded reality became also the believer's perception of it. As such, perception was in itself an actual reality. This gravitational primacy of a person's mental perception eliminated the physicality of the natural world's reality regarding the latter as secondary. As such, the mind's virtual perception, ideas, illusions and delusions, rational and irrational feelings, superstitions and phobias all interplayed to reaffirm personal idealism. Secular idealism has simply replaced the idea of "God's divine mind" for the idea of the "power" of the human mind. Substituting one idea for another idea was a simple mental process. Now, the religiosity of "spirituality" is more often used to mask ancient or primitive superstition.

I want to make something clear: in the last thirty years or so, technological advancements have created a new term called "virtual-reality." Virtual reality is not an actual physical reality, but an artificial image of it. The human brain's mental processes are "virtual" related to any actual external physical motion or potential material circumstances. Virtual images created in image-projecting instruments are real-time virtual images of tangible objects or hypothetical conditions. The technology of virtual imagery within computer simulations is used in airplane pilot training, medical training, and architectural designs etc. It's very commonplace today. There is no confusion between the projected virtual image and the physicality of the object itself.

In children's picture books, images of talking animals, metaphorical descriptions of "good" or "bad" witches, tooth fairies, and magical places are part of long-established naïve idealism and the cultural expression of an explicit and implicit mimetic value system. Parents who read bedtime stories to their children know these are metaphorical stories–they have no literal foundation. Children, of course, have not yet developed a mature intelligence to recognize the difference between the metaphorical and the literal, and between the virtual and the physical reality. So, children believe what they see in these children's books and what they hear from their parent's storytelling. This I call children's "Naïve Idealism" which is shared with adults when dealing with Santa Claus.

However, there is a fine line between naïve idealism and destructive religious/secular idealism. Such a fine line is determined by cultural norms and perceived social conditions. For example, during World War II and the Vietnam War, a number of Hollywood movies were made showing heroic secular images of American soldiers fighting and killing the "other" bad guys in the "good" war. War is about the killing of men, nothing more! In the religious fundamentalist version of Islam, the killing of the "other" is justified based on an equally destructive idealism of delusional mental perceptions. Practicing violence under religious or secular justifications is "destructive idealism." The heroic sagas of Alexander the Great, the Vikings, the Mongolian hordes, the Crusaders, the Jihad suicide bombers and the Japanese kamikaze are part of the "idea" of greatness in secular/religious destructive idealism. Nationalism, patriotism, ethnic and racial superiority, and killing in the name of "God and Country" are some examples.

I remember as a child attending Grade Two or Three watching two pictures on my classroom wall above the blackboard. One of the pictures showed King Constantine, the other a man's black bearded face. The King's face was "angelic" and the background scene was a light blue colour. The bearded man's face was a dark colour. I've always wondered who these two men were. One day, the teacher explained to me that the first picture was the "good" King and the "other" face was of a "bad" communist. Because of this explanation, every time I've looked at the King's picture, I have had the sense of a "good" feeling. For a long time, whenever I came across any man's bearded face in the street, a sense of fear would overcome my body.

Some years later, I was travelling through the Black Sea coastal countries and a sense of being uncomfortable in "communist" nations persisted. I visited universities, museums, parks, stores, and I saw mothers and their children, couples holding hands, etc, The delusional fear of secular destructive idealism of the "communist" was so embedded in my mind that it took a personal effort to overcome it. The fear that secular destructive idealism caused in my mind of the "other" was imbedded on the same delusional base that virtual-reality is formed. Secular naïve idealism–the King's face–and secular destructive idealism–the communist's face–were both delusional images. In short, this was a case of a virtual perception of reality, of good and bad, caused by the delusion of "Mind over Matter."

Technological advances have led to the development of advanced technology in the fields of computer science, communications, exchange of medical information, and the Internet. The power of mass communication encompasses a very impressive global scope. For example, medical procedures can be viewed and directed from far away by medical experts to surgeons performing complicated operations. Experimental designs can be created and modified for mechanical devices and structural entities. Professionals planning their building projects can easily print out their blueprints to speed the pace of physical work needed to complete a project. A blueprint, therefore, is the literal interpretation (or application) of a pending project. Such a literal interpretation includes: first, the structural (or real/literal) and second the aesthetic (or metaphorical) parts of the project itself. The mechanical dialectical process of the material reality projects the *gravitational directional force* in implementing the ideas along the various stages.

The aesthetic part of the physical project includes metaphorical designs depicting themes appropriate to the overall scheme. In a children's park, for example, various games and play structures are designed first to meet *physical specifications* and then are painted or decorated with designs to please the children's metaphorical imagination (naïve idealism). Naïve idealism of the park's metaphorical designs would imprint on the children's brain a metaphorical thinking that stays with them during their childhood. At a certain age, mature children would conclude that such childhood themes are not real but are metaphorical. Thus, as these children become adults their naïve-idealism's metaphorical image of the park's depicted animals would be gradually negated by the external reality of the real beauty of actual animals, magnificent natural environments and landscapes. The concept of beauty then is gradually transformed from metaphor/naïve to literal/real, from illusion of the secular naïve idealism to the reality of the dialectics of nature. This in turn, would repeat the dialectical mimetic process of transmission of a set of cultural memes of secular naïve idealism from one generation of children to the next. The children's naïve idealism—outside the park's mimetic influence–would include a childhood phenomenon of the "imaginary friend" which can form a natural lead into religious beliefs.

The imaginary friend of childhood is an example of naïve idealism–an illusion of normal children who have a complex make-believe world. It can be Winnie the Pooh or Smoky the Bear or any other childhood hero. In my family's case, I watched my daughter Melissa befriend "Charlie" who was her doll and a close friend. Until Melissa was five years old, "Charlie" was the only one who would listen to her complaints.

At some point, I noticed that "Charlie" was left behind when Melissa would take a walk on our farm. Later on, I found out from my wife that Melissa had a new imaginary friend, a boy named "Glorio." For safety reasons, I would follow my six-year old daughter when she was taking off for her walk in the forest. If she saw me following her, she would insist that I should leave her alone, which gave me an opportunity to find another tree to hide behind. Because of the distance, I could not hear the lively conversations she conducted with "Glorio."

These casual walks lasted until she was eleven years old. At some point I simply gave up my hiding attempts; I was simply not very good at it. Over the years, I found that "Glorio" was Melissa's companion, confidant and confessor about whatever problems a girl has at her age. Her naïve idealism caused her no psychological harm. We had no religion at home for a possible replacement of her naiveté with religious destructive-idealism. When "Glorio" was no longer around, her personal diary became her new confessor.

My point is that Melissa's childhood dependency on the imaginary friend "Glorio" is similar to a vulnerable person's dependency on an imaginary "God"–a companion, a confidant and confessor. Does a religious believer's dependency on God–as imaginary friend, confidant and confessor–indicate a fixed state of cognitive underdevelopment at a childhood psychological level? Can this childhood phenomenon of imaginary friends be used as a point of departure for analyzing people's theistic belief in God, as an imaginary protector, confidant and confessor? Even better, since an imaginary friend or God displays such an ever-ready patience, unlimited attention, and devotion to listen to the sufferer, can this explain the persistency of the God-meme and its holding strength on believers? Even when shown their view of the imaginary God to be false, far from recognizing the fallacy, believers rant by intensifying the fervor of their beliefs!

There seems to be no doubt that secular naïve idealism is quite evident within a large section of the adult population. The basic characteristics are identical to a child's secular naïve idealism– a belief in the invisible entity, in the influence such an entity has over their lives, and the "supernatural" abilities they can exhibit. Let's look at some of the most popular concepts that are based on secular naïve idealism as the dominant force.

"Paranormal" beliefs refer to what are "beyond" scientific explanations–or not in accordance with scientific evidence or determined by the laws of nature. I am not sure whether the term "beyond" refers to a specific place on Earth, in the sky, or neither of these. The thing that I do know for sure is that above us the Material/Natural Universe encompasses planets, solar systems, and space objects that include new and dying stars and planets. A dialectical premise is this:

- *Anything that has occurred within the infinity of the Natural Universe was necessary, normal or natural.*

- *If it is normal or natural, then it has occurred.*

❖ *If it did not occur then it does not exist.*

The fact that the "free thinker" naïve-idealist finds comfort in "paranormal" beliefs does not speak very well about his/her desire to seek dialectically objective truth. In short, the belief in the "paranormal" is the art of being well deceived. The term "paranormal" refers to the mental process that goes into seeking the non-physical and the extrasensory–ghosts, haunted houses, the Bermuda Triangle, UFOs, etc. Because of a lack of scientific evidence, notable scientists don't support the naïve idealism of "paranormal" beliefs.

Belief in Astrology and in Horoscopes is a belief that the planetary positions have an influence on the course of earthy occurrences in human affairs. Astrology is often ridiculed as medieval superstition. Astrology, unlike astronomy, is not a scientific study and has been much criticized by scientism. Anyone who has taken a casual investigation into astrology will have noticed that the metaphorical language of "astrology horoscope" is well constructed, grammatically correct, and characteristically convincing. Yet, scientifically speaking, this proves nothing because secular naïve idealism simply separates/isolates ideas in the mind from their respective related realities. This is plainly a delusion of "Mind over Matter."

Secular believers of such nonsense evidently share a common characteristic. They place the gravitational primacy on the ideas-in-mind, instead of having their ideas determined by external material conditions as the *directional force*. Physical or psychological harm to humans by naïve idealism may be very minimal, other than setting a mimetic pattern or habit of accepting the metaphorical "existence" of non-existent entities. Other area where secular naïve-idealism is quite evident is in Tarot card reading, tea-leaf reading, palmistry, reflexology, numerology, graphology, etc. However, these "arts" do tend to make victims of others as part of the deceiving industry of "psychics" and other charlatans.

The dialectical/natural opposite of naïve idealism is, of course, secular *destructive idealism*. This kind of idealism is quite different from naïve-idealism, because it negatively affects human affairs. In other words, it is not naïve or harmless! Racism is, for example, a secular destructive-idealism. It is a belief system which maintains that race is the primary determinant of the human characteristics of intelligence and capacities. Also, it holds that racial differences produce an inherent superiority or inferiority of a particular race. It is an ideology which states that humans are divided into separate and exclusive biological living beings called "race" and that there is a causal link between inherent physical traits and traits of personality, intelligence, morality, and other cultural behavioral features. In my book *For God, Country and Drug Prohibition*, I quote the first director of the Bureau of Narcotics, H. Anslinger:

"Marijuana influences Negroes to look at white people in the eye, step on white man's shadows and look at a white woman twice."

"There are 100,000 total marijuana smokers in the US who are Negroes, Hispanics, Filipinos...This marihuana causes women to seek sexual relations with Negroes... the primary reason to outlaw marijuana is its effect on the degenerate races."

An old form of racism is *anti-Semitism*. One variety of anti-Semitic racism was the emerging 19th century racism that later formed the basis for the Nazi's so-called "scientific racism." This was different in essence from the Christian racism of anti-Jewish prejudices. *Aryanism* was the mental delusion of the Nazi's 20th century destructive-idealism proclaiming their superiority. This dogma of "Aryanism" expanded and became the destructive ideology of Nazi racial delusions during the time of Hitler's political terror.

Racial segregation is the physical and cultural segregation of different racial groups in daily life. Segregation–as it was practiced in South Africa–may be enforced by law and military force or by social custom influenced by destructive idealism. It is based on religious or secular idealism. It is destructive because it creates real social victims through death, torture/lynching or by discrimination in education, health care and work opportunities. It is advocated and perpetuated through discrimination during hiring practices, in the rental or sale of homes, in education, in interracial marriages, and in medical treatments. Racial/ethnic segregation has appeared in many parts of the world where there were, and still are, multi-racial communities. India is an example of where religious and secular destructive-idealism is propagated in daily social/economic life. The profane *Sanskrit* literature propagates a destructive idealism by segregating *Hindu Aryan* culture from the *"untouchable" Aryan Dravian* culture. Light-skinned Indo-Aryans are forbidden by rigorous segregation from contact with the dark-skinned indigenous and "untouchable" Dravian tribes. Secular destructive idealism has formed the Indian caste system.

In Europe, Jewish segregation was enforced through laws or by social pressure. But it was also advocated by religious destructive-idealism. Jewish communities were segregated in the *ghettos* and in *shtetls* (small towns). The religious fanatic Martin Luther in his book *On Jews and their Lies,* Part Two (1543) advocated a religious destructive-idealism which was put into practice by Hitler and his Nazi henchmen. This included Luther's instructions to *"take their gold and possessions, burn down their business and property, remove Jewish men, women and children, and then kill them."* He wrote that anyone who does God's work should feel no remorse because *"We are innocent of [their] blood."* Here is a real example of Luther's extreme religious destructive-idealism:

"What shall we Christians do with this rejected people, the Jews? Since they live among us, we dare not tolerate their conduct, now that we are aware of their lying and reviling and

*blaspheming...I shall give you my sincere advice: First, to set fire to their synagogues or schools and to bury...them...This is to be done in honour of our Lord of Christendom, so that God might see that we are Christians...Second, I advice that their houses also be razed and destroyed. For they pursue in them the same aims as in their synagogues...that they are not masters in our country...Third, I advice that their prayer book and Talmudic writings in which such idolatry, lies, cursing, and blasphemy are taught, be take from them. Fourth, I advice that their rabbis be forbidden to teach henceforth **on pain of life and limb**...Fifth, I advice that safe-conduct on the highways be abolished completely for the Jews...Sixth, I advice that...all cash and treasures of silver and gold are taken from them."*

(Typical of idealists in general, religious advocates have always deliberately isolated the **Idea** of religion from the **Practice** of religion–the **Idea** that "God loves all children" from the **Practice** of pedophilia by religious pedophiles).

The point is that human relations are particularly susceptible to secular or religious destructive-idealism. This can be noted in the notorious event of *Kristallnacht* (Night of Broken Glass) which took place as an anti-Jewish pogrom in Nazi Germany on November 9, 1938–on Martin Luther's birthday. In a coordinated attack on German Jews and their property, 110 synagogues were destroyed, 91 Jews were murdered, and 30,000 were arrested and deported to ghettos and concentration camps. Religious idealism is by its core essence destructive, threatening, full of hatred and fearful of the "other." It promotes anger towards anyone who does not fit into the mental delusion of "Mind over Matter."

Distortion of material reality–whether by naïve or destructive-idealism–is just that, a distortion by means of applying to it a "virtual" perception of one's own choosing. Thus, delusion in social concepts–like racism–is aimed toward the cultivation of the "idea" of a personal self-image of racial superiority. This involves the mind's mental processes, rather than the physical consequences of applying it to social acts. The idealist motto "Out of Sight, Out of Mind" diminishes the reality of the material consequences of destructive human activities. So, a Nazi killer who finds a mental justification for murdering an innocent "other" is also a victim of secular destructive-idealism. It is because the **"idea"** is what counts as a directional force not the killing—which is the reality's gravitational consequence. In the religious destructive-idealism of present day Jihadists, it is the **"idea"** of God's command which provides a *directional force* when killing innocent people. An equal delusion–without physical consequences–is the secular belief in naïve-idealism which is imbedded in the popular meme of "It is the thought that counts" i.e., Mind over Matter.

The metaphoric term "virtual reality" lures careless persons by means of delusion. As people take this metaphor literally, they imagine an "experience" of virtual-reality as a solution for anything. Such a person, as long as he/she "experiences" or "believes" in virtual-reality, does not care that an illusion or an ideal cannot change the laws of nature. True enough, careless followers of "virtual reality" are not usually psychotic or hallucinatory–although some are. They are just not able to distinguish the delusion of "virtual" from external material reality. They are aware that there is a humdrum world of real humans, physical objects, and cultural relations driven by the natural laws of material reality. But they find the make-believe system of "virtual-reality" to be fascinating precisely because it does violate their own ordinary cognition about the reality of the world. In short, when the external objective reality does not correspond to the mind's virtual images or thoughts, or, when the mind's thoughts or virtual images do not correspond to the external objective reality, religious or secular destructive delusions can take control of the mind. This clouds the physical importance of humanist reality.

Let me for a moment present you with another example of secular naïve idealism. Until the time I was ten years old, my parents would frequently send me to my grandmother Angelica's farm for a break. This was an adventure in itself. My favored activity at the farm was climbing trees and sampling their fruit. One such was an apricot tree. I spent most of my time climbing this tree and eating its fruit. It was a huge tree, and to climb it was quite a task.

At the age of twelve my family moved away, which made my visits to my grandmother's farm impossible. During my absentee years, I had many pleasant thoughts about my favored apricot tree. At the age of twenty, I re-visited my grandmother's farm. I remember well that I could not wait to climb that huge apricot tree and eat its fresh fruit. The moment I arrived at the farm, I asked my grandmother for the location of the apricot tree. When she pointed it out, my first reaction was: this cannot be my apricot tree. The one I was looking at was a relatively small tree compared to the "huge tree" that I remembered from my childhood. My wise grandmother reminded me that as a child of ten years old, the apricot tree must have appeared huge. My disappointment was not easy to overcome.

So, what had happened with my virtual perception of the tree? During eight years absence my mental image of the real apricot tree had remained fixed. Mental images do not distinguish the difference between subjective and objective thoughts. My image of the apricot tree was not based on the external objective reality of the tree itself. The physicality of the real tree was changing under the natural laws of nature, but my mental image of the virtual tree was just that, a virtual reality of my mental process and nothing more. I tried to fit my virtual reality of the tree itself to the reality of the actual apricot tree because I used my idea-in-the-mind as *a directional force* for my belief, delusion or illusion of the tree itself. I had placed a gravitational primacy on my mind's thought over the external reality of the physical changes that take place in the natural world. Thus, when I protested to my grandmother that "this is not my apricot tree" what I was in fact doing was imposing my idea upon an external reality to match my mind's virtual reality. To paraphrase a 19th century philosopher: *"It is not our ideas that determine an existence, but the other way around."* In my case, the material reality of the tree was not in gravitational primacy–or a directional force–but it was the other way around.

To return to our main subject, we can say that secular naïve and destructive idealism place ideas in the mind as primary and the external reality as secondary. Therefore, material reality does not always correspond with naïve or destructive mental perceptions of it. Human relations are not simply manifest with wishful thinking, naiveté, or destructiveness. More often than not, the attempted imposition of ideas or ideals on external reality results in personal difficulties. The ideas of the "perfect man" "perfect woman" "perfect love" "perfect job" the "American Dream" "perfect family" or "I can have it all" are fixed ideas we attempt to impose on a world that is not fixed. Such an imposition is based on the logical fallacy in which a belief or wishful thinking is assumed to be in primacy over reality. Following a preferred personal belief, a belief from personal incredulity, is the same as following a belief derived from ignorance. Wishful thinking–which is distinct from hope– is the formation of ideas and beliefs that maintains that a person can make life's decisions in accordance with what might be pleasing to the "mind's eye" rather than by appealing to reality's achievable possibilities.

Promoters who benefit from secular or religious idealism interpret facts, reports, events, perceptions etc., according to what their social agenda dictates. It is done intentionally and without regard to objective truth. Their basic premise or goal is to control the public's idealism which, in turn, would direct people to designated mental and physical behaviors. For example, commercial advertisers know how to implant suggestive ideas in the public's mind to purchase a product or service, regardless of the obscurity of the service or the lack of usefulness of the product. The ideal "shop until you drop" is an implanted image in the mind of an idealist consumer, which is relatively an easy task. Advertisers know how to sell to the consumer the "idea" of the product **first**–since the idea is primary to the consumer and the practical/material usefulness of the product itself, is **secondary**.

The dialectics of the natural world show that reality is completely independent of our virtual perception of it, because reality is external and objective and does not depend on what we think or believe. This means that physical reality is measurable and verifiable, and we can base our mental conclusions and decisions correctly upon it. This also means that what we think of our social surroundings has no effect on reality itself, but our physical/practical actions do. For example, whether we think the natural world is in *constant change*–matter in motion–or static in accordance to our thoughts, has no impact on the lifecycle of the world's motion and change. This means that our "virtual" perception of reality is at best at a constant level of "trial and error"–a motion and change in itself–which can also be called personal or life experience. Our dialectical experiences shape our capacity to deal with our natural and/or social world through passive or active observations of it. The best that we can do is to dialectically perceive reality as accurately as possible, recognizing that human participatory mimesis is included so that we can make the best possible personal decisions. Our virtual perception does not create objects or things nor does it change the laws of nature but rather it is the external natural and social reality that stimulates our thoughts i.e., *Matter over Mind*.

Grammatical structure is the primary basis of either naïve or destructive idealism, which often uses the term "believe" or "believes" as a substitute for evidence and an investigation of reality. The term "believe" of course, is a non-investigatory term. Taking an action based on a belief is simply a delusion motivated by idealism's fallacy of mind over matter. Secular idealists are trapped in their own belief bubble, where one's subjective beliefs can "create" or manufacture a degree of false objectivity. For this person, reality and praxis are secondary. For example, going to work everyday is not based on the reality of the external necessities for producing the means of your daily subsistence. The falsity lies in the delusion that it is one's beliefs that are the directional force and that one's physical actions are simply part of his/her mental process. With the misuse of language, mental processes can be re-directed and the term "material reality" substituted to mean "perception" of it. Thus, the terms "believe" and "reality" become synonymous to mean "my reality," "your reality," where each human being–of the earth's six billion–has and can live in "his/her" own reality. This implies that the natural universe–external reality–exists in the mind only and that reality is only what you believe it to be (unless one has to go to the bathroom where thoughts alone do not count). Idealists contend that one's beliefs do not need to be tested or verified because this would be pointless. Those beliefs do not require evidence since your beliefs are "self-proving"–your beliefs should be trusted because you are the "creator" of those beliefs.

Secular idealists carry on the religious idealists' mental framework regarding the illusion of mind over matter. Both believe that mind rules over matter, or the physical is ruled by the spiritual, or that the physical laws of nature are actually governed by the mental processes of the mind. It follows that the physical laws of the universe are governed by a universal or infinite mind. This infinite mind turns out to be God's superior mind. This God's superior mind determines what the physical laws of nature are or are not. I often ponder whether a religious idealist who believes in such absurdities will attempt to defy the physical laws of gravity by jumping off a tall building to

Prisoners of our Ideals

prove that "mind rules over matter." Will his mental consciousness control and avoid undesirable consequences? Will his reality "within himself" defy the external reality or will mental thoughts literally control external reality?

The problem which idealists face today is that they are open to mental abuse. This is because they believe in the primacy of their ideas. This is the core intellectual weakness that is exploited by ideologues of all sorts who implant the "right" ideas in people's minds in order to entice them to behave in a particular way. Predatory mortgage lending is promoted by financiers who sell the "idea" of easy mortgage terms. Ponzi schemes are successful because the schemer sells the "idea" of "above average" profits to those who place the primacy of the idea of quick profits over the material reality of financial conditions. Commercial advertisers sell the "idea" of the product attached to mental sentiments/vanities instead of the affordability/practicality of the product itself.

One can envision a materialist and a naïve idealist looking at the same advertised product–a car for example. An idealist would be influenced by the image formed in his/her mind of the car and by the wishful thinking of the "ideal" benefits from it. A materialist may also like the fancy car, but he/she would also look at affordability, payment structure, mechanical services, safety record etc. If we look further at the housing crisis of mortgage foreclosures in the US during 2008-2010, most people "liked" the house based on the delusion of the "aesthetics," the "feeling" of owning a house or of being part of the "American Dream." These people bought the house based on the primacy of mental satisfaction–and lost the house because they could not afford it. While these good people were "victims" of their naïve idealism, they were also victims of destructive idealism practiced by the real estate/mortgage agents. They bought the "idea" of owning a house because they were impressed by the illusionary image, the delusional benefits installed in their minds by those who knew the power of destructive idealism. This is a common delusion of "Mind over Matter."

In religious circles, well-paid zealots, televangelists, fanatical cultists and gurus of all sorts also practice destructive idealism by implanting various delusional beliefs or fears, false morality and clone behavior for all. The "inner world" is taught to be the only one worthwhile; the outer physical world is secondary or of no importance. Fear of birth control is another example: Catholic dogma opposes birth control because the outdated Bible's Genesis 1:22-28 states that God told man to go "forth and multiply." Threats of violence and actual killings of doctors practicing abortion, dangers to women's bodies and health, and overpopulation in many Catholic-influenced societies becomes non-issues for believers of this dogma. One needs only to look at the brutal actions taken against medical personnel by those who kill in the name of an invisible God. The "idea" of killing in the name of God is primary; the physical human tragedy caused against the "other" is secondary. Thus, destructive idealist beliefs (ideas) are the *directional force* of believers whose actions cause environmental and human consequences.

Destructive idealism includes economics as a belief system. Economics in our contemporary society functions not as a science serving humanity's needs, but as an activity of a secular faith. The theory of perpetual economic growth is based on faith, not whether it is true or false, harmful to human health or harmful to the environment, or that multinational corporations destroy the indigenous production of local food supplies and manufacturing. In place of genuine scientific research, disinterested aggressive special interests are employed–against the public good–to support the delusional pride of the CEOs who bring it about. It is hardly fitting that they should be celebrated for their "courage" and "intelligence" or for their faith in globalism, while not realizing that their destructive idealist principle of "ever-growth" applies only to terminal cancer. We all share the responsibility for the destructive idealism and for the justification of economic activities that assumes that eventually there will be harmony between their corporate interests and the public good.

Observation of facts shows that achieving equilibrium between normal profits and optimal resource allocation for millions of employed persons has not been achieved. When corporations become "too big to fail" they tend to wield great economic and political power. They tend to distort and manipulate their financial products to a point bordering on legalized fraud at the expense of many unsuspecting investors. Recognizing the illegitimacy of this trend is to bring about recognition that the present economics, as a belief system, is not politically and socially neutral. This belief system is an integral part of an overall tendency to persuade the rest of us to avert our eyes from the reality of material consequences.

Another area that needs genuine scientific investigation is the effects that destructive-idealism has upon children and youth, especially regarding "entertainment" in the "virtual reality" of deadly electronic games. Multimedia violence portrayed in violent games on the Internet and in home consoles, such as Play Station is associated with the highest level of youth delinquency. This is the expert conclusion of 650 professors, school teachers, youth counselors and parents at the 2009 conference *"Computer Games and Violence"* sponsored by Munich College for Applied Sciences. The central conclusion of all these expert studies shows that an alteration of one's emotional stability, beliefs, feelings, and attitudes takes place via the violent games played on the computer.

The "virtual reality" of these games that moulds a youth's belief system is a destructive idealism. Young people are affected by the frequent re-enforcement of aggression. A youth's brain has not developed to the stage of knowing the aftermaths or consequences of violent acts such as killing another person. The scientific community no longer debates this issue related to youth violence. Their evidence puts any doubt to rest. Violence is aggression that aims to harm another person intentionally, whether at home, on the street, or at war against the "other." The destructive-idealism of the virtual reality of games which glorify violence constitutes a learning process and teens learn and believe what they are taught.

Learning processes take place by means of reading, writing, studying, viewing, and experiencing. Humans employ different means of learning depending on the intended task. For example, the military embraces electronic "virtual" war games as a means for training new army recruits. Combat soldiers "fight" in a virtual Afghanistan and Iraq as they remain in a safe environment at their training stations. For many new recruits under virtual reality combat training, it often seems like the closest thing to being in real combat.

Most recruits who grew up on popular consumerist virtual war games have a "natural" familiarity with the war games in army training and can easily adapt to them. As recruited soldiers, they learn better skills to virtually kill an enemy under combat situations. The army attempts to prepare recruits mentally for their task ahead. There is a genuine excitement in playing war games in the increasingly realistic virtual reality of "killing" the enemy. Or is there? Some military trainers express their professional concerns that the more the electronic games seem like war, the more the real war may be seen as a game. The more delusions virtual reality strengthens, the more believable, they say, it becomes. For example, LT. Gen. William S. Wallace, the commander of the Army V Corps based in Kuwait, noted that the guerrilla tactics of the Iraqi resistance groups was "different from the ones we war-gamed against." The point here–for our purpose–is that the destructive idealism of virtual reality war did not fit in with the external reality of the Iraqi or, in fact, the Afghanistan guerrilla war tactics.

Here we have a classic case of the contradiction between idealism and realism, or a contradiction between the metaphorical assumption of war and the literal interpretation of war. Destructive-idealism takes hold on the soldier who is so habituated to the "games war" that the external reality of war is equated with the artificial or virtual. This may result in his/her death because he/she is not actually game-warring from the safety of the training school.

Moreover, since the soldier is a product of an idealist system of thought, he/she becomes a trained soldier under the impact of delusion brought about through virtual reality. When the real war does not fit with the idealist war game, he/she will just keep trying to make the reality of the war correspond with the virtual reality of the game. Remember, "virtual reality" is an idea-in-mind that, for the idealist, is primary—*and a directional force*—that must be fit into reality (because the real world is regarded as secondary). The effects of destructive idealism on the soldier's mental confusion—or trauma—can be long-lasting.

The contradiction of war's external reality and the twisted virtual or ideal perception of it would increase the soldier's psychological anxiety. This is the beginning of post-traumatic disorder or, as the older soldiers used to call it "shell shock." It is an emotional reaction to an extreme psychological trauma. As a result of so many soldiers suffering post-traumatic disorder, in the summer of 2009 USA Army brass adopted "reality" psychological training to help soldiers strengthen their mental capacity. Of course, "reality" training is not simply educational, but a dialectical training of life's material processes. It remains to be seen how these military courses on reality will open the soldier's eyes. A large proportion of war casualties occur due to the fact that soldiers are essentially trained to fit a virtual reality in to the material reality of war where nothing is simulated. The only way a soldier can learn about war is by practicing his/her skills while in real war combat. This is the only way to become mature or battle-tested soldiers, and these soldiers are more likely to survive. Such soldiers have been tested by reality's experience of trial and error during combat.

We must note that computer virtual war games do not teach the recruit how to walk and camouflage through thick grass, what to think while walking through thick grass, or the relative precautions needed to be taken while walking through thick grass. In addition, in virtual reality it doesn't hurt when a soldier gets shot. It's a simulation. It's a mental image of "something" that does not exist. War is about the physical reality of the killing of men, not about hitting a command with a keyboard and a mouse.

Idealism, whether naïve or destructive, is about the distortion of material reality. The "goodness" or "badness" of both can be discovered objectively. How? Planning, analyzing, thinking, proposing, imagining, feeling emotionally attached and most other emotional sentiments are mental images. These need to be tried out because they are the complementary opposites of external reality. Future thinking processes must be worked through on the basis of their material consequences first, and how these mental conclusions benefit or harm one's person or humanity at large. A balanced thinking process occurs as follows:

A dialectical materialist system of thought starts with an external premise balanced by mental opposites. To lean extremely strongly upon one or the other, would cause the negation of one or the other. Acting and thinking must be reciprocal to thinking and acting. Any changes that are required must be necessitated by the effect of external conditions upon mental thoughts, and not the other way around. Believing in something does not make it true or false.

Naïve idealism practiced by children and most artists is qualified as "beneficial" within the realm of the mental imagination. This means that naïve idealism is secondary to the infinity of the elegance of reality. In the arts, no amount of imagination is worth a penny while it is "housed" within the artist's brain alone. There is no such a thing as "pure" art that can only exist within the brain's functions. This is because the "mind" is not a separate entity from the brain. The largest imaginary world an idealist can build in his/her mind can never be larger than the size of the grey cells in the brain.

The term "mind" is a metaphorical and consolidated word. The "mind" is not a literal, observable entity; it is not a fluid or a solid; it is not measurable; does not have a temperature, shape or color nor does it occupy space. Idealists have failed to recognize that when a single concept like "mind" becomes so broad as to include worlds which do not exist, like Hell and Heaven, God and Angels, Saints and Satan, and, in short, to encompass everything "spiritual," then the concept becomes meaningless. One must remember that metaphorical concepts are mental concepts, for they are abstract concepts making idiomatic translations nearly impossible. So, when you and I use metaphors when speaking or writing, we need to remember that the "price of a metaphor is eternal vigilance."

Naïve idealism entices children to think creatively, to imagine pleasantries that construct friendly metaphorical entities. This is a natural starting point where the material world provides the bodily identity of imaginary things. For example, the metaphorical concept of "Santa Claus" is built upon the bodily identity of a real man, with a white beard, who passes gifts to all the world's children in a single night. He knows "if you've been bad or good," and so on. Without a real bodily identity and function–matter in motion–the metaphorical concept of "Santa Claus" is "mentally pure," and thus meaningless and non-existent.

Literally speaking, we know that the naïve-idealism of "Santa Claus" is a distortion of reality. When we look at the concept more closely we see that parents do maintain a natural balance between the opposites of naïve idealism vs. the bodily reality of a man. This balance of opposites is beneficial and non-destructive because it does not extremely lean on one opposite or the other. This balance is cultural more than it is social. It is an integral part of the cultural aesthetics of childhood.

The same principle applies to metaphorical storytelling in areas of dancing, writing, painting, or in pictorial weaving. Secular naïve idealism, therefore, is essentially cultural. It is not social or political, for it does not dictate behavioral manners or lifestyles, does not have governing laws, and does not demand obedience under the threat of punishment. The latter describes destructive idealism.

When does cultural naïve idealism become socially destructive idealism? Destructive idealism is an all inclusive mix and match of delusional anti-humanist, semi-cultural, and socio-political propagations with an irrational agenda. It is singular and extremely one-sided. It negates nearly everything that is in balance with a related opposite. I sincerely hope, metaphorically speaking, that this very brief analysis has raised legitimate questions in the way you and I use or (God forbid!) believe in how metaphors are real, whether in naïve or destructive idealist thinking.

3

CONSEQUENCES OF DESTRUCTIVE IDEALISM

"When did I realize I was God? Well, I was praying and I suddenly realized I was talking to myself."

Unknown

"Our [religious] ideals, like the gods of old, are constantly demanding human sacrifices."

George Bernard Shaw

One important question we must ask before analyzing the effects and destructiveness that religious idealism has on our natural environment is this: Are organized religions and cults culpable for acting upon what they believe to be God's laws, even if such laws cause enormous human suffering and environmental destruction?

In male-dominated religions such as Christianity, Judaism and Islam, women and children were historically regarded as possessions of the household patriarch. When these religions became the dominant socio-political power in their respective societies, the point that a religious justification for bondage polygamy was fabricated is difficult to deny.

Let's investigate a set of polygamist cults. In the *Buffalo News*, Oct. 23, 2008, a former member of the Fundamentalist Church of Jesus Christ of Latter-day Saints (FCLDS), Sara Hammon, told reporter Barbara O'Brian:

"There are 95 people in my family. Seventy-five children and 19 mothers, and my father. We were nothing like the normal, average family....On his deathbed, my dad tried to sexually abuse me..."

She further stated:

"My father's last marriage, when he was 68, was to a 17-year old."

Rulon Jeffs, president and "prophet" of the FCLDS, is married to 19 wives and has fathered more than 60 children. Warren Jeffs has 22 wives and 60 children. Winston Blackmore, leading member of FCLDS, has 26 wives and has fathered more than 80 children. In Tel Aviv, Israel, Goel Ratzon has 32 wives and 89 children. These five men have fathered 364 children in total.

Polygamy is rampant in the Christian Bible. For example, it is stated in Genesis 26:34 that *"When Esau was forty years old, he married Judith, daughter of Beeri the Hittite, and also Basemath, daughter of Elon the Hittite"*, in Genesis 4:23-24: *" Lamech said to his wives, Adah and Zillah, listen to me; wives of Limech..."* and in **Kings** 11: 1-3, King Solomon is described as having 700 wives of royal birth and 300 concubines.

The Qur'an in Sura 4:3 says:

"And if you be apprehensive that you will not be able to do justice to the orphans, you may marry two or three or four women whom you choose."

Muhammad, of course, had the power to marry more than four wives. He was married to nine wives, one of whom entered his household carrying her toys because she was only nine years old. In Sura 4:129**,** the institution of polygamy is further entrenched with this passage:

"Allah made it clear that the husband cannot literally keep equality between two or more wives because they themselves cannot be equal in all respects. It is too much to demand from a husband that he should mete out equal treatment to a beautiful wife and to an ugly wife, to a young wife and to an old wife, to a healthy wife and to an invalid wife, and to a good natured wife and to an ill-tempered wife. Those and like things naturally make a husband more inclined towards one wife than towards the other."

There is a common perception among social thinkers that the institution of religious polygamy was instituted to deal with an excess of females in the population. This overpopulation was the result of (predominantly male) war casualties. Widows and unmarried women within a tribe might still be cared for by their immediate families, but giving them away in marriage was preferable to bearing the cost of feeding and protecting them.

Thus, a social system of multiple wives was encouraged and dressed up by religions as being blessed by God. Religious idealism accommodates external reality to its "ideals." The Christian and Hebrew Bibles and the Muslim Qur'an contain myriad stories illustrating the system of polygamy. Since women and children were regarded as the property of the patriarch, wives were signs of wealth and power and were also the objects of negotiations. Marriages were negotiated and arranged between families or between competing tribes to strengthen land claims and political ties. Those ties were often sealed by the higher leading classes, such as kings and heads of multiple tribes. The patriarchs of ancient Israel–Abraham, Isaac, Jacob and Joseph–were all polygamists.

While polygamy is the legal inclusive definition of multiple wives, there is also a religious history of the widespread use of mistresses, as in (among others) the case of King Solomon's 300 concubines. While religious institutions morally blessed marriages between a man and multiple wives, those same religions condoned the morality of sexual activities outside of marriage. Any official sexual restriction that limited conception to faithful marriage was a well-entrenched double standard of morality. There was public understanding that religious institutions condoned the extra-marital sexual activities of men. Those were not regarded as cardinal sins. In 2009, this double standard of religious morality is very much entrenched within polygamist offshoots of Mormonism, in that sexual activities with under-age females is permitted and encouraged, with resulting pregnancies viewed as acceptable. There are approximately 100,000 Christian polygamists in the U.S.A alone.

The over-breeding that once deeply infused tribal religions in pre-Islamic regions and the Middle East was subsequently adopted by the Roman Catholic Church. The Vatican's holy fecundity policy has had an overwhelming impact on struggling families throughout the Latin world and other parts of the globe, as birth after birth is endured by males and females devoted to their religious dogmas. The teaching of unprotected procreation as God's divine command is simply contrary to any sort of artificial birth control aimed at subduing over-breeding.

Religious traditions have contributed to humanity's over-breeding by propagating the "Word of God," which commanded believers to be *"fruitful and multiply,"* but disastrous environmental results were not expected. It has always been the tendency of all three major religions to encourage large families. The believers, who were the majority of the earth's population, were thus urged by the Torah, Bible and Qur'an's main message to be fruitful and multiply. For example, God's favoured believer, Jacob, was singled out to receive special breeding instructions:

*"I am God Almighty: be fruitful and multiply; a nation and a company of nations shall be of thee, and kings shall come out of thy loins." (*Genesis 35:11*)*

Jacob's multiplication of sons and daughters yielded the twelve tribes of Israel and in accordance with Exodus 1:7, *"they were fruitful, and abundantly increased and multiplied, and waxed exceeding mighty; the land was filled with them."*

Religious apologists have suggested that the word "multiply" has been misinterpreted by humanity, whose over-breeding levels were and are critical, and that to multiply does not relate to God's command because it is only a figure of speech. This begs the question over the true meaning of the message; the disastrous and far-reaching implications for the planet can be blamed on the propagators of the Word of God, which commanded the believers to multiply.

Another obscure religious claim for humanity's over-breeding levels is based on the supposed ignorance of believers that the mathematical concept of multiply was not understood as an increase of offspring, because numbers were not known by believers. In any case, in a tribal family and community, multiply (growth or increase) has resulted in over-breeding, and it is ridiculous to suggest that the unrestricted increase in the growth of offspring resulted because believers could not count.

Are contemporary religious institutions responsible for their criminal ignorance in their obsession with the inability to tell their meek and gullible believers about the legitimacy of birth control? Can anyone in the three religious institutions say that the Word of God has had a disastrous consequence that has brought about environmental destruction due to humanity's over breeding? Is it not time that religious leaders of all three major religions raise the issue of consequences such as the destructiveness of the earth's environment at a terrifying cost, and that such terms as unrestricted as "be fruitful and multiply" are no longer valid?

Religious advocates propagated God's first command to multiply. Be fruitful and multiply was intended to drive the message home to humans that they are the dominant force over all other animals and plants and that they could subdue them at will. What do those words mean to contemporary people who obey them? What is the human experience that is drawn to obey God's words to continue with over-breeding? Why has such an absurd message gained so much power that religious believers still believe that God has commanded them to continue to be fruitful and multiply? Granted, the message to be fruitful and multiply has, over the last 3,000 years, diminished in urgency. But the environmental consequences of humanity's over-breeding are still relevant.

According to various anthropologists, by 1560 CE the human population on earth was just over one billion. It then took about

400 years for the population to reach, by the mid-1930s, the 3 billion mark. By 2009, human population reached over 6 billion. Such an explosion in human population has forced cultivated land to be overproduced, per acre or hectare, in order to meet the ever-growing demand. We are forced to use chemical fertilizers to revive productive land. We use tractors and combines and overuse irrigation systems. We are concerned about the ever-increasing organic and non-organic waste, chemical spills and smog in our atmosphere.

Overpopulation has indeed been overwhelming, as a brief look at human history will reveal. Human beings have dominated the earth to the point that our numbers have expanded in every direction of the globe. We have forced the agricultural land to produce more and more. We have developed large agricultural machinery to extract more products faster from the land itself, with signs of nutritional exhaustion showing. We have then found ways to "revive" the land with a variety of dangerous fertilizers. We have created a complex highway system to accommodate the demand for cars, trucks and RVs. We use combustion engines for all of the above, as well as for lawnmowers, leaf blowers, recreational snowmobiles, golf carts, small airplanes and helicopters.

In order to meet the demand for more food, we have genetically modified products of livestock, poultry, fish and vegetables. These expanding human activities that are related to land production and the environment are performed under a biblical calling. This calling's **mimetic** religious message was transmitted from and hosted by both religious and secular idealists who believed that human life was the only kind that needed to be preserved at the expense of all other forms of life.

By today's standards of rapid economic growth, China and India are accelerating their manufacturing capacities to meet not only their national demand but also the global one. Environmental disasters are common occurrences in the mining sector of the Chinese economy. Also, air pollution is caused by burning dirty coal that the Chinese use to generate production in factories. So much for their ideal of "Worker's Paradise." The Chinese and Indians want a standard of living equal to that of Western consumerist societies. They desire cars, electrical home appliances, phones and computers that are available in the West. Our ever-excessive Western lifestyle has demonstrated our dominance on our side of the earth, and leaves us with little or no moral grounds to demand that the developing nations curb their own appetites for consumer goods.

At the peril of appearing an alarmist, I wish to ask whether we have the ability and willingness to take the drastic steps necessary to avoid the upcoming environmental disaster, before the only earthly home we have is pushed over the edge the destruction. Can such environmental and human tragedies be averted? Are we willing to place a limitation on human overbreeding? Are we willing to influence the educational system to begin teaching our children about the dangers of obeying the Word of God, and the supposedly divine command to be fruitful and multiply? Are we willing to describe the current environmental destruction as human genocide? Are we willing to teach our children that the religious idealism of the Word of God has been, and still is, a terrible and destructive message disguised as divine and holy? The "World of Humanity" must be an inclusive text of conservation of the earthly environment and of all that lives in it. This will save us from an upcoming disaster.

The natural world is reacting against the destructive attitude and practice of a single species that has acted to be fruitful and multiply and to dominate the earth. The human race has practiced the religious ideology of destruction and has regarded the world as if its exclusive existence was to provide comfort and wealth to human beings. Our current secular idealism, without religiosity, continues to propagate the dominance of the earth to the point of exploitation beyond which there is no possibility of recovery. God's chosen leaders of ancient tribes who lived in comfort and wealth have today been replaced by secularism's chosen multimillionaires and billionaires. They hold the same view and position that says that the natural world is at their disposal because they can afford to pay and over-consume the earth's resources.

DESTRUCTIVE-IDEALISM AND THE HUMAN SOCIAL ENVIRONMENT

The ideology of religious destructive idealism has had enormous consequences for the human race. The Judeo-Christian and Muslim ideology has never demonstrated any environmental concerns for the natural world. Their religious ideology was and is still focused on Man himself. It treats him as a separate entity from the natural world, which only exists in order to be dominated by him. Such a focus on Man was not based on a benevolent set of ideas, but on his self-degradation. Man's life itself was sinful and unworthy. Man, who was created by God, was born in sin and was a fallen creature. There was nothing good or decent about him, and thus, Man was and still is in the perpetual need of being rescued by God's representatives on earth. Everything about Man is regarded as bad and evil, and the only "good" a man can do is by being religiously domesticated and obedient to religious dogma. That being so, every effort must be made–by atheists and humanists–to educate the public about the cancerous growth of religious sickness and about self-destruction.

Religious ideologies written in the Bible, Torah and Qur'an have always regarded the natural world and Man himself primarily through divine revelation. That is, God who rules this earth from a position outside the boundaries of the natural universe is divine. This biblical claim is that God is not of this world. Man also is not of this world, because Man was created in the divine image of God. Thus, God's command to Man to subdue this natural world was justified, since Man was not part of it. Believers, who viewed the divine world (heaven) as being God's world, viewed Earth as an enemy that needed to be subdued. Only an alienated species from this world would regard earth as unworthy or of any consideration. Since the "other world" is where all believers will be invited to live an eternal perfect life, this natural world and its entire species is a temporal one of no real value. Periodically, this supernatural God would invade this world in a "miraculous" way in order to control the weather by flooding the earth for 40 days, or by taking a strategic position against the Egyptians, the political enemies of His chosen people of Israel.

So powerful was this misleading biblical description of the human situation on earth, that ultimately it prevented people from seeing the myth of the miraculous virgin birth of a God-infused human, Jesus. Since this God-infused human was not of this world, he was launched by resurrection-propulsion back to the other world above the clouds and into the cosmic sky.

This **mimetic** religiosity was transmitted from father to son, from mother to daughter, from tribe to tribe, from visitors to travelers, and was hosted by the ignorant, the meek and the dominant classes. The latter took advantage of people's fear and inclination towards obedience. Their sense of security needs "survival" and nothing else would do as an alternative to submission. Today's human beings recognize that there is no supernatural God that exists in the other world. Yet, the same people may still believe in the belief "just in case." My grandson, for example, tells me that he does not believe in organized religion, yet he "believes" in the one God, although this monotheistic God was invented by organized religion. He simply separates the idea-God from the religious institution of the Church, and it is by this claim that he is able to speak of God without having to explain the notoriously bloody history of the Church. As such, the idea-God remains immaculately clean of any crimes committed in His name. This interplay of ideas-in-the-mind is fundamental to idealism. The divorce of one idea from another with no inter-connectivity and process between them is its basic delusion.

In fact, this divorce between the idea-God and the **praxis** of religious authorities has been used by apologists to justify crimes committed in the name of God. For centuries, practicing Jews, Christians, Muslims and Hindus, as well as believers of other faiths, have committed the most atrocious war crimes in the name of their God and their own religious brand of faith. Not only that, but they have often done so by divorcing their acts from what their sacred texts (ideas) dictated to them as the correct way in which to live. The extermination of Muslims in Jerusalem in 1099 or in Srebrenica in 1995 or the Islamist imperial conquest and domination of North Africa and Spain are acts that separate the idea of the benevolent, the compassioned and the all good God from the **praxis**-of-war crimes. For Christians, this is hardly compatible with the Ten Commandments, two of which command people to love their neighbours and not to kill. Muslim warriors were perpetually on the march while conquering new territory from 632 to 1683. This period of more than a thousand years was related to conquering and the hoarding of wealth rather than to introducing their compassionate God to others. In fact, Islam is, and always has been, a religion of power. Hindu fanatics periodically kill Christians or Muslims in India.

Believers tend to accept the delusion that their God will always be on their side. Religious authorities get away with excessive claims that they can speak for God with certainty, in order to keep human doubts in check. Their job is to recreate God and seek a more adequate definition to justify new claims. Thus, the once supernatural God who lived beyond the natural universe is no longer external and of the other world, but internal. Does this mean that all believers, whether Jewish, Muslim, Christian or Hindu, have their own individual kind of God within themselves?

Religious idealism throughout history has directed believers to look upward for a God above the sky. Intelligent people know that our infinite natural universe does not house supernatural invisible Gods or saints. So why does idealism redirect believers to shift their attention to a new "housing" of God within the framework of our natural world? Are religious authorities attempting to "fix" our natural world by re-introducing "God's good religion" as being a part of the solution to our current grave environmental situation which they had once contemptuously deemed worthless?

Destructive idealism is also directed against women and children, and it is not limited to the Muslim and Judeo-Christian sects alone. What is necessary to point out, however, is that **misogyny** was channeled through religion and has entered other secular segments of our human environment. This realization revives the fact that there is something ingrained within the religious core that fuels discrimination against women and children. **Patriarchy** (and gender bias) has been practiced by religious schools (known as madrasa) in the Muslim world and by secularist idealists for many centuries, and young males are being taught to be hostile towards women. One of the leaders of 9/11, Atta, wrote, in his final letter to his parents, that he did not wish women to visit his grave.

Ancient Greek idealists have probably best stated the universality of anti-gender notions against women. Socrates, for example, is recorded as saying:

"Do you know anything at all practiced among mankind in which the male sex is not far better than the female?"

The idealist Xenophon said:

"The ideal woman should see as little as possible, hear as little as possible and ask as little as possible."

In Islamic societies we know that a woman is regarded as "half man" and that *"forgetfulness overcome the woman...they are inherently weaker in rational judgment."*

In legal issues, a woman who has claimed domestic abuse against her husband must have four male witnesses to a man's requirement of only two. In Jewish religious prayers, boys are taught to pray:

"Blessed be to God who has not created me a heathen, a slave or a woman...It would be better to burn the words of Torah than to entrust them to a woman."

There are a variety of theories as to why secular Greek philosophers or religious idealists have had such overwhelming negative views of women. Ideas may vary, but the mistreatment of women was, and still is, a reality. Some anthropologists who have studied ancient traditions suggest that there was a time in human history when fertility gods were the source and sustainers of tribal life. In time, the male image of God, who lived beyond the sky and had impregnated the passive fertility god, set out a new relationship between tribal males and females. The thrusting of the male organ into a female partner was identified as a powerful male act of the sky god, whose strength was modeled after male-dominant roles in tribal societies.

One of the most prominent anti-female advocates was Saint Paul, who claimed that the Word of God led to the "rightful" treatment of women. Paul's advocacy is little more than a guiding text for women's oppression. In fact, Paul plagiarized the words from Genesis 2:20-23, an ancient Jewish source, to support his pervasive views of women and construct an anti-female base within the New Testament. It was man, NOT woman, who was made in the image of God, for woman was made from Adam's rib. All three major religions fail to consider a woman an independent person. Since this has been such an integral religious view, its influence continues to be strong in defining the sexes to this day in our secular society. One tribal story in a tribal society has resulted in real human consequences that are felt throughout our secular world.

Furthermore, God put Adam in charge of all the animals that were his subjects and of Eve, who was a part of his body (his rib). Adam had named her, as he had named all of the earth's animals. Since all animals and the woman Eve were NOT made in God's image, the man-Adam held his dominant status because of his divine image of God. The animals and the natural environment were to be dominated by man and so was the woman. She was taken out of his body; she was kin (the animals were not); she was his playmate and an obedient and subservient being, which accepted his male sperm into her and relieved his sexual desires. So this was the beginning of the hierarchy and patriarchy, institutions in accordance with biblical narrative law in the relationship between the sexes. Theirs was a **mimetic** relationship of the dominant male to the submissive female, the superior to the inferior, the master of the household to the servant. This was the religious structural order, which was regarded as God's order and purpose. This is all that believers needed to obey for not violate or modify God's plan.

So the stage was set for a second religious system that followed the path started by the Judaist ideology of **patriarchy**–Christianity and later Islam. Islam installed centuries old **mimesis** of discrimination and misguided suppositions onto the human population. Females were taught to be submissive and that their only purpose in life was to fulfill the purpose given to them by God. Thus, a woman's role was to obey the superior man, to accept punishment from the patriarch, to accept that she was much less intelligent than her master and not capable of being educated. Taliban's laws state that women do not to have equal social and legal rights to those of man.

Secular laws that guarantee legal rights between the sexes cannot, as yet, sway away the traditions set by religious institutions so many centuries ago. This is true even today as those religious definitions are still propagated by religious institutions whose stronghold over their believers is reflected by its impact within secular society. Preachers and priests, evangelists and televangelists, polygamists, cultists and rabbis, imams and Hindu holy men, Catholics and Protestants, still sound the Words of God and verses of their holy books to keep intact the active holy laws regarding male superiority and female inferiority.

This **mimetic** propagation slowly but surely turned **patriarchy** into **misogyny** in Latin American nations, Afghanistan, Pakistan etc., where women of all ages are still dealing with its effects. Can those religions be permitted to propagate against universal human rights and define women as sub-human or second class by religious definition? Should those tribal religions of the once ancient tribal societies be allowed to go on? Should such ignorant tribal religions continue to regard women as being "created" by a ignorant tribal God that blames women for every human sin?

RELIGIOUS BIGOTRY AND FEMALE SEXUALITY

Every major institutionalized religion has degraded women's existence as viable human beings. This has been the case from the ancient desert tribal communities to 20th century religious groups. Pat Robertson, a leading right-wing evangelist, in his 1992 fundraising letter to his supporters wrote:

"The [woman's human rights] agenda is not about equal rights for women. It is about a socialist, anti-family political

movement that encourages women to leave their husbands, kill their children, practice witchcraft, destroy capitalism, and become lesbians."

Religious bigotry against women has always been about their sexuality, about being dirty because of sexual contact with men and about being guilty because of Eve's "original sin," which every woman on earth has inherited. That is, all women except the Virgin Mary. The basic lie is of an immaculately conceived virgin who delivered the Son of God. Yes, such a myth can be found in other religions before Christianity. The Greek god Perseus was born when his father, the God Jupiter, visited Danah who had a virgin birth. Buddha was not delivered through a virgin birth, but through his mother's side, between her rib and hip. The God Attis was delivered by his virgin mother Nana, and so was Genghis Khan. Krishna was born from the virgin Devaka. Mercury, Horus, Romulus and others were all born from a virgin mother.

Christian religious bigotry against women revealed the Virgin Mother Mary as its ideal woman. All other women were to be compared to her. Since it is quite impossible due to a woman's biology to be both a virgin and a mother, tribal and contemporary women are, by religious definition, not as ideal as the "virgin" Mary. Such a pervasive contradiction does not have a rational solution because, on the one hand, mothers were bearing sons and daughters to fulfill their biblical duty. On the other hand, they were bearing children by biological necessity, which meant that their virginal purity had to be destroyed. With the ideal of "Virgin Mother," all other mothers were incomplete, unfulfilled and carriers of the original sin.

In destructive-idealism, whether religious or secular, every ideal claim is possible, because the emphasis is on the idea and belief rather than on its physical reality. In Galatians 1:19 in the Bible, James is identified as being Jesus' brother, and in

Mark 6:3, Jesus' brothers are identified as James, Joseph, Judas and Simon. Some sisters are also identified. So the virgin myth that was developed by Christianity in the ninth decade (90 years after Jesus' birth) by Matthew and Luke has inflicted real pain on women for the last 20 centuries. The Catholic Church's obsession with the ideal virgin-birth can be witnessed by the forceful demand on its believers NOT to question such a stupid claim. Pope Pius IX, in 1854, set the ground rules saying:

"We declare, pronounce and define that the doctrine which holds that the Blessed Virgin Mary, at the first instant of her conception, by a singular privilege and grace of the....God, in virtue of the merits of Jesus Christ,...was preserved immaculate from all stain of original sin...and therefore should firmly and constantly be believed by all the faithful."

But how was the next step to be taken in explaining the virgin myth when Mary was not of immaculate birth herself? Mary, like all women, was a child of Adam and Eve's original sin, in which the world's women were regarded as fallen. The deceptive trick was to present Mary as **de-sexed** as possible by over-propagating her holiness and by emphasizing her "extraordinary" birth. This extraordinary state was "established" by the Church's conclusion that Mary never died but was lifted into heaven in a god-like manner. By Mary's bodily "assumption," she escaped from God's punishment for the original sin. What about the rest of womankind that could not be divine or de-sexed? They could not be helped because religious bigotry has always regarded women as the source of evil.

In a male-dominated religious world, women have been blamed for many things. The ancient Hebrew, Greek and Muslim myths and sacred books have described women as having no intellectual abilities and having no interest in interpreting God's creation of life. Thus, women were intentionally excluded from cultural activities, socio-political decision-making processes and from explaining how the natural world worked. It is quite common even today in the majority of Muslim countries to blame women for everything bad that happens. If a male or a group of males rape a woman, it was because she has tempted him/them with a provocative attitude or appealing dress. Two things can happen in the case of rape. The woman can take the rapist to court with 4 male witnesses. She can face the deadly consequences of an "honour killing" for dishonoring the family by "allowing" a rape to take place. A rape can be prevented by having the woman wear a **burkha** to cover her body from head to toe. In a case where a woman dares to show modest flesh, public flogging is not uncommon. In Iran, a woman cannot touch a man's hand in public because the watchful eyes of the **morality police** will force her to follow "correct" behaviour. If a husband, brother or male relative abuses a female family member, it is because she brought it upon herself by irritating her male abuser.

For many centuries in Muslim Africa, young girls have been and still are subjected to the cruel act of circumcision or infibulation. This is outright child abuse. Female circumcision is without a doubt an extremely hideous painful act that involves the slicing off of the labia and the clitoris to prevent sexual pleasure in women. This mutilation is often performed with a sharp stone or unhygienic metal object. It is followed by the equally painful stitching up of the vagina's opening with strong yarn. This twine will stay in place and not be removed until it is broken by the thrust of a penis on the bridal night.

This act of female circumcision is a crime against humanity, human torture, a humiliation, and misery exceeding all imaginative cruelty against women. One thing is sure; no secular or atheist society would tolerate such a humiliating practice, for only in a religious society can this act be sanctified. One can accuse me of being a cultural imperialist for not respecting an ethnic culture and may feel that we must not interfere when a Muslim culture mutilates the female body.

I do not give a second thought about their "right" to bring up African girls in their own way. Human suffering is human suffering and I do not care under which religious and cultural justification it happens. No society should tolerate foul practices under any nonsensical religious claims.

The religious cult of Christian Science is known to deny medical care to its young children. Jehovah's Witnesses have constantly refused to allow their young children to have blood transfusions, even if they would die without one. Polygamist cults such as Mormons force their underage daughters to marry much older men who are already married to older women who have more than the normal number of children. The Muslim fundamentalist Shia, under the Iranian theocracy, allows girls of nine to marry and follow Mohammad's previous wife into his household. These pre-pubescent brides often brought their toys with them. Hindus in India can take child-brides who are frequently abused by being flogged, raped or burned alive. In the past 40 to 50 years, pedophile Catholic priests in Canada and the U.S.A have sexually abused aboriginal children on Indian reservations and residential schools. Other priests in large and small parishes were shielded from the law or were transferred to other parishes where new grounds for pedophiliac "pickings" of young children were an "inspiration" for those priests. The Catholic Church, whose powerful political influence is unimaginable, has prevented its priests from going to jail by spending over 500 million dollars for their defense or by paying off victims' parents for their silence.

The Muslim Taliban of Afghanistan are known to be against any improvements for girls and women. Typical of religious bigotry and anti-female attitudes, Muslim Taliban flog girls and women in public. During the Taliban's rule in Afghanistan from 1996 to 2001, girls were banned from attending school and from receiving public education. On November 14, 2008 in the Taliban's birthplace in Afghanistan, no female students showed up at Mirwai Mena's public school of 1,500 because religious believers attacked 15 girls and teachers with chloride acid. These religious attackers squirted the acid from water bottles at the girls as they were walking to school. Most girls were injured and left with scars on their faces and one teenager still cannot open her eyes after being attacked. On January 14, 2009, a schoolgirl named Shamsia Hussein and her sister were walking towards their school when a Taliban religious fanatic approached them asking if they were going to school. When the girls said they were, the man pulled off Shamsia's **burkha** and sprayed her face with burning acid. Jagged and discoloured scars have now spread across her eyelids and left cheek.

Judaism, Christianity, Islam and cults of all sorts have historically been and remain the greatest enemy of women's emancipation. In the Jewish-Christian Western world, the Old and New Testament verses in particular sum up their inferior position. In Genesis 3:16 it is stated:

"I will greatly multiply thy sorrow and thy conception in sorrow thou shalt bring forth children; and thy desire shall be to thy husband, and he shall rule over thee."

In the Bible's New Testament, 1.Tim. 2:11-14 decrees:

"Let the woman learn in silence with all subjection. But I suffer not a woman to teach, nor to usurp authority over the man, but to be in silence. For Adam was first formed, then Eve. And Adam was not deceived, but the woman being deceived was in the transgression."

The darkest side of Christianity was during the Reformation because of the severe physical oppression of women during witch-hunt persecutions. The Reformation did not try to convert Europeans to fundamentalist Christianity through preaching alone. It was a period from the 15th to the 18th centuries where between 200 and 500 thousand women accused of being witches were tortured and/or burned alive. The Church's **misogyny** was fully implemented in **theory and praxis** in an attempt to destroy what Christianity had been preaching for 1,500 years: an elaborate concept of **evil worship.** Devil and Satan, saints and purgatory, punishment and suffering, denigration of women and the justification of human slavery were all Christianity's form of educating its delusional believers. As a result, a mass delusional hostile ideology was established that was directed against any deviational worship, which was also fed by the Bible's misogynist advocacy.

The witch-hunts were an eruption of fundamentalism that for hundreds of years explained why Christian women deserved their inferior status as human beings. This religious ideology became institutionalized, as the **Inquisition.** The Inquisitors wrote a manual of torture, "The Malleficateus Malaficarum, ("The Hammer of the Witches") which "explained" why women were more than likely to become witches than men. Its premise was that women, because of their sexuality, were an impediment to God's strict demands of renunciation of physical pleasure and:

"Because the female sex is more concerned with things of the flesh than man."

The stupidity of the book's message was spread among the ignorant believers.

The basic belief of Christianity's primitive witchcraft was a confirmation of an older pagan tradition of the desert people. Witchcraft was institutionalized by Christianity in its style of worship, its devotion to supernatural power, its customs and rituals to the magical power of the miracles and the power of the Devil. In fact, some Christian witchcraft cultists considered the worship of the Devil a "logical" function, based on the twisted logic that since the Devil was bad, it was better to worship and please him (so as not to be harmed by him) than the "good" God.

One of the fundamentals of witchcraft is linked to the "art" of foretelling the future and seeking the aid of supernatural powers. Tea leaves, coffee cup readings, Tarot card readings, Chinese Tao-chi and other divine pagan traditions were part of humanity's delusional attempts to make sense of the material world.

My Aunt Margaret was a well-to-do woman within her own rights. She was a walking encyclopedia of home-based remedies from healing to…whatever. She was a fortune-teller, a tea and Turkish-coffee cup reader, a card reader and so on. Rich and poor, young and old, mostly women, came to seek the good-witch who could predict an individual's future. For 40 years, good old Aunt Margaret's advice and "predictions" were based on her personal knowledge of the visitor's life, family, rumours and wishes.

Most of Aunt Margaret's clients wished for information on his/her future love, money and health. Based on the visitor's personal or rumoured information, Aunt Margaret was able to "help" the. Although she sincerely believed in the "power" of her reading material, I could not be convinced of her having a mysterious gift for foretelling the future. One thing I can say about Aunt Margaret's "spiritual" idealism is that she never used God, Satan, saints, heaven or hell or any other kind of religious- threatening witchcraft. This was not the case with my far-removed cousin Kristos (Christ in Greek), who claimed to be the reincarnation of Christ and exploited the villagers' naïve and ignorant religious beliefs, until the Greek authorities put him in a jail's mental ward. This type of delusional person is common where religiosity is strongly integrated into a society's social fabric. In fact, "miraculous" appearances of the "virgin" Mary, a crying icon of the "virgin" Mary and all sorts of "miracles" happen only in those societies. Miracle-networks of the wealthy televangelist in the U.S.A. and Latin America are also an example of religious fraud against the meek. Years ago while travelling in Haifa, Tel Aviv and Jerusalem. I encountered a number of individuals who wanted to exhibit their divine power to forgive my atheism. In Jerusalem, those "reincarnated" Christ wore the garment style of the ancient world. I considered those individuals mental cases that represented a special danger to themselves and others.

There are deluded mentally-ill people who suffer from the same delusion as the rest of religious believers. It is a type of maniac illness that cannot be easily recognized by the external calmness exhibited by such nutcases. They see themselves as the new Messiah, the Prophet who has come to announce the end of the world. It is a typical Chiliastic message that proclaims a religious apocalyptic end of the world as we know it. Some of us who have seen religious destructiveness in a variety of cultural and ethnic social environments are convinced of the close connection between religious faith and mass mental disorder

I'm not a trained psychologist, but if someone claims that he or she has killed a child or a witch-woman and that same someone believes he or she is the biblical God, I would have no hesitation in saying that the killer is not guilty by reason of insanity, which should land him or her in a mental institution for the criminally insane. But if a suicide bomber, or Jim Jones (of the 918 mass suicides on November 18, 1978 fame) has been taught by a preacher of an institutionalized religion to happily inflict death on innocent people, a person who claims to have heard voices (God's, Allah's or Abraham's) to kill his or her children as a divine mercy, I would say that it is murder encouraged by a religious instigator. Witch-hunting was propagated by religious instigators who were motivated by centuries-old ideologies in which women were held at fault on all sorts of counts.

Christianity has always regarded women to be impediments to the Church's dogmas of demanding strictly demands a renunciation of physical pleasure. The Hammer of the Witches explained:

"Because the female sex is more concerned with things of the flesh than men; because being formed from a man's rib, they are only "imperfect" animals and "crooked" whereas man belongs to a privileged sex from whose midst Christ emerged."

Other preachers of the time:

"...denounced women on the one hand for...the lascivious and carnal provocation of their garments, and on the other hand for being over-industrious, too occupied with children and house-keeping, too earthbound to give due thought to divine things."

Throughout its history, the Church slowly but surely persuaded society's males and females that women were inclined towards evil, and that women no longer should be thought of as benevolent healers, teachers or wise people. Women were portrayed as heretics who were prone to become witches and organize themselves into *"...small clandestine society engaged in anti-human practices, including infanticide, incest, cannibalism, bestiality, and orgiastic sex..."* The Church also projected its own hierarchical framework onto this new anti-feminism by promoting into its ranks its most **misogynist** males. Between 1574-1669, two of the most notorious Inquisitors, Kramer and Springer, made sure their torture manual, The Hammer of the Witches, was reprinted 16 times in order to have it available to every European priest and thus ensure the rescuing of the Church of Christ from female witches.

Underlying all of the above, the persecution of female witches was also a money-making proposition. The Catholic Church's inquisitors prolonged the profitability of their institution to secure its financial future. This is similar to the Nazi persecutions of rich Jews in order to confiscate their wealth. Religion and corruption have been exclusive historical partners. The Bible's saying of *"Thou shalt not suffer a witch to live"* was put into practice to the point that inquisitions against wealthy families accused of witchcraft left some regions economically destitute.

One of the Catholic inquisitors dared to complain that *"In our days there are no more rich heretics...it is a pity that...[our] institution... should be so uncertain of its [economic] future."* In short, by adding witch-hunting to the crimes it persecuted, the Catholic Church exposed a new source of revenue through its organized crime. For 300 years, the Catholic Church and its Inquisition committed atrocious crimes against women and took every advantage of the opportunity to enrich their coffers. Once a person was accused of witchcraft, it was nearly impossible to escape death unless the victim's family bought out the conviction. In fact, as more and more trials for witchcraft happened, all other types of heretical trials were ignored or stopped.

The irony of this human tragedy can be summarized by the cliché *"If you can not defeat them, join them."* Fundamentalists such as Calvin, Knox and, later, John Wesley (the 18th century Methodist founder) declared that God's Bible was in favour of women practicing witchcraft ! ! ! *"The giving up of witchcraft is in effect the giving up of the Bible."* Other apologists of the Church's hideous crimes against women were no longer sceptical of paganism:

"To deny the possibility, nay, actual existence of Witchcraft and Sorcery, is at once flatly to contradict the revealed Word of God in various passages both of the Old and New Testament."

There you have it! It took hundreds of thousands of burned-alive women, the torture of others and the robbing of large fortunes for the Catholic and Protestant killers to finally accept that the pagan-witchcraft was NOT any different from the religious witchcraft that their churches were practicing. The pagan witchcraft would NOT drive their business away but in fact would re-enforce their institutionalized religious ideology of witchcraft: Christianity. Women healers, herbal oils or ointments *"in healing of man and beast, by the power of God taught to [a witch] by the...fairies, be both godly and good"*. This belief successfully joined witchcraft delusional religious practices. One has only to travel through Latin American countries including Peru, Bolivia and Ecuador to witness the close relationship between the Roman Catholic Church and local witchcraft **curanderos** who practice their craft while also holding the religious icons of the Virgin Mary. The lesson to be learned is that over a period of two thousand years, the Christian religion and its institutions have killed, tortured, oppressed and brutalized millions of human beings in an attempt to enforce its delusional beliefs upon humanity.

THE PROPHET'S OWN WORDS

The sayings of the Torah and the Old and New Testaments about sexuality, women and children are ill-founded and grossly inconsistent. The Qur'an's message is also immoral as are many of the other 'good books that so many delusional believers think to be the Word of God. The last **mimetic** recipient of God's message was Muhammad and his Qur'an. In it, there are vast sayings in Suras, Verses and Hadiths of doubtful learning value. Its written anecdotes were built upon the same blood-soaked primitive tribal stories of their desert predecessors. "Revelations" were selected to turn the illiterate into converts. How could Muslim mullahs present the Qur'an's Word of God to an illiterate tribesman who in turn could not possibly hope to **mimetically** pass on the unaltered words? The

Muslim fundamentalists found those illiterate people with their extreme simplicity to be fertile ground upon which they unleashed the unverifiable and falsifiable claims of the Qur'an's sacred texts. Oral transmission of the Qur'an into different Arabic dialects and into more everyday speech, plus the unchangeable traditions and tribal rituals, were all combined and used as "proof" of the text's divinity.

Muhammad himself was an illiterate merchant and a tribal warlord with the power to incite bliss and rage among the followers of his large tribe. Unlike other religious prophets, the figure of Muhammad has, by contrast, more evidence of his life's activities. As with other schizophrenic prophets, Muhammad was also in touch with spirits while he was asleep or in a trance. He heard a voice commanding him to attack other tribes in order to establish his power base

The essayist Gore Vidal best describes the three religions' loathing of women thus:

"The great unmentionable evil at the center of our culture is monotheism. From the barbaric Bronze Age known as the Old Testament, three anti-human religions have evolved–Judaism, Christianity, and Islam. These are sky-god religions. They are, literally, patriarchal - God is the Omnipotent Father - hence the loathing of women for 2000 years in those countries afflicted by the sky-god and his delegates."

Muhammad's newest Abrahamic desert religion carried on with the other two anti-female tribal religious obsessions with sexual restrictions and patriarchal ethical systems. Among the three religions, their differences are much smaller than their similarities, as the readers can see in the following:

Qur'an 4:3

If you fear that you shall not be able to deal justly with orphans, marry women of your choice who seem good to you, two or three or four; but if you fear that you shall not be able to do justice [to so many], then only one, or [a slave] that you possess, that will be more suitable. And give the women their dower as a free gift; but if they, of their own good pleasure, remit any part of it to you, eat it with enjoyment, take it with right good cheer and absorb it [by your wealth].

Qur'an 4:11

Allah directs you in regards to your children's (inheritance): to the male, a portion equal to that of two females,–these [divisions] are settled portions ordained by Allah.

Qur'an 4:43

Believers, approach not prayers with a mind befogged or intoxicated until you understand what you utter. Nor when you are polluted, until after you have bathed. If you are ill, or on a journey, or come from answering the call of nature, or you have touched a woman, and you find no water, then take for yourselves clean dirt, and rub your faces and hands. Lo! Allah is Benign, Forgiving. [Islamists believe that women are unclean].

Qur'an 33:59

Prophet! Tell your wives and daughters and all Muslim women to draw cloaks and veils all over their bodies [Burkha is the garment that covers women's body from head to toe, allowing one or two eyes to see directions]. That will be better.

Qur'an 4:15

If any of your women are guilty of lawless, take the evidence of four witnesses from amongst you against them; if they testify, confine them to house until death [by starvation or beating] claims them.

Qur'an 24:31

Say to the believing women that they should lower their gaze and guard their modesty; that they should not display their beauty except what [has to] appear; that they should draw their veils over their bosoms and not display them except to their husband.

Qur'an 24:34

Force not your slave-girls to whoredom [only] if they desire chastity, that you may seek enjoyment of this life. But if anyone forces them [rapes them] then after such compulsion, Allah is oft-forgiving [of the dreadful act of rape].

Qur'an 24:1

[this is] a Sura which we have revealed and made obligatory and in which we have revealed clear communications that you may be mindful. For the woman and the man guilty of adultery or fornication, flog each of them a hundred stripes. Let not compassion move you in their case, in a matter described by Allah. And let a party of the Believers witness [in public] their punishment.

Qur'an 24:6

And for those who launch against their wives, accusing them, but have no witness or evidence, except themselves; let the testimony of one of them be four testimonies [swearing four times] by Allah that he is the one speaking the truth.

Tabari IX: 113

Allah permits you to shut those [women] in separate rooms and to beat them, but not severely. If they abstain, they have the right to food and clothing. Treat women well for they are like domestic animals and they possess nothing themselves. Allah has made the enjoyment of their bodies lawful in his Qur'an.

Tabari 1:280

Allah said; It is my obligation to make Eve bleed once every month as she made this tree bleed. I must also make Eve stupid, although I created her intelligent. Because Allah afflicted Eve, all of the women of this world menstruate and are stupid.

Tabari VIII:62

Ali [Muhammad's adopted son-in-law, and future Caliph] said, 'Prophet, women are plentiful. You can get a replacement, easily changing one for another.

Tabari VIII: 116

Ishaq: 511 So Muhammad began seizing their herds and their property bit by bit. He conquered home by home. The Messenger took some of its people captive, including Safiyah and her two cousins. The Prophet chooses Safiyah for himself.

Tabari IX: 3

Since the Hawazin and Thaqif had marched with their women, children, and flocks, Allah granted them as booty to His Messenger, who divided the spoils among those Qurayah who had recently embraced Islam.

Ishaq: 327

Allah said, A prophet must slaughter before collecting captives. A slaughtered enemy is driven from the land. Muhammad, you craved the desires of this world, its goods and the ransom captives would bring. But Allah desires killing them to manifest the religion.

Ishaq: 511

When Dihyah protested, wanting to keep Safiyah for himself, the Apostle traded for Safiyah by giving Dihyah her two cousins. The women of Khaybar were distributed among Muslims.

Ishaq: 584

Tell the men with you who have wives; never trust a woman.

Ishaq: 185

In Hell I saw women hanging by their breasts. They have fathered bastards.

Ishaq: 469

The Apostle said, Every wailing woman lies except those who wept for Sa'd.

Ishaq: 496

"Ask the slave girl; she will tell you the truth." So the Apostle called Burayra to ask her. Ali got up and gave her a violent beating first, saying, Tell the Apostle the truth.

Ishaq: 593

From the captives of Hunayn, Allah's Messeger gave [his son-in-law] Ali a slave girl called Baytab and he gave [future Caliph] Uthman a slave girl called Zaynab and [future Caliph] Umar another.

Muslim: BIN142

O womenfolk, you should ask for forgiveness for I saw you in bulk amongst the dwellers of Hell. A wise lady said: Why is it, that women comprise the bulk of the inhabitants of Hell? The Prophet observed: You curse too much and are ungrateful to your spouses. You lack common sense, fail in religion and rob the wisdom of the wise. Upon this the woman remarked; what is wrong with our common sense? The Prophet replied, Your lack of common sense can be determined from the fact that the evidence of two women is equal to one man. That is a proof.

RELIGIOUS LAWS: SHARIA

Sharia literally means "the path to a water hole." It is basically a Muslim religious code of living in the same way the Christian fundamentalist Church dictates to its followers a total way of life. Because by definition Muslim nations are theocracies, Sharia's text is law and thus applicable to society. Sharia courts are essentially religious and judges are usually imams of the local Mosque. They are involved not only to impose the literal interpretations of ancient Muslim traditions and desert tribal customs, but also to supervise the guilt penalty. Iran, Saudi Arabia, Sudan, Nigeria, Afghanistan under the Taliban and in remote tribal areas of Africa and Asia, Sharia laws apply to all areas of life and reach deeply into the control of the personal and moral life of the people who are bound by it. It is basically a patriarchal law directed to control women's personal and public behaviour. For example, under Sharia Laws:

- ❖ It is forbidden for post-pubescent women to expose their faces in public.

- ❖ The use of alcohol and the consumption of pork are prohibited.

- ❖ **Blasphemy** is punishable by prison or death.

- ❖ The penalty after a fourth conviction for a **homosexual** act is death.

- ❖ **Adoption** is not permitted. Guardians can take care of a child but can not adopt it.

❖ In 2003, a Nigerian Sharia court sentenced Animan Lawal to be stoned to death for having a child **out of wedlock**. The man named as the father denied responsibility, and as a result, the court dropped charges against him.

❖ A Pakistan teenager, Bariya Magazu, testified that she was raped by three men and became pregnant as a result. Because she had sex outside of marriage, a Sharia court sentenced her to one hundred lashes, even though seven people corroborated her story. The men accused of the rape received no punishment.

In this section of the book, I have brought to the readers' attention that many Catholic and Protestant Christians, Jews and Muslims (who have blind faith) may well believe that religious violence is practiced by other religions but not their own.

However, because violent verses against women in the Old and New Testaments and the Qur'an are still continuing to inspire violence as well as individual murders, stoning, mass murder, genocide, anti-female and anti-gay behaviour and female genital mutilations, I am all for criticizing those propagators of human suffering. One simply cannot deny that violent verses in religious texts continue to motivate violence in the 21st century.

Muslim, Jewish, Christian, Hindu and Sikh religions, through often in conflict with each other, in the 21st century are all largely closed, immutable, alienated and frozen. Their verses or sayings are embedded in their holy books, which their religious followers accept as the Word of God. However, there are contradictions and conflicting messages in the Old and New Testaments, Torah and Talmud, Book of Mormon, Qur'an, the Hindu Upanishads and the Sikh Adi Granth. Their claims are, simply put, unverifiable.

Proponents of specific religious texts falsely attempt to present their holy books as a reliable authority that is **mimetically transmitted into the minds of believers in their specific**

religions.. When such delusional beliefs are adopted, they become a way of life that affects every aspect of family, social and cultural personal decisions. These holy texts supply their own fixed-frozen answers to ultimate questions, demanding and imposing a way of life that is based on desert-tribal clannish ties, and commands moral principles that are alien to 21st century secular societies.

This means that while a given holy scripture is commonly accepted, willingly or unwillingly, by followers within its closed community, it is disregarded outside that community. This does not apply to theocratic Islam. Muslim theocratic leaders seriously believe that the Qur'an Sharia Laws must be obeyed by all of their citizens. In accordance with theocratic imams, the rigidity of their Qur'an is the only true Word of God. All other holy books have lost their original message and thus, their originality.

Religion is based on blind faith and this faith is re-enforced by not allowing any rational scrutiny based on a healthy degree of verification. While educated secularists, humanists and atheists interpret these religious verses, they examine them based on contemporary social standards. On the other hand, religious propagators impose out-dated verses that were written over many centuries of time by desert-tribal men (Jewish, Christian and Muslim) who regarded animals and women as men's property and who had the power of life or death over them. All such holy books were written not by their prophets, but by corrupted writers whose biblical messages were based on their own political, economic or cultural agendas and tribal alliances.

We have to bear in mind that no-one is *"an island unto himself."* No one is isolated from the historical setting of society. Therefore, many of the religious verses bear the imprint of the time in which they were written. All of them were formulated in a pre-scientific age and were based on superstition, naïve assumptions, ignorance, false beliefs and prejudices that were part of the social structure of the customs and traditions of the time. These ancient **tribal moral codes** were followed at the time but the present secular age finds them inhumane and offensive. The claim that the Word of God is of religious origin is difficult to verify when the scientific background of this claim remains non-existent. A particularly vigorous defense of a believer's ignorant status was mounted by the Catholic Church in the Syllabus of Errors in which Pope Pius IX declared the proposition:

"The method and principles by which the old scholastic doctors cultivated theology [how about God's authorship] are no longer suitable to demands of our Times and progress of the sciences..."

Indeed, this must be condemned. Believers are still being asked to accept on blind faith the revelations that were "created" within the Abrahamic era of some 5000 years ago. In the Abrahamic religions of Judaism, Christianity and Islam, the images of violence against women, calls to warfare and patriarchal exploits project the religious false hope of "doing good." Religion is a negative force and the secular world has no specific safeguards to prevent its abuses in such tragedies as described in the Qur'an of many centuries ago. The Jonestown mass suicide, the Branch Davidian cult's juvenile pregnancies, deaths in Waco, the Solar Temple suicides and the Heaven's Gate deaths fall under the same umbrella.

Only the Word of God texts and its verses of offensive commandments can continually promote violence across ethnic and racial boundaries. These ready-made pretexts for all sub-sections of Christian, Jewish, Muslim and Hindu fundamentalists with their righteousness lead to violent actions which they consider just. Only religion can "justify" the destruction of innocent human life under the pretext of holy piety. Only the religious meek can blindly downplay the problem of religious violence in so-called holy books. Humanists, secularists and atheists must continue to expose the violence-of-God tradition in the Jewish Scriptures, the Christian New Testament and the Muslim Qur'an if humans have any realistic hope of constructing a peaceful world.

4

IDEALISM IS A MENTAL ILLNESS

"If religion is not a mental illness, then a disease is a health."

Unknown

"The most deadly form of insanity is the Obsession Neurosis commonly called "religion." This aggressive and contagious mental health disorder has caused more death than any other communicable disease. At the root of this disease is the delusion that impossible creatures and worlds exist–angels, gods, saints, hells, heavens, etc…and that these imaginary beings demand mind deadening obedience."

Emmelt F. Fields

Philosopher Bertrand Russell wrote:

"Religion is based... mainly upon fear... fear of the mysterious, fear of defeat, fear of death. Fear is the parent of cruelty, and therefore, it is no wonder if cruelty and religion have gone hand in hand... My own view on religion is that of Lucretius. I regard it as a [mental] disease born of fear and a source of untold misery to the human race."

Religion is highly addictive and makes believers want others to join them in their addiction. Religion induces obsession and compulsion in the believer: those are mental disorders. Also, let me put it in non-ambivalent terms: believing in "God" is psychotic, and religion is an institutionalized by-product of induced psychosis.

Before we go any further, let me say that I view "mental illnesses" from a non-psychological point of view. That is, from the simple premise of ideas-in-the-mind and praxis. This is my dialectical materialist base. It maintains that "mental disorders" are ideas-in-the-mind that don't reflect reality. It is expressed in terms of the physical well-being of the person's relationships. Secondly, whether we call ideas-in-the-mind delusional, misleading, confusing, destructive, dangerous, or distortional, it is of no consequence unless the person that "houses" those ideas puts them into praxis (acts in any manner). For those devoted religious believers, whose religiosity was induced by powerful religious institutions, mental illness is the end product. Although no validated studies exist in support of the notion that religious beliefs and practices induce mental illness, my premise, as stated above, remains intact. Generally, when delusional beliefs are organized into a consistent worldview that is logical, even though it may be based on an improbable foundation, they form the basis of institutionalized mental disorder. They are disguised as religious beliefs.

So, it all goes back to that old saying (somewhat modified) that "religion is the opiate of the believer." Most devoted believers are people who appear to be unable to cope with the harsh reality of life without something seductive to keep them from thinking and acting rationally. Religion is such a seducer. Instead of learning (ideas) to act (praxis) in the natural world that we all live in, they prefer to "live" a lie because they can't handle the real world. When believers feel driven to perform, they must do so according to religious rules that must be applied rigidly (aimed at preventing some imagined dreaded event). Although adhered to in order to reduce fear, compulsive behaviour (praxis) and mental delusions or impulses (ideas) do not solve real life's problems.

The majority of religious participants use religious beliefs and activities to cope with life's daily difficulties or frustrations. They are devoted to religious escape and use of coping mechanisms, with prayers being the most frequent activity. Specific religious coping activities, such as praying or reading the Bible or the Qur'an, are associated with more severe symptoms, frustrations and greater delusional impairment. The more time spent with religious escaping and attempting at coping, the higher the level of frustration. I maintain that religious activities and beliefs tend to compel the more devoted Christian, Muslims or Jewish believers to advanced symptoms of delusion! Religion serves as a pervasive and potentially ineffective method to create a socially productive life.

Delusions (idealism) are irrational beliefs, held with a high level of conviction. They are highly resistant to change even when the delusional person is exposed to direct proof that contradicts the belief. They see nothing wrong with the way they are thinking or functioning. Religious delusion arises from the distorted ways biblical books have of explaining life to believers. The most prominent problem that develops out of the Biblical explanation of life involves the manner in which religious believers accept delusional conclusions about other people's cultural behaviour (such that are not prescribed in the biblical texts).

To think that other people's cultural behaviour is "wrong" is in itself harmless, but acting (praxis) upon these religious delusional dogmatic conclusions (ideas) against millions of "others" can be very harmful indeed. This is concrete evidence of mass mental illness. Since the people draw rigid conclusions without considering alternative explanations, they tend to view life as a continuing series of threatening events.

The "others" who are non believers, "blasphemers," "gentiles," "witches," or "atheists" are evil because the "Word of God" says so. They must be killed, tortured, and burned alive or enslaved as war booty. To cause such extensive human death and destruction just because the biblical books demand it could only be practiced by normal, everyday people with a mental illness. This mass insanity has been induced in believers by insane propagators: Moses, Abraham, and Muhammad. They could hear in their own heads (schizophrenia) "God's voice" demanding believers to kill and destroy human life.

Let us take a non-legalistic explanation of what constitutes insanity or mental illness. Often we read or hear of someone killing another person, and the killer is found not guilty by reason of insanity. The killer, "John," kills his neighbour "Peter" because "John" believes that "Peter" is evil. An evil witch has placed a "bad spell" on "John." A typical claim would be that "John" should not be held accountable for delusional thinking (ideas) or his action (praxis) because "John" has a certain mental illness that interferes with his capacity to reason. Whether or not we grant insanity or mental illness a legal distinction, the fact is that mental illness is culturally motivated. The Bible, Torah, and the Qur'an systematically instruct their believers in Satan's influence, the evil influence of witches, and in the evil of non-believers who must be destroyed. I am talking about the socio-cultural consequences of religious indoctrination in children, the vulnerable, the meek and the born-again believers.

An important aspect of recognizing religious delusional beliefs is to identify the form of the delusion. The most common biblical verses or "sayings" are of the paranoid type. Their message instils fear of "others," irrational ideas about the bodily function of menstruation, and a conviction that a woman's body is dirty and that it emits a foul stench after sex (according to the Qur'an's verses). These induced mental illnesses may arise from the distorted ways the church or cult leaders have explained life to themselves and to their followers.

Religious delusions are manifested into *mental delusions* which, in turn, lead to *mental illness.* Religious delusions are taught in Islamic Madrasas. They are places of "learning" *hifz,* the memorising the Qur'an in its entirety, the Islamic religious Sharia law and the *Hadiths* which are the recorded "sayings" (ideas) and deeds (praxis) of Muhammad. Some alleged ties between Madrasa and Al Queda indicate that these religious schools promote Islamic fundamentalism and the distortion of reality to fit in with the delusional religious curriculum. It should be noted that the religious Madrasa schools in Pakistan, Bangladesh, Egypt, Lebanon, and Afghanistan are at the primary and secondary levels. The children are from 5 to 18 years of age and are the most vulnerable to delusional religious teaching. In general, Madrasas offer a religion-based curriculum well beyond the instruction found in basic religious tenets. But along the Afghanistan-Pakistan border Madrasas promote an extremist form of religious delusions and teaches young Muslim students to fight and kill non-believers. It stands contrary to the moral "decadence" of the western world. Students are instructed to reject "immoral" and "materialist" western culture, and are encouraged to preserve an "authentic" Islamic heritage.

Most of the graduates have only had access to a limited type of education. As such, ignorance creates faith. Due to their educational limitations, these graduates are only employed in religious sectors as prayer leaders or imams. After going through the static role of Quar'anic memorization and mental delusion, these men are neither skilled nor prepared for the modern workforce. The only thing they can propagate to the general populace is their religious Quar'anic delusions of keeping Islam "pure" from the "pollution" of the infidels, that Islam's religion is the way for all of humanity, and that the world must live under the *compulsion* of religion in accordance with the Qur'an.

The preaching of the imams is often associated with violent behaviour. They instil the delusional mentality that Muslims have a distinguished role that is "inspired" by the supernatural divinity of the Qur'an, and that they will enjoy some extraordinary religious benefit in the afterlife. These delusional messages are mimetically transmitted day after day to all people from young children to adults. They form an irrational way of viewing "others," women in their villages, and people of different ethnic ties and races.

To a graduate of the Madrasa religious school (perhaps now an imam or a prayer leader), those beliefs are not considered delusional because the content of them is common to his society's mass delusional religious culture. One must remember that a person with religious delusional beliefs or distorted reality does not appear to be obviously odd, strange, or peculiar during his or her active life with mental illness. In our western societies, televangelists, priests, cultists and other sorts of preachers are raving and yelling at the top of their lungs that the rest of us are all going to hell unless we submit to their delusional beliefs. My point is that the rest of us have come to accept their preaching as "normal" behaviour, tolerating their mental illness as harmless. Yet, another religious person might make dreadful choices in day to day life because of his or her religious mental illness. Expanding on the previous example, one or a group of Muslim would-be "martyrs" who suffer from religious mental illness believe that they have a religious duty to kill infidels. They become suicide bombers, killing themselves and as many "others" as possible. Only a mentally ill person would take such tragic action against humanity.

Religious mental illness is not exclusive to Muslims. Christianity has also had its share of crimes against humanity. An example involves the case of the religious mentally ill leader who led 850 mentally ill believers, culminating in the Jonestown religious mass suicide on November 18, 1978. The delusional religious cult leader Jim Jones established the People's Temple and moved his vulnerable followers to Guyana, South America. He was regarded as a "divine-healer" who performed "miracles." A reincarnation of Jesus, Buddha, Lenin and Father Divine, Jones was paranoid and a compulsive controller of his followers. He imagined enemies within and outside of his cult. He was accustomed to subjecting his followers to middle of the night drills called "white nights" in order to prepare his delusional followers to "defend" themselves against an invisible enemy. His drills rehearsed a commitment to mass suicide. A survivor of the Jonestown tragedy writes:

"A mass meeting would ensue...we would be told that the jungle [of Guyana] was swarming with mercenaries...we were given a small glass of red liquid to drink. We were told that the liquid contained poison and we would die within 45 minutes. We all did what we were told."

We all did what we were told!!

Religious beliefs generate notions of dread and fear that lead, in time, to a compulsive disorder which can be classed as mental illness. It affects believers by making them believe that by doing some sort of strict religious ritual like praying, fasting, reciting verbatim the Qur'an or the Bible, sacrificing an animal to appease God, the saints, or Lady Luck, they can avoid harm to themselves and others. The tragic People's

Temple religious cultists believed that the "world in the afterlife" was much safer than this physical or natural world. Practicing the ritual of "drinking poison" essentially led to a mass suicide, the poisoning and murdering of their 300 children. They did not connect the practicing of this act (praxix) with any perceived harm.

Any rational man or woman (i.e., not affected by religious delusions) might have come to judge that such ritual behaviour would bring about some negative or destructive event: the death of themselves and their children. Yet, the believers were "sure" that this "poison-drinking" ritual was fending off the "enemy" within or outside of their group, and that "something bad will happen" if they did not strictly obey the ritual. So the statement of "we all did what we were told" eventually did take them to the world of the "afterlife."

Seeing any gray in their lives leads such religious mentally ill people into a disastrous sort of despair. Religious mental illness via ritual induces the mentality of "all or nothing" conclusions for its believers. "Relations" are viewed in black-and-white terms: be an object of failure if they stay in this world, or be a complete success if they choose the "after life." In its extreme religious delusional form, paranoia–the perceived threat or fear where the enemy are "infidels" or "jungle mercenaries"–slides into the realm of mental illness. The more fundamentalist the religion is, the less there is room for doubt the less it has to do with reality.

The deadly religious mental illness of the self-proclaimed messiahs–Abraham, Moses, Jim Jones, Muhammad and David Koresh–is self evident. All had declared that God would destroy the enemy and vindicate their religious flock. The Branch Davidians, consisting of 77 men, women, and children, met their deaths on April 19, 1993. This event is worthy of our focussed attention on religious mental illness.

The Branch Davidian religious cult was presaged by the Old Testament's King David. This religious cult can be traced back to Seventh Day Adventists, a millenarian church that emerged in the 1800's. It is a millenarian church because of its embedded conviction in end-time events (eschatology). Its own expression of Christianity is considered by them as the only valid one (a typical "black and white" conviction). Millenarian delusional religious movements are common throughout history. They simply "predict" the end of the world at a specific day and time. As a child, I witnessed one such gathering of millenarian believers in Athens, Greece. When their "prophecy" failed, the group disintegrated.

Davidian cult religious leaders taught and enticed young girls into becoming sexual partners by naming them "wives." By divine declaration, they confirmed that these girls had been chosen by God to multiply mankind. In brief, David Koresh was a Messiah-delusional who believed that just as King David ruled over God's people, so he also was a "type of Jesus" who would rule over God's people, and, eventually the whole world.

Just as Cyrus was "anointed" by God's mandate to rebuild the temple of Jerusalem (Isa 45:1), so was David Koresh also "anointed" by God to "create" the perfect human family with prepubescent girls to restore God's rule over the world. All adult males of the Davidian religious cult acted as paedophiles. Sex was used as a powerful delusional lure with which older men compulsively controlled all 140 "wives" who were available for sex with every male in the cult. The reader may wish to further investigate this bizarre religious cult.

In the western world there is a growth in the religious industry propagating mental illness in apocalyptic teachings with pseudo-science, eastern religions, prophecies of all sorts, speaking in tongues, catastrophes, death and destruction, fear, and paralysis. In 1995, the Roman Catholic newspaper "Queen of Peace" (Pittsburgh Centre for Peace; Spring, 1995) said:

"The time has arrived...the long awaited 'Era of Peace' predicted at Fatima in 1917 is said to be about to occur...The Virgin's words indicate that the face of death will be transformed...some nations will even vanish...the Church will reign, Evil will be paralysed, and like an old well, it will dry up and almost vanish from the face of the earth."

Religion and its delusional culture do not prevent mental illness! True enough, mental illness exists with or without religion. Yet, religion exhibits the same delusional distortions of reality, paranoia, impulsiveness, and obsession-compulsion identical to common mental illness. In addition, religion is a major contributor to people's distortion of reality based on fear and threat. This propagates anxiety, paranoia, justification for rape, paedophilia, polygamy, killing, looting, the oppression of women, the promotion of a culture of the despairing, and delusional hopes of the afterlife. It also promotes the unworthiness of our natural world in exchange for the nonexistent "other world."

Religious beliefs influence mental health and behaviour. The effects are likely to spill over into other areas of people's lives with some influential factors embedded in social and economic lifestyles. Both behavioural and social determinants are relevant to the religious mental illness that guide or influence people's behaviour "for or against others" with no consideration of alternative solutions.

Religious mimesis is an integral part of people's code of immoral social conduct. Religion is a system of thought, a delusional school of social conduct, based on idealism rather than on materialism or reality. It distorts the reality of human nature, its relation to the natural world, the value in preserving a healthy human lifestyle for the collective benefit of all ethnic or racial groups. The irony of religious mental illness is expressed by Robert T. Carroll: "A delusion held by one person is a mental illness, held by a few is a cult, held by many is a religion."

Delusional people believe in "things" that do not exist, and in "events" that have not taken place. They have derived delusional conclusions either by some sort of brain-chemical imbalance, by their own misinterpretation, by how the natural and social world works, or they were taught to view things in a delusional way. This religious delusional system of thought has become an integral part of the delusional believer's system of misperception and misinterpretation of human life. Religious mental illness, then, can be caused or imposed, or it can be taught or induced by an institutionalized socio-cultural power.

Fantasies and delusions are equally mental distortions of reality whether they are derived through religious beliefs or by "obedience" to a psychotic voice in the head of an imaginary God or Allah, residing in some magical place that does not exist. People are given medical treatment with brain-chemical balancing drugs in order to control their mental health. There are community organizations dealing with mental illness. The social structure exists to provide helpless people dealing with religious delusions with assistance to maintain their personal sanity. Why is it then that the current psychology supports the use of religious delusions as a cure for mental illness rather than recognizing that religion is the main mimetic cause of it? When people profess a delusion as a religious "experience" why then do psychologists not treat them? Religious "experiences" are the most intense beliefs about "things" that do not exist (e.g., demons, Satan, saints, God, Allah, heaven, hell). Yet, these vulnerable people are regarded as religious believers and not mentally ill.

Evident in the Bible's and the Qur'an's messages, are underlying examples of delusional beliefs (demons, Satan, heaven, hell etc) that involve several elements and symbols suggesting the interconnectedness of all such things. Such binding occurs through forces and powers that transcend both the physical and the cultural. Religious delusional idealism invests special power and forces in many symbols.

Jewish, Christian, and Muslim believers are convinced that there are real connections between symbolism and its referent, and that some real power flows between them. One of many symbols is the act of praying. For example, if a believer is praying to recover from a sickness and has the good fortune to recover, he or she will associate the act of praying with the recovery from illness–both events will be causally linked together. To a religious believer, delusional symbolic acts may seem believable at face value, and the believer may appear normal as long as someone does not question the connection between the symbolic act (praying, fasting, alms-giving, or the act of confession) and its referent (unrelated beneficial results).

Another mental delusion may result if the religious person believes that he or she has some great insight or a special relationship with God. The believer would begin to exhibit strong symptoms of schizophrenia. He or she may hear "God's voice" or sense "God's presence" commanding acts–against abortion clinics, infidels, non-believers, sex-education, atheist-communists, same sex relationships–and develop a gloomy mood as a reaction to his or her delusional beliefs.

The term "religious paranoia" describes a disturbing mental state of deeply held beliefs that are rigid, inflexible and maladaptive. They are further directed toward the "other's" moral code of conduct. In addition, religious paranoia can result in a sufficient level of fanaticism so as to cause a significant unwarranted tendency to suspect the religious or secular beliefs of "others" as being deliberately demeaning. Christian fundamentalists may suspect or regard "liberal" Christians as immoral or decadent. They may present an immoral influence *vis-à-vis* the strictly fundamentalist moral code of conduct. Muslim fundamentalists are paranoid of western cultural influence upon Muslim women, their property and marriage rights, their desire to educate themselves. To kill or destroy all infidels appears to be the only preventable solution, in accordance with the Taliban's and Al Qaeda's religious paranoid believers.

I maintain that religion is an institutionalized propagator and inducer of mental illness due to:

(1) distortion of reality,

(2) punitive nature,

(3) disregard for human life,

(4) delusional persistence in claiming the existence of the invisible and the unattainable.

Victims of religious delusions suffer a mental disease that may last an entire lifetime. These victims are the religious believers who tend to express their beliefs with an unusual persistence. Their beliefs can exert an undue control and influence over their lives. They can alter the reality of their material and cultural life to conform to their psychosis. Yet, despite their exhibition of strong religious fundamentalism, their mental illness causes them to suspect anyone who dares to question their beliefs in a serious or humorous way. Even when their delusions are logically constructed and linguistically sound, it is when their hostile behaviour occurs that one can see how such is directly related to their religious mental illness.

According to James Randerson, writing in New Scientist, May 2002:

"The notion that a strict...God fearing, upbringing may contribute to obsessive-compulsive disorder has been boosted by a survey which discovered that devout [religious believers] were more likely to show symptoms than less religious people."

What do the religious mentally ill actually have control over in their lives? Maybe they are not sure of anything, so they invent things and control their behaviour in order to exert influence over their circumstances. This gives rise to delusion, superstition, and mental illness. Over centuries, these beliefs have controlled them. Religious biblical and Qur'an verses aptly demonstrate that religious practice is obsessive and neurotic. There are many examples of such activities: the prescribed recitations of the rosary, praying towards Mecca five times a day, fasting for 40 days, offering the stipulated number of genuflections, chanting and reciting Buddhist sutras several times in the morning and evening, and the importance of doing things in sets of four as it is practiced among the Lakota and other Native American and Canadian tribes.

Religious believers of institutionalized or non-institutionalized bodies engage in these behaviours as a way to ease their irrational fears and anxieties or to prevent punishment from evil spirits, God, or Allah. Obsessive behaviours such as praying, fasting or other such repetitive religious acts are irrational attempts to give meaning or control to future events, the environment, or a myriad of other circumstances. Why do religious believers find it so hard to let life happen? Why do they have such difficulty with live and let live. Religious ritual and repetitive choreography encourages delusional beliefs and espouses practices that are contrary to healthy human life. Controlling one's personal environment is not possible when a religious mentally ill person is infatuated with fear and irrational behaviour.

The problem with religion is that it speaks of "truth" and this "truth" has become (over the centuries) imbued with layers of neurotic dogma. The "truth" is then nothing more than a delusional non-existent entity. So, religious believers invent "truths" in rituals to deny their neurotically-based fear and to fill a mental gap between the elegance of cultural reality of the natural world. The boundary between delusional and rational beliefs must be drawn by appealing to rational deficits of the delusional believers. Religious mental illness reflects abnormal expectations. Deluded believers suffer from bizarre "experiences" such as God's presence, God's voice etc.

IDEALIST MENTAL ILLNESS IN CHILDREN'S EDUCATION

Education of children is one of the most important socio-cultural tasks of all human societies. The way each nation regards its young generation is reflected first and foremost in its educational system.

Here I will try to picture children's education as it affects their relationship with each other and their view of the world. I will examine religious indoctrination as it relates to boys and girls, and the effects it has on the whole community. In strong religious societies like those in South America, Catholic Europe, Iran, and Saudi Arabia, religious indoctrination has been imposed on children. This causes them to hold fixed beliefs and religious values. Religious indoctrination is a delusional mental process aimed toward destroying a pupil's rational and cognitive reasoning. In the indoctrination system, the religious power structure attempts to persistently teach the youth delusional "truths" about the existence of God, hell, heaven, miracles, and that religion is the only source of morality and other "truths." In such societies, the impact of religion on everyday life and in the educational system is far from trivial.

Religious rituals reinforce mental distortions on the impressionable young ones who lack an alternative cognitive option. Religious-led institutions have a major impact on grade school education and in the general direction of the whole system. Children are taught that belief in religion and obeying biblical laws by living according to strict codes, norms, and thoughts are the necessary preconditions for receiving God's protection. Biblical indoctrination and learning verses is compulsory throughout the primary, secondary and post-secondary schools. Propagators are pretend teachers who are selected from within the religious institution. Such individuals know the Bible from cover to cover, including prayers and delusional religious thoughts. Religious mental illness is taught and practiced systematically. Free thought and questions expressing doubts on religious claims are suppressed. Religious superstition, medieval rituals and customs form a learning mental illness that has affected children and young adults from kindergarten to religious universities. This has propagated a fixed, stagnated, and unscientific mimesis from one generation to the next. It should be noted that religious indoctrination is a brainwashing process and it is thus an inflicted mental illness.

Religious mental illness deprives children in their homes, in Sunday-schools, and in Churches from learning and experiencing scientific advancements about the origins of human life and the existence of what is real and possible. Social and cultural acts must be validated within the human society. Religious brainwashing creates a mental illness that distorts the creativity of young minds and replaces natural curiosity and a desire for further learning in all aspects of social life.

For twenty centuries or more, religion has advocated the degraded state of young girls and women. This is one of the most devastating social mental illnesses that have ever been embedded into the rest of the social structure. There is indoctrination of school children with the idea that girls are inferior to boys, and that a woman is equal to only half of a Muslim man, and that females belong to men. This massive social attitude is a mental attitude held by both religious leaders and their followers, and has corrupted the rest of the social structure to the point of spreading a massive religious mental illness.

Children are born without religion, and without absurd rituals, traditions, and prejudices. They have not joined any religious cult. They are new human beings who, by sheer coincidence, are born into a family with specific religious delusions and rituals. They grow up in a family whose religious beliefs are not of the child's choice or free will. They automatically learn to accept religious delusions and repetitive rituals as the norms of life. It is not their choice, and indeed to speak of the children themselves choosing to believe in eternal punishment, hell or heaven, is plainly absurd.

Certain religious schools, mainly Catholic, Evangelical and Adventist, are the biggest, most lucrative, and most prestigious ones that exercise a strong form of mental child abuse. As stated previously, I assert that early childhood religious indoctrination is a deadly form of brainwashing on vulnerable youths long before they reach the age of reason. The Catholic and Adventist Sunday schools propagate outrageous absurdities presented as "truths." Dogmatic religious books are full of malicious tribal fairytales and idiotic dogmas such as creationist myths, praying to an invisible god, worshipping marble, stone or wooden idols, and kissing the hands of guys with funny hats and silly costumes.

This religious mental illness is now at epidemic proportions. It affects today's youth and propagates an elaborate system of mental child abuse. Children should be protected against the mental illness of religion, transgressions of their social and civic rights, and from religious paedophiles. If the reader is a parent, how do you view your children? Do you think that your children are individuals just like you, only a bit smaller, that must be loved, rather than creatures whose main task it is to obey mindlessly? Please do not let anyone poison your children with toxic religious memes.

During 2006-2008, I travelled to various South American countries, investigating Evangelical and Seventh Day Adventist religious institutions. The most noticeable and politically well-connected was the Church of the Adventist. While my investigation was going relatively well, I still did not have a well-founded "insight" into the Church's social structure, their daily base of operation, and their educational methodology, etc. While staying in Lima, Peru (as my "luck" would have it), I was in an accident and a friend took me to a privately-run hospital. The hospital was operated by the Adventists. During my recovery, I noticed how well the hospital functioned, how friendly the staff was and that their medicine was genuine and not counterfeit. It had the structure and management of a well run multinational corporation.

Fortunately, I went to live in the largest educational Seventh Day Adventist University in Latin America, located a short distance from Lima, Peru. I rented a small house within the university's housing compound. This location gave me the opportunity to be in close contact with other single or married residents who were professionals in various occupations within the university. During the daytime, the total number of people residing, working, or attending classes was about 4000-5000. Within the university compound there were shops, restaurants, a bakery, a printing facility, a dairy production, sports facilities for both boys and girls, and a large library. Within the compound and its perimeters there were guards who were in contact with the two main entrances where the control centre was located. At night, the perimeters were watched by armed guards with guard dogs. They were responsible for preventing thieves from climbing the walls and stealing whatever they could.

The villages around the university were typical of South America. They were poor, unhygienic, drug and crime infested, and corrupted. But the most notable item of all was that 99% of the people were extremely religious. I use the term "extremely religious" because the social environment was infested with churches, with icons on building walls, and in vehicles, and open markets. Idols of saints were in nearly every corner; religious graffiti was on nearly every wall. There were weekly open-air religious gatherings and evening sermons. People gave the sign of the cross everywhere, and they uttered a standard "May God help us," or "Thank God" during even brief conversations. Saturday is the Adventist Day of Rest and more than 80% of the stores in the villages were closed. Devoted Adventists kept their stores closed all day while other

Adventists kept them closed until 6 in the evening. Primary and Secondary Adventists schools in the nearly villages were also closed every Saturday. Among the Adventists themselves, women and men were addressed as "sisters" and "brothers."

Within this extremely religious culture, there were a number of "spiritualists" who exploited the ignorant, the superstitious, and those who were seeking love, money, and health. Signs were posted on posts and walls, advertising their special "powers" to cure everything from cancer to ingrown toenails. Religiosity in one form or another was present in every level of people's daily life. Competition among small and large "evangelical" religious institutions and spiritual charlatans was quite evident (with the exception of the Catholic Church which has "embraced" all the others except for the Adventists). Catholicism is the predominant religion and the influence of its Church is evident on all social, political, and economic levels.

Every time I left the town and entered the University campus gate, I entered into a different world. It was a world which was clean, where no garbage could be seen, and where building walls were clean. The workers wore the clean uniforms of their industry, and there were no beggars, thieves, prostitutes, and pick-pocketers. A patrol guard was visible every 40 meters. Students, pastors, and staff would greet each other as they passed one another.

The power base of this institution was its pastors. They were well-paid, each had a new black car, and each had a cell phone. They were given their own housing facilities, and each one had control over the Church's subsidiary in various parts of Peru. This control included the printing of the Church's classroom reading material, sport activities and the general socialization of students in extra curriculum activities. Students were joined by their parents in these activities, and mid-week and Saturday sermons. I lived right across from the students' eating facilities, and I had a chance to watch and listen to the pastor's short sermon during each breakfast, lunch, and supper. All the employed men and women were Adventists which meant that Saturday was their obligatory day off from doing any sort of work, except for the patrolling guards. I suppose God forgives their Saturday work sin!

All Adventist believers, young and old, that I met during the 115 days of my stay had a notably submissive timidity towards the Church's rules. Every sermon that I witnessed was an orgy of fear and threats. I watched the faces of these men, women, and children leaving the sermon halls in a defeatist manner, faces imprinted with fear. The name of Satan! Satan! Satan! was broadcast with the loudspeakers was so intense, that even I (a declared atheist) looked over my shoulder for Satan to appear!

At no time did I hear a sermon teach the believers about love, human dignity, and helping those outside the university's compound who lived in extreme poverty. There were no sorts of community works projects, no building of housing, and no organizing with the locals to clean up the rotten garbage that threatened the drinking water supply. Further, there were no provisions of shelter for the children living in the streets, nor was there any protection against child labour and sexual exploitation.

True enough, the Adventists were not the only corporate religious body who looked after *numero uno*. Various nun-run monasteries of German, French, and Belgium nationalities were there behind their 10ft. perimeter walls, producing and selling fine dairy and grain products to support themselves. In short, they all lived as "islands" unto themselves, surrounded by an ocean of crime, drug addiction, exploitation, economic misery, environmental pollution, and political corruption. Yet, the "islanders" appeared to be living "happily ever after" holding daily sermons and telling the poor and destitute that God was there for them. They nonetheless insisted that Satan and their sins were the root cause of their daily human misery.

The whole structure and purpose of the Adventist institution was about itself (as the means and an end). It was a well-run corporate body whose main managerial-pastor's function was to maintain the power structure of organized religion. The guards and unskilled labourers in the ground works, cleaning, laundry and kitchen were paid miserly wages and lived outside the compound, while the managerial and skilled personnel and their families (including the pastors) all lived safe within the perimeters.

This was indeed a corporate church of a strictly organized religion, whose bottom line objective was its own perpetuation. All social and sports activities or cultural celebrations involved only other Adventist schools from across Peru. I never heard or saw a single athlete or a group of local athletes from nearby villages invited to participate in any of the open-air social activities.

Just imagine a child entering an Adventist religious school at the age of 6 and finishing his or her secondary education at the age of 18 before entering post-secondary education. That person would have had a minimum of 12 years of religious brainwashing, resulting in an institutionalized mental illness. How do you think that young person would view the rest of the "others" who were not like him or her? I think that I can answer my own question by stating that he or she (looking at the local dreadful human and social environment) instead of looking outwards for real solutions would be looking inwards, in prayers, using the tenets of "morality." That person would rely on blind faith, hearing voices that no other human could hear, and build an over-inflated self-esteem based upon the delusional mental imagery of the "Word of God."

I avoided telling anyone in the University that I was an atheist, for I assumed that if I had told them, "they" would have kicked me out of the compound. Instead I declared myself a "spiritualist" rather than an atheist. I was asked about my parents and told them that they were Eastern Orthodox.

Conversations with some of the most interesting people that I encountered had ways of turning topics to the subject of religion. They specifically aimed to convert me from a "spiritualist" (which really I'm not) to a Seventh Day Adventist (which I could not possibly become). The fact that I was a writer was a big plus, for should they have converted me, they would have gained another "skilful" person to serve their objectives.

One of the most fundamentalist Adventists that I met was Juan, who took it upon himself to show me God's "truth." I can summarize his long speeches to me in just a few words. Juan viewed the natural world and the human race as being evil. Every natural disaster, every "evil" within the human race, and every disease was the work of Satan. Satan was everywhere, working tirelessly from day to night, never resting one bit but always doing his evil work! The world was going to end in Hell and Fire! Doomsday scenarios were evident in every aspect of human life!

In fact, now that I think about it, Juan did not see any love, honesty, decency, goodness, or show any admiration toward another human being or human act. These human qualities were alien to him, and the concept of honesty did not appear to be a part of him. He was corrupted to his very core. He was taking payments "under the table" to do some printing work for me. To my genuine surprise, one day Juan came to say goodbye. He had 24 hours to pack and move himself and his wife to another Adventist settlement some 1200 km away in the Peruvian jungle. When I asked him why, he simply replied that he and all other Adventists were under orders from the Church to go (at short notice) anywhere they were commanded to serve. Disobeying the Church's orders was not an option. Speaking about this as a totalitarian state or a fascist regime is an understatement! The high degree of indoctrination was, without a doubt, evident in the extreme obedience to the church's rules, and the lack of questioning of its authority. In this sense, the religious indoctrination was the foundation of the mental illness. My experience with the Seventh Day Adventists showed me firsthand that individual mental illness was perpetuated by a system of total indoctrination.

Am I suggesting that religion is an inflicted mental illness? Yes, I am. This is because a lot of religious symptoms are indicative of mental illness. For example, when a religious believer says that "God told me this…," or that "God told me that…," or "I felt God's presence," or "I can hear God calling me to…," or "I felt Jesus calling me to…," such voices in the believer's mind are labelled religious schizophrenia. There is an old cliché that goes "When you talk to God, it is called religion, but when God is talking to you, it is called schizophrenia!" This is not a question of which one comes first, a person's schizophrenia or the religious mental illness of schizophrenia.

Religious schizophrenia, sense of fear and paranoia is an inflicted mental illness. This is not a "chicken and egg" question. This is about an inflicted mental illness developed over the passage of time, one that is primarily caused by a person's delusional belief in "God's existence" and, thus, in the "existence of God's voice." When a religious believer maintains the delusional beliefs of Satan, life after death, hell and heaven, and fear of God (and once such beliefs become an integral part of that person's system of thought), the delusional thoughts direct his or her irrational behaviour. Thus, religion is schizophrenia!

The fear of God is another characteristic of the mental illness of religious paranoia. This is the case when believers believe that they are constantly being watched. An adult (parent, teacher or preacher) religious paranoid teaches a child that angels or God or Allah are watching over that child. A child is told that "Santa Claus knows if you've being bad or good," and that Jesus or God is with the child everywhere, and that the child must not do anything "bad." In time, the child develops a tendency to think or feel that God or Jesus is always watching.

This kind of religion-induced thinking process would constitute a religious mental illness. In other words, if a child believes that he or she must blend in with others to "wash away" the "bad" or the "immoral" things he or she has done or is thinking of doing, this child is in danger of developing a religious obsessive-compulsive mental disorder. When children follow their religious parents' example of imagining drinking (Jesus') human blood and eating (Jesus') human flesh when it is taking communion, they are inflicted with delusional behaviour.

Do churches function as mental institutions where religious mentally unbalanced people are gathered? Are churches there to reinforce people's religious mental illness? It isn't hard to imagine a psychiatrist visited by a person who hears God's voice, and the psychiatrist recommending treatment and counselling. What would we think when that same psychiatrist attends a church and hears a preacher, a pastor, a priest, or a believer saying that they also hear God's or Jesus' voice commanding a "religious" act? I would suggest that any good psychiatrist would cast doubt on the mental health of any religious person "hearing" God's voice and would recommend some form of therapy to address the person's schizophrenic symptoms. I would also suggest that when another person believes that he or she is followed by an "evil spirit," the same psychiatrist would conclude that the person is mentally unbalanced (i.e., paranoid). What would a psychiatrist conclude about a Muslim suicide-bomber who believes that his enemies must be destroyed because "they" are evil and pose a threat? Whether the "others" are real or imaginary is immaterial for the act of religiously motivated suicide is the delusional behaviour of a mentally ill person.

Jewish religious historians and politicians propagate the "heroism" of the mass suicide at Mount Masada in the 1st century. Jewish religious rebels resisted Roman dominance from their mountain fortress of Masada. After nearly eight years of continuous assault, the Romans found a way to capture Mount Masada. The Roman Legions approached Masada with their assault ramps and prepared for their final assault on the Jewish fortress. The Jewish religious rebels then decided to commit mass suicide rather than be captured. Their leader, Eleazar Ben Yair, ordered his most devoted followers to start killing men, women, and children. The remaining rebels were to kill one another, and the last one would commit suicide.

Books and documentary movies propagate the "exemplary" act of mass suicide/killing of Masada rebels as an example of religious faithfulness and righteous courage. How does one compare Masada's mass suicide/killing of the 1st century with the mass suicide of 918 believers in Jonestown in 1978? Do we see any similarities? Jim Jones believed that there were evil enemies who were preparing to attack their religious camp. Jim Jones chose mass suicide rather than being "captured" by his enemies. The most devoted religious followers killed by poison their co-believers and committed suicide as a final act of religious delusional behaviour and defiance. The scenarios between the two religious camps appear to be similar. Religious induced-mental illness made their mass suicide a "comfortable" act.

In the Old and New Testaments and the Qur'an there are examples where God has commanded someone to sacrifice and kill innocent people. Reading Genesis, we find that Abraham hears God's voice commanding him to kill his son Isaac. In 2003, Deanna Laney, a devoted religious woman, killed her two young sons and claimed that God commanded her to do it. The jury found her not guilty for reasons of insanity. But what or who had inflicted her with such a dreadful insanity? Believing that God commanded her to kill her two children, I would suggest that she also believed the Bible's story of Abraham's willingness to kill his only son.

Was Deanna Laney sitting in church listening and believing the preachers who constantly talked about obeying God's commands? Is it rational to suggest that this devoted religious believer (who could hear God's voice and commands) suffered from religiously inflicted schizophrenia? If such murderous mimetic imagery was constantly transmitted and hosted by religious believers, then can Christians count on Christianity tolerating murder if killing your innocent children is a form of religious obedience to God? What would be a jury's verdict of Abraham? Would he be found guilty or not guilty for reasons of religious insanity?

The question is:

Are there legal grounds for class action lawsuits against religious institutions that inflict, through their religious indoctrination, mental illness?

It is not too difficult to identify religious mental illness, even if one argues that cultural differences, subjective assessment, and competing psychological theories do not provide one with an absolute legal definition. What could possibly be more mentally damaging to a young child than repeatedly telling him or her that there are monsters under the bed? Yet, Christians send their children to Sunday schools and to church, telling them that there exists an invisible man called God who is unwilling to prove he exists yet he is watching you every second of every single day. This invisible man in the sky can read any child's thoughts, and if he or she does not believe in this invisible God, he or she will go to Hell to be tortured and burned for eternity.

The indoctrination of religious delusions is one of the most serious inflictions of mental illness today. It propagates to religious believers an *inability to face the material reality of life, growth and the finality of death.* The more pathetic, empty, purposeless, and desperate a person's life is, the more likely that person will believe in God. Religious beliefs constitute a mental illness because it gives false hope, a distortion of reality, and a delusional explanation that there is a higher meaning to sad, non-creative, and pathetic lives. Indoctrinating children to believe in the three in one god- God, the Son, and the Holy Spirit, is no different than having them believe in the big three of Santa Claus, the Easter Bunny, and the Tooth Fairy.

What I have tried to convey here is that religion is a superstition, and a belief in supernatural beings is a mental illness. Superstition is a belief in magic, magical trickery, an illusion of "something" existing beyond the bounds of nature or outside of the natural universe. Thus, a religious belief is a superstitious belief, and acting upon such beliefs is a mental illness. The common factor in religious mental illness is the delusion of the afterlife, resurrection, or eternal life. However, the historical and scientific fact is that not one of us is coming back. When all of us recognize that religion is an inflicted mental illness, then we can surely begin to find a cure for this disease.

Religious destructive idealism is used to spread hatred and intolerance. There is much that has been said about the relationship between religious idealism and mental illness. You may question: "Why are delusional beliefs that have religious themes closely related to people diagnosed with schizophrenia?" Is it because schizophrenia is a vivid delusional and dramatic religious idealist disorder? Religious persons who believe and "hear" God's commands that no one else hears; those who believe that their priests or pastors have some special ability to communicate with God; these people suffer from the mental illness of religious destructive idealism.

5

FOR THE LOVE OF SUFFERING

"Through me the way into the suffering city,
through me the way to the eternal pain,
through me the way that runs among the lost
justice argued on my high artificer;
My maker was divine authority,
the highest wisdom and the primal love
before me nothing but eternal things were
made,
And I endure eternally.
Abandon every hope, ye who enter here"

The Gates of Hell -Dante's Inferno

"Religious suffering is, at one and the same time, the expression of real suffering and [peoples] protest against real suffering. Religious [pain] is the sigh of the oppressed creature, the heart of a heartless world, and the soul of soulless condition. It is the opium of the people."

Karl Marx -1818 - 1883

During the development of human civilization, religions of all sorts have played a dominant role in moulding the civil and national character of society. Though it is beyond the scope of this book, it is worth pointing out religious dogmas to the reader. Metaphorically speaking, Religion is like an old general country store. The store's (church) stock has something for everyone and caters to every need; from drugs (or snake oil) to magic cures, and all sorts of gifts for every occasion. So long as its position is dominant, the store's services will be in its rudest and crudest form. The proprietor (God) is so dull and ignorant of his customers needs that his prescriptive services remain fixed, sterile, and, most repulsively, lifeless. The church kept its religious followers sick day and night for twenty centuries by bleeding them, torturing them, enslaving them, burning them alive, ordering them to commit acts of genocide against indigenous people, and submitting women to subjugation.

In times of war, the church would bless the arms and guns of its followers. Nationalism and patriotism would become an extension of religion—love for country, flag and honour, and a blessed duty to kill the "others." Blessed are the meek that will conquer the world. Sometimes, when materialist reality conflicts with his meme-dogma, the believer is motivated to revolt against his oppressor, but he doesn't dare—he "knows" better. He knows that his Maker would find out his secret thoughts–the Maker of the world sees and knows everything that goes on; the believer's excommunication and punishment in Hell is predetermined. And how dreadful that would be! The mere thought of his being discovered brings chills down his spineless body. Isn't it curious, how he knows it to be true?

A believer very seldom fights a winning fight against the Holy Ghost. The odds too highly favour the great invisible. Religious dogma, so the believer believes in his own mind, has been fire-tested and proven in his mind. As for the human corpses lying on the plains of Guyana's 1978 Jonestown suicide pact of 850 believers, they were simply shop-rejected products. When alive, did they know just when and how their convictions came about? The dreadful results show they didn't care. **"Theirs was not to reason why, theirs was to follow and comply."**

So long as the believer was with what seemed the majority—which was his most important identity, the safe place to be, the comfortable thing to do—he was blindly imitating others. The small herd follows the larger herd, then all believers follow what they supposed was the divine order of the majority. In Jonestown, all 850 women, children, and men died without putting up a fight. Their benevolent God could only kill his own believers, and that is what He did. When all His healing and comforting "snake oil" medicines failed to result in anything (other than to be used as debilitating poisons), it made Him abandon His flock to Hell and damnation altogether.

For two thousand years, religious love, comfort, charity, and compassion were comforting opiates administered to the meek. The storekeeper was proven to be a quack for his cures were no more than repulsive purges and tortures to destroy flesh and scientific thought. The believer's incurable sickness was evolution, which has been the materialist truth ever since the natural universe has been in existence.

For believers of African-American descent, your religiosity has been very curious–your dogmatic devotion to the very religious institution which bought and sold your tragic ancestors. In all the centuries of the existence of the Roman Catholic Church (and much later, of the Reformist Church), it has owned, bought, and sold for profit African slaves. It authorized and encouraged its merchant-believers to trade them.

How could any African-American know with absolute certainty that the inhumane treatment of their forefathers was not in accordance with God's will and design? Surely you would not doubt God's specially appointed representative, the sole voice of God's word on earth? After all, with the written Bible that you obey today, the infallible expounder of Him, His message cannot be mistaken, and its meaning cannot be distorted. It was His will for His divine church to be on the side of trade in human beings. But do not despair, the new religious knights are kneeling before the same God and proclaiming forgiveness to the sinners, who destroyed African homes, ripped children away from their mother's bosom, split families, and broke human hearts. It was done in the name of the merciful redeemer and the holy gospel of the meek. It was done to build glorious churches, with elegant stained glass depicting a prophecy of the apocalyptic Second Coming.

The Biblical prophesies still remain and the religious practices have been refined. Idealism has helped our hearts to grow soft. We were able to disconnect religious delusion from the material reality of human tragedy. But the holy work of the church's meek (nurtured by blood and human suffering) needed a new procession of blood: the burning of the live human flesh of those who believed in another God. They needed to be destroyed because the Bible said so. The Bible has always been misogynous, so burning 50,000 "witches" alive was in accordance to God's commands.

Throughout human history, our ancestors depended on pagan witches to explain the mysteries of the cosmos, give reasons for the reoccurrence of natural disasters, such as floods and tides, and to give offerings to the mysterious forces governing the material world. Science was still in its infancy. The power of natural forces was overwhelming and the witches' prophecies provided a way of dealing with collective ignorance. This placed the pagan's spirituality in direct competition with the church's divine monopoly over the workings of the natural world. Therefore, the church's priests who were specialists gathered up the tools of their trade: halters, thumbscrews, hot-irons, and shackles. They set out to perform their holy work with earnestness and conviction. So much so, that they imprisoned, tortured, burned, hanged and annihilated entire colonies of mostly female "witches" in their quest to rid the Christian world of dissenting voices.

Our social conversion came when social thinkers began to rise against their holy oppressors. Their combative and innovative writings in both France and England fought a strong and stubborn fight against religious dogma. The proverbial "Pandora's Box" was, at last, open. Secular opposition was clearly defined against religion's coercive and abusive force. The religious slogan that life is sacred proved incapable of standing before the social scrutiny of religious persecution, religious wars, religious inquisitions, the endorsement of slavery, and the oppression of women.

Religion was born out of ignorance regarding how the social and natural world works. Contemporary apologists of Christianity want us to "forget and forgive" the church's atrocities and destructiveness and separate these things from the idea of God. For the church's followers, the only requirement was (and still is) to believe. Any acts against humanity were placed squarely on the shoulders of individual priests and other members of the church, but not on the church itself. Praxis (acts) was separated from the mental (idea).

This delusion alleviated Christian believers from the burden of cognitive reasoning. This was by means of not associating mental thought with praxis and praxis with mental thought. It proved to the institutional church that idealism works with blind followers, the ignorant, and the vulnerable. Any passing second thought could always be defused by sermons, exquisite music, and a constant supply of mimetic beliefs, since the believer's primary wish is nothing more than an overwhelming search for security.

Capitalizing on such a basic sense of insecurity, Christianity's dogma encouraged the vulnerable to dream, worship, and expect the "real life" that would occur in heaven, thus diverting their focus away from this Earth. Not having any responsibility for its care, protection, and harmonious transformation, the Earth was seen as hostile and evil, a temporal place, in the salvation from which the meek would escape to heaven. In the belief system of Christianity, Judaism, and Islam, heaven is not for the unworthy. Earth is the place where demons, evil, sinners, Satan, sickness, poverty, wars, and ecological disasters live or occur. Heaven, on the other hand, is perfect, everlasting, and dreamlike.

Acting upon these mimetic religious delusions, grave environmental disasters were inevitable. The Bible teaches the meek (Genesis 1:28) that their purpose on earth was, and still is, to be fruitful and multiply. Also, the meek must subdue and have dominion over all living things. Any sort of birth control was regarded as a sinful act and against religious dogma. The most serious environmental abuse of overpopulation (a real material effect) was placed secondary in importance to the dominant idea: God.

To obey the church is to obey God. Failing to obey and believe is to face the church's darkest and most destructive power. In the process, organized religion revealed ever so clearly that its primary goal was, and still is, its dominance over the blindly faithful. In doing so, it compels its minions to kill adherents of other religions. Christians are against Jews who are against Muslims who are against both. Protestants are against Catholics, true believers are against false believers, Gentiles and atheists. All serve a mythical range of messianic ideas of God.

Who is this messianic God? In accordance with religious tradition, God is a divine being who rules this world from somewhere outside this natural world. It is because He comes to us from outside life that this God, by divine command, can subdue this world's animals and plants, control the weather, and also its ecological events. Why does this God want to subdue the earth unless He is angry at it? Why else would He send the rains for forty days and forty nights to achieve the divine punishment of the Earth's sinful? Why else would He destroy Sodom and Gomorrah to punish the homosexuals, or inflict the Egyptians with the plague, for daring to disobey His divine command to free the Hebrews? Why would He cause the Katrina floods in 2005, or the Tsunamis in the Asian coast off Thailand?

Why has this angry God created man to carry on with his divine destructiveness and punishment against the earth, other humans, animals and plants? Why such an environmental hatred and arrogance? God's orders for man to obey and follow, in accordance with the Bible are:

(1) to subdue the Earth

(2) to have Dominion over all living things

(3) to be fruitful and multiply

To subdue the earth signifies that religion places the human as central where the natural world revolves around his selfish wants and needs. This is fundamentally an anti-earth attitude which has been adopted by believers of Judaism, Christianity, and Islam. The mimetic phrase "subdue the earth" entered the religious vocabulary and has been transmitted to the rest of humanity as a form of secular idealism. It has made its way to all those who believe that "anything goes" because we are *"numero uno."*

Uncontrolled consumerism, an idiotic entitlement, has transformed us from human beings to corporate clients. We are consuming products, self-images, music, video games, fast food, love and happiness: all for a price. To have dominion over all living things has resulted in environmental disasters of over- fishing, daily destruction of the Amazonian rainforest, the pollution of land and water, and the extinction of numerous animal species. Geological natural resources as well as renewable (but not inexhaustible) resources are placed at the whim of consumption and waste.

The most destructive human act and most idiotic mimetic-phrase is to be fruitful and multiply. This is strongly followed by Catholic believers, various cults and Muslim polygamists (some of whom have up to 60 children). The cultural attitude where a man's social worth is measured by the number of children he has with different women continues to plague many third world societies. Ignorance of birth control, by any legal method, has led to overpopulation in Africa, India, and China. The overall consequences include the scarcity of food resources and the spread of HIV.

Overpopulation is human abuse. It has the most serious form of environmental impact on both the earth and the ozone layer. It is this ozone shield that has made life possible on our planet. Its continued depletion is occurring in the Southern Hemisphere over the southern part of Chile, New Zealand, and Australia. While living in Peru for several years, I had the opportunity to briefly travel in the southern part of Chile. In the summer months, I saw young children playing, running, and engaging in their games and normal children's activities. What was not normal, however, was that those children were all wearing some kind of hat and all of them were wearing sunglasses. Harmful UV rays of the sun from the "ozone hole" destroy the pupils of the eye and cause skin cancer. In specific Chilean areas, such as Punta Arenas, the human population is exposed to UV radiation that is above normal and unhealthy.

While it is beyond the scope of this book to provide an extensive analysis of environmental disasters and their causes, it is still important to understand the cause and effect of these destructive practices. For more than two thousand years, humans were influenced by and followed a cultural mimetic set of religious beliefs directing them to be fruitful and multiply. All the while, economic activities have increased in the last 500 years. While economic activities and trade are normal human social traits, excessive consumption is not.

Excessive consumption leads to the excessive production of manufactured items. Developed and industrialized nations have been forced to admit this reality, in that industrial waste is partly responsible for global warming. While it is customary to blame the industrialized nations for global warming, environmentalists shy away from criticizing the corrupt relationships between third world businesses and their national governments. Foreign and national mining companies, fish-meal producers, smelting furnaces, and transportation by dirty diesel causes blood mercury levels in Peruvian children to be extremely high. In addition, asthmatic diseases are present in 30% of Lima's Incan population.

I have witnessed the effects of pollution on the city of Lima, where the air tastes and smells like diesel fuel and your eyes are hurt by toxic gases in the air. Mexico City, Jakarta, Beijing, and most cities in India, suffer from the presence of chemical toxins. I have been in Peruvian and Bolivian mining villages where metal smelters and open air furnaces operate with no chimneys or chemical control systems. I have witnessed protestors, both workers and environmentalists, fighting against such unlawful acts but to no avail. Corruption is widespread between businesses and governmental institutions. So much so that no one can protect the people and the environment. Radical groups thrive in Latin America because of inequalities of monetary distribution and institutional corruption.

Admittedly, environmental consequences are also evident in the coal burning stacks in North America. However, the top polluting nations are also the most deeply shaped by Catholic religious dogma. Biblical traditional attitudes which regard the Earth as a hostile place can be witnessed in Latin American attitudes towards the environment. Religion and corruption are not necessarily against each other, for various biblical stories tend to validate exploitation of the meek, the trade of slaves, and the subjugation of women. Raw exploitation of the environment and the weak is elevated by the strong religiosity evident in the population's anti-earth attitudes. While I made efforts to convince them about cleaning the raw garbage in their village and explained its negative effects on their health–it truly felt as though they did not understand the message. Taking care of the environment was not part of their daily thoughts. But when the conversation turned to God, Satan, and heaven, they seemed to be well-versed on delusional beliefs. The religious dogmatic hold encouraged them to worship and believe in a perfect world where there is no raw garbage, no flies, no bad odours, no poverty and no earth for which to have any responsibility for its care.

Idealism and its effects are so evident. Even the secular idealists were having a hard time accepting their environmental mess due to their deep sense of nationalist pride. In conversation after conversation I had with villagers over the span of an eight year period. I discovered that people believed that the soul lives on after death, that the local *curandero* (witch-doctor) can change the physical world, and that the earth's illness and "bad luck" are caused by spirits, ghosts, fairies, angels, demons, devils and angry saints. In fact, these villagers are no different in their beliefs than the 25% of Americans who believe in the existence of witches, 45% who believe in ghosts, 50% who believe in the devil, 50% who believe that the Bible is God's true word, 68% who believe in angels, and 75% who believe that Jesus was raised from the dead.

The mimetic transmission of delusional beliefs has been embedded in the believer's mind and provides a comfort zone against anything real that does not fit into the perfection of the invisible. For two thousand years, the propagation of religious mimetic beliefs passed from one generation to the next, resulting in delusional thoughts of a benevolent shepherd. This raises the question of why a person finds concordance in delusional beliefs which he or she can obviously see are false. The Bible is believed to be the benevolent God's true words, yet it contains instructions for rape, genocide, and the destruction of families. Religion has encouraged believers to stone, murder, take part in holy wars, inquisitions, Islamic jihads and fatwa, to become suicide bombers, and to be members of cults that have mass suicides. All of this in order to reunite in heaven. The French philosopher Blasé Pascal (1623–1662) wrote:

"Men never do evil so completely and cheerfully as when they do it from religious conviction."

This is quite evident from the fact that all 19 suicidal men so willingly went to their graves during the 9/11 destruction of the World Trade Centre.

Let's focus on a common thread shared by all religions and spiritual cults: praying. Religious believers and spiritual cultists use the act of prayer as a method of success of the spiritual or mental over the material natural world. They ask that the Laws of Nature be negated or annulled on behalf of a single person or group of petitioners. Praying is a desperate mimetic delusional belief to beg gods, saints, spirits, cosmic energy etc. to cure sickness, help one to win the Super Bowl, find love, communicate with the dead, find a good job, win the Lotto 6/49, win the war in Iraq and Afghanistan, and bless the guns that would kill the crusaders and infidels. What kind of delusional person would do something as idiotic as inventing ghosts and ask or petition them to act for social change or good weather?

Religion has habitually promoted ruthless and useless activities that endanger the lives of its meek individual followers. Throughout religious history, thousands of people have been punished and have suffered in the name of God. Punishment, or the threat of it, was part of a system of social control, and suffering became accepted and imprinted in the minds of those who were being punished. In time, a culture of accepting suffering was propagated through the church's writings, all to convince believers to endure pain, punishment and suffering.

Learning and accepting suffering became a way of life, and the mimesis of such a custom passed from parents to children.

Reasons for enduring suffering were numerous, from punishments of all sorts to the consequences of not obeying the church's orders. Suffering is in the core of Christianity's dogma:

> *"The voice of Christ: I came down from the heaven... and took upon Myself your miseries,...out of love, that you might learn to be patient and bear the sufferings of this life without repining....From the moment of my birth,...suffering did not leave me,...I suffer great..."*
> (J. Sponge)

From its beginning, Christianity has defined humanity (Adam and Eve) as sinful and fallen creatures. They were punished and suffered for their sins. Religion inspired habits of everlasting suffering. By calling the Bible the "Word of God" church leaders reserved to themselves the right to interpret the idea of punishment and suffering. So, who is this God who caused the punishment and suffering of the entire human race— with the exception of Noah's family? Who is this God who caused the punishment and suffering of the entire population of the city of Sodom (except for His chosen family! So who is this God who sent the Angels of Death across the land of Egypt, with the brutal task of murdering the first born male in every Egyptian family?

His chosen people are contemporary religious fundamentalists (e.g., televangelists) who are punishing and causing suffering to their vulnerable believers by saying that *"God wants you to give [your money to us] till it hurts."* Whether they are Catholic or Evangelist fundamentalists, they continue to set the tone for the way their church's power relates to human life. Constructed around its presumption of divine power, the authority to inflict punishment such as excommunication or group shaming becomes a necessary prerequisite for the maintenance of their institutional power.

Endless rituals and rules abound with their emphasis on religious duties. Failing to adhere to those solemn obligations would bring a proper punishment from God. An endless stream of causes and the acceptance of suffering are so integrated in religious life that it has developed a yearning for sadomasochism. Acts of self-mutilation (flogging) exemplify this as a justification of suffering because believers believe that they were "born-in-sin."

My own grandmother Angelica never travelled further than 50 miles from the village where she was born. The only "crime" that she committed during her 93 years of life was to, from time to time; kill one of her own chickens to feed her guests or family. As a child I could not understand why she cried during the preparation of the chicken. Much later, I was told that it was because she felt guilty for killing her chickens Every Sunday, my grandmother attended church to hear the priest's "fire and brimstone" sermons against sinners, who were doomed to suffer forever.

The concept of punishment and inflicting suffering is so broad and flexible that it is unavoidable for believers not to be affected by the religious expectations of inflicting pain on themselves and others. The Martin Luther 1543 writing, *On the Jews and their Lies,* is a blueprint of Jewish obstinacy. It says that synagogues should be burned, Jewish literature confiscated, Jewish teaching forbidden, and vengeance taken upon them for being "Christ-killers." Luther had a destructive, anti-Semitic fanatical hatred. His demagogy about the Jews was unbelievably hostile. For Luther, Jews were nothing short of evil by nature, greedy money lenders, lacking redeeming value and saving grace. He railed against the Jews, publicly and privately, propagating that they were, by their very being, demonic sinners who had compromised their right to live, and that the Christian world would be well served by their death.

Such a religious delusion (idealism) was imposed upon the reality of the human race. On November 9, 1938, Luther's birthday, Nazi leader Adolf Hitler unleashed his Kristallnacht (Night of Broken Glass) of Nazi minions who smashed windows in homes, shops and synagogues in Germany's Jewish communities. This has been mirrored in the destruction of the World Trade Centre by the religious suicide bombers of 9/11; Israel/Palestinian killings and bombings; Sudan's Muslim genocide against African-Sudanese; Ireland's Catholic/Protestant killings; and the Taliban's public flogging of women who dare to show an inch of female skin. These are just a few more examples of religion's infliction of punishments and suffering.

Christian, Jewish, and Muslim religions define humans as fallen creatures because of their long list of eternal sins. The original sin is found in the story of Adam and Eve which set the tone for human's need for suffering. These two were doomed as human beings the moment they disobeyed God's command. As the definition of the human as a fallen creature developed within the church, it became an ideological base, in which humans—who were not perfect—embodied a sense of guilt as sinners who needed to be punished and rescued at the same time. Human suffering entered the Christian, Jewish, and Muslim religious traditions, which re-enforced the idea that humans were not what God intended them to be. Such religious tradition, were aimed at subduing the uniquely human characteristic of freedom of choice. Our biblical ancestors simply disobeyed God.

The Bible presents the picture of God as a judge. God distributes punishment causing humans to suffer the eternity of hell. (Mark 9:43–48, 82–85). At other times, God—who was occupied with other things—would send angels with powerful swords to do His deadly deeds. In time, such angels became the church's priests, holding power over the meek who, in turn, felt sinful, guilty, and ready to accept punishment and suffering. Once believers accepted their own guilt as fallen sinners, the priests, imams and rabbis portrayed humans as wretched and miserable creatures who, to win a full pardon, needed to suffer the church's or self-inflicted punishment.

Torturing the human body as a way to gain salvation is well documented in some Catholic and Muslim fundamentalist sects. Believers flog themselves with chains which cause bleeding, and this is hardly a healthy act. Delusional believers tend to do great harm to themselves, clearly based upon the belief that they deserve to suffer. The Peruvian 1671 Catholic saint, Santa Rosa of Lima, is well-documented to have inflicted pain and suffering to her body by wearing a metal spiked crown, iron chains about her waist, and pouring hot red pepper (aji) in her eyes to imitate Christ's suffering. The American televangelist Oral Roberts used God's threats of death to encourage his followers to raise 10 million dollars for his church. Former President G.W. Bush claimed that it was God who told him to invade Iraq—so he did—causing death and suffering to thousands of Americans and Iraqis.

The religious slogan "Jesus died for my sins" is a commonly repeated expression used in some form or another in every religious circle. That was and still is the core of religious belief, which makes it easy to understand why the disobedient child would stand before a righteous parent prepared to be punished. It is not uncommon for religious believers to raise their children with the mimetic customs and styles that are modelled after the traditions of organized religion. Such violent traditions of inflicting suffering—*"Spare the rod, spoil the child"*—is sadistic and continues to pass on from one generation to the next the irrational need to suffer. Christianity, Judaism, and Islam are about pain and suffering and the destructive attitude of denying life. An Episcopalian hymn partially reads:

> *Before thy throne, O God, we kneel....*
> *What're the pain and shame may be,*
> *Bring us, O Father, nearer thee ...*
> *Warn us and train us with thy rod:*
> *Teach us to know our faults, O God*

One can imagine the scene projected in this hymn where the message is that we are all "born in sin" and that we are all in need of the Lord's mercy, after the punishment is administered. Tell me, are those words not those of a quivering meek person who seems to be obsessed by guilt and asking to be punished? Are those words not a standard feature from which torture, whippings, burnings, and excommunication are administered to God's chosen people, the Christians?

The Bible describes and reduces human beings to the animal level—sheep and goats—who depend on guidance from the "Good Shepherd," the priests themselves. From this diagnosis of the state of humanity, the entire Christian dogma is directed at believers to forfeiting their humanity and to accepting punishment and suffering as part of their dehumanised piety, which is clouded in forms of worship. Is this healthy? Does dehumanising a person through punishment and suffering enhance life and personal growth? The Bible's focus on human suffering is not yet visible to religious believers. The followers of Protestant fundamentalists, hearing their preacher's fanaticism describing their sinfulness, then feel an irrational dependency on the preacher's divine "power" to extract their sins. At the end of the sermon, believers go home satisfied that the verbal abuse they just received, and the money they gave, has alleviated their guilt and suffering.

The most profound human suffering that religion has inflicted upon its followers is that upon women and their daughters. Pro-male or anti-female bias has resulted in women's suffering under religious and secular idealism that can be traced back to ancient history.

Hindu religious texts advocated women's suffering that goes beyond mere pro-male of anti-female bias:

"It is the highest duty of a woman to immolate herself after her husband's death."

In the Hindu laws of Manu:

"In childhood a female is subject to her father. In youth a female is subject to her husband. When her lord [husband] is dead, she shall be subject to her sons. A woman must never be independent."

Today, many Afghani women are forced to live under strict Islamic restrictions that reflect the depth of female deprivation and suffering. It is not an overstatement to say that Taliban religious fanaticism treats women worse than animals. The infliction of human suffering is at the core of the Taliban's treacherous and filthy crimes against 50% of the population of Afghanistan, and it deprives them of a humane existence.

Afghani women and their daughters suffer in many social areas. There is a complete ban on women's work outside the home. No female teachers, no female engineers, no female professionals are allowed. Some female doctors and nurses are allowed to take care of women and their children only. Outside the home, there is a complete ban on women's activities (unless accompanied by a father, brother, son or husband). Social activities for women are permitted under those restrictions; however, they must wear a long veil (burka). In open market areas, women are not permitted to deal directly with male shopkeepers. They cannot be treated by a male doctor, nor are they allowed to study in schools, universities, or any other educational institutions. For a more detailed list of Taliban restrictions on female activities, you may wish to visit: http://www.rawa.org/rules.htm.

The causes for these overwhelmingly destructive attitudes towards women are based on a religious and secular idealism which regards women as being the "weak sex." The term "women and children first" is associated in our western secular idealism with the notion that a mother and child are bonded in weakness. This is a state in which they could never escape their "destiny." I am staunchly against the secular idealist vulgarity behind the male expressions "f--k" and "screw" or the pervasive idea that "sex sells."

Where organized religion and secular idealism are strongly embedded in any given society, a mimetic attitude finds its expression in social activities that have been advocated for many centuries. Passed from one generation to the next, delusional mimetic beliefs (secular or religious) have been propagated by leaders as an imposition of their ideas upon the external world, with dehumanizing consequences. Somewhat milder is the practice of secular idealism that promotes a mimetic attitude of "the stick and the carrot," the attitude of punishment and reward towards an opponent. When religious influence began its decline (due to public education and people's rejection of religious beliefs), the Holy Book's social attitude was mimetically transplanted to secular idealism which carried on the stereotypes of what women can or cannot do. The secular ideal of women does not correspond to objective reality, in that, secular idealism clouded the reality of women as real human beings.

Instead of the religious oppression of women, secular idealism rejected religiosity but retained similar domestic violent attitudes towards them. It took women's liberation in the 1920's and 1960's to bring about protests against such oppression.

I want to assure the reader that we are not fallen or sinful creatures as it is described by religious priests, imams, or rabbis. We do not deserve to be punished and to suffer under any religious rules and traditions. We must recognize that religious believers are frightened and insecure people who are not able to achieve a clean break from religious shackles. These believers must learn to celebrate the creative nature of humanism and atheism. We all must acknowledge that we are part of this human race and that we are not alone. Classified as Christians, Jews, or Muslims, we are humans together in every race, colour, or creed. We all must acknowledge that Earth is our only home, that there are no "other worlds." Delusional senses of guilt, judgment of others who are different from us and the dogma of righteousness are religious idealist products of irrational fears. A vicious and bloodthirsty biblical God would never make believers feel like safe, fearless, and reborn humans. We need to empower ourselves not with idealism and delusion, but in a deeper and fully human way. We must pursue the quest for an even more profound sense of what it means to be human, a real human who is connected to the elegance of the reality of our natural world.

Believers often tend to become disappointed at God's silence. They are not protected from normal life's pain and injuries. One can witness the valuable gifts offered to the Virgin Mary, the saint of Guadalupe, or any other of the 6,000 saints within the Catholic Church for some miracle. Believers' prayers, offerings and ecclesiastical pleadings for curing diseases and physical traumas become almost incoherent. One hears hysterical pleas for God not to allow us to receive pain and suffering. When all else fails, we hear the priests comforting the believers about how God never asks them to bear more pain and suffering than they can endure. At times, priests scold believers that they actually deserve the pain and suffering that has been inflicted upon them. Does a believer with HIV seem particularly sinful? Does God designate those who were victims of the Holocaust, genocide, ethnic cleansing or drug-related executions to suffer in this matter? Does God designate the Third World poor to die of hunger and sickness? Are we humans already conditioned by religious idealism to prefer to live in a world of make-believe that we cannot outgrow? Have we been conditioned by thousands of years of obeying delusional beliefs to live with false hopes, expecting an invisible entity to function in accordance with our whims, instead of actively altering our lives to save ourselves and our environment? The point is that if this invisible entity can control the weather patterns, bring rain when farmers pray for it, stop the hurricanes, or flood the earth and kill all of its inhabitants—except his favoured believer Noah—could this God also prevent all diseases from happening? Could He vacuum away the polluted atmosphere and restore an environmental balance?

6

RELIGION AND SLAVERY

"…you may purchase male or female slaves from among the foreigners who live among you. You may also purchase the children of such resident foreigners, including those who have been born in your land. You may treat them as your property, passing them on to your children as a permanent inheritance."

Leviticus 25: 44 -46 NLT

"The delegates of the annual conference are decidedly opposed to modern abolitionism and wholly disclaim any right, wish, or intention to interfere in the civil and political relation between master and slave, as it exists in the slave-holding states of the union."

Methodist Episcopal Church, 1836 General Conference, Cincinnati

Among the most damaging of religious crimes against humanity is the biblical sanction and regulation of slavery (Doulos in Greek). Beginning with the Hebrew Scriptures of the Old Testament, the sanction of human slavery is based on the 10th Commandment. More on this will be discussed later.

In an apparent attempt to edit or disguise the religious practice of human slavery, Jewish and Christian translators of the Old and New Testaments substituted the term slave with ambiguous words like: servant, bondman, maid, handmaid, manservant, etc. However, the first correct use of the term slavery appears in Genesis 9:25 where Noah cursed his grandson Canaan: "Cursed be Canaan! The lowest of slaves he will be to his brothers." In **Genesis 9: 27,**

"Blessed be the Land, the God of Shem! May Canaan be the slave of Shem. May God extend the territory of Japheth: may Japheth live in the tents of Shem and may Canaan be his Slave."

These two Biblical verses set the future grounds for ancient theologians who wished to justify slavery in Judaism and Christianity. Later, any Protestant or Catholic owner of slaves in England, Spain, Portugal, Holland and American, were only implementing God's commands by owning humans as slaves.

These verses (as theory) and the praxis of slavery are considered immoral by today's secularists, and by religious apologists who are aiming to redefine and recreate a "good" religion." The brave Bishop J. S. Spong is one of them. In his informative book, *The Sins of Scripture* he states:

"The Bible has been used for centuries by Christians as a weapon of control. To read it literally is to believe in a three-tiered universe, to condone slavery, to treat women as inferiors creatures, to believe that sickness is caused by God's punishment...that mental disease ....epilepsy are caused by

demonic possession. When someone tells me that they believe the Bible is the 'literal and inerrant word of God,' I always ask, 'Have you ever read it?"

This human abuse, such as the capital crime of murder, and regarding a woman as property (as is the case with Saudi Arabian women today) is evident in the following verse from the Revised Standard Version of the Old Testament, **Exodus 21: 20-21.**

"When a man strikes his slave, male or female, and the slave dies under his hand, he shall be punished. But if the slave survives a day or two, he is not to be punished, for the slave is his [property]."

A notion of morality, including Islamic theory and its related praxis is put forward by all three major religions. These appear to be a blueprint for universal morality. However, it is not freely chosen by individuals for their own behaviour, but imposed upon the populace.

I strongly advocate that any institution, group, or individual who propagates a "good morality" must have reasonable social credibility. Such a social credibility must underlie a code of conduct that perpetuates freedom from oppression and endangerment of life. Social credibility is a framework by which we judge someone's advice or action as being "good" or "bad." Does he or she (or an institution) have the social credibility to "give" advice or encourage an action? For someone to say, for example "John has committed many violent crimes, but inside he is a good man" does not hold water. Morality then cannot be just an idea or sentiment. Morality is a credible code of social conduct. Does a religious institution which sanctions slavery have the social credibility to be described as "good" religion? Let us see if this is so!

Prisoners of our Ideals

To begin with, neither the founder of Christianity nor any of his Apostles have ever been recorded as saying or taking a stand against slavery. The institution of slavery was very much active and had a long history before Christianity was invented. The Old Testament was fully adopted by the "holy book" of the New Testament. A prominent Jewish Rabbi, Raphall, is quoted as saying, in 1861, that *"receiving slavery as one of the conditions of society, the New Testament nowhere interferes with or contradicts the slave code of Moses..."* Let us see if such a statement holds true, taking notice (as previously mentioned) that the term slavery has been replaced by less "offensive" words.

Matthew 18: 25 states *"But for as much as he had not to pay, his lord commanded him to be sold [as slave] and his wife, and children, and all that he had, and payment to be made."* This is a case where a husband and father were in debt, and he, his wife, and his children were sold to pay the lender. How difficult is it to assume that the British and American debtor's prison, which was still active until 1869, carried the Hebrew-Christian social code of morality? Such an assumption has a good deal of credibility because the priests of this religious code of morality were slave owners themselves. According to **Mark 14: 66**, *"And as Peter was beneath in the palace, there cometh one of the (slave) of the high priest."*

To strengthen my point further there are the Gospel of Luke; infamous instructions of how to carry out an abuse by slave-owning Christians:

Luke 12: 45-48

"The lord (owner) of that servant [slave] will come in a day when he looketh not for him, and at an hour when he is not aware, and will cut him in sunder, and will appoint him his portion with the unbelievers. And that [slave], which knew his lord's will, and prepared not himself, neither did according to his will, shall be beaten with many stripes. But he that knew

not, and did commit things worthy of stripes, shall be beaten with few stripes for unto whomsoever much is given, of him shall be much required: and to whom men have committed much, of him they will ask the more."

What a religion! The writer apparently saw no social evil in the institution of slavery, or in the immorality of a Christian master owning a man or woman as a piece of property to be bought or sold. In fact, of all the Christian apostles, not one is recorded in the Old or New Testament as condemning slavery and its associated abuses. In addition to propagating the institution of slavery to Christians, St. Paul also directed his immoral preaching to the slaves to obey their owners in the same religious way they obey Jesus Christ!

Ephesians 6: 5-9

"Servants (slaves), be obedient to them that are your Masters according to the flesh, with fear and trembling, in singleness of your heart, as unto Christ; Not with eye service, as men pleasers; but as the servant of Christ, doing the will of God from the heart; With good will doing service, as to the Lord, and not to man; knowing that whatsoever good thing any man doeth, the same shall he receive of the Lord, whether he be bond or free. And, ye masters, do the same thing unto them, forbearing threatening; knowing that your Master also is in heaven; neither is there respect of persons with him."

So far we have seen that both religions of Judaism and Christianity institutionalized slavery. Biblical Laws were regarded as the "Word of God." Secularists insist that the Old and New Testaments were written by tribal religious zealots in ancient times that were propagating their own socio-political agenda and views of the world. St. Peter and St. Paul were the prominent religious fanatics among many within the Hebrew society. They instructed laws and actions on social issues like slavery, genocide, and homosexuality, oppression of women and children, incest, the execution of non-virgin brides, and the stoning and torturing of prisoners. Those primitive tribal laws and actions were carried out for many centuries. It makes little difference to the victims whether the Old and New Testaments' religious laws were written by "God" or by fanatics who established and perpetuated those religions. Because of this, real human abuses have occurred throughout history, in the name of Judaism and Christianity. Slavery, as a religious moral code of conduct, was mimetically transmitted to Islam.

SLAVERY IN ISLAM

Muslims in general are very sensitive towards any criticism of Islam and in particular of the Qur'an, the "Word of God" and their "holy book." Any form of criticism of their moral code of conduct is regarded as blasphemy, a serious religious offence directed against their nationals or foreign believers. It should be noted that the majority of practicing Muslims are non-Arabs and do not speak Arabic. The largest Muslim population today is in Indonesia with 198 million, Pakistan with 135 million, Iran with 65 million, Turkey with 65 million, India with 90 million, and other countries–mostly African–with a combined Muslim population of about 150 million.

Fundamentalist Muslim leaders believe that the Quar'an, as it has been passed on from one generation to the next, is quite simply the most perfect, timeless, and unaltered "Word of God." In short, every Sura or Hadith that is written between the covers of the "holy book" of the Quar'an is the perfect "Word of God." A Hadith is an oral tradition relating to Muhammad's words and deeds which were written down by his close associates and are traditionally passed on as an important tool to determine the Muslim moral code of conduct. The Sura is one of the 114 sections into which the Qur'an is divided. Suras are subdivided into Ayat (verses). Muslims believe that the Qur'an Suras were given to Muhammad by God to perfect the "sayings" of Abraham, Moses, and Jesus.

For theological reasons slavery persists in various Islamic societies in the 21st century. Examples include: Mauritania, Sudan, Djibouti, Ethiopia, Sri Lanka, and India. Slavery was "officially" abolished in Saudi Arabia in 1962, but there are reports that it still continues today. And why not? Slavery was institutionalized in the Qur'an in an equivalent way to the Judo-Christian religious texts. It is the foundation of theocratic societies like Saudi Arabia. It is also a cornerstone in the oppression of non-Muslim migrant workers who, throughout Islamic history have often been enslaved by their Muslim overlords. The following is an example:

MALI: Iddar Aq Ogazide: *"They like to enslave the children early"*

GAO, 14 July 2008 (IRIN)-Iddar Aq Ogazide, a black Tamasheq, was born in 1973 at Tinahamma near Ansongo in northern Mali, 1350 km north of Barmako. His family has been owned by the Toureg Ag Baye family at Intakabarte for several generations. In March this year Iddar finally decided he had enough and made a dramatic escape:

"I was born into slavery because my mother was a slave. My owner's family had bought her grandmother, so that made our whole family inheritable slaves.

It is not a real life, the work is very hard. I had to do everything in my master's house. I looked after the large flock of sheep alone, collected the water and did all the heavy domestic work. I worked day and night and I never received any money.

I never went to school. As I got older I got used to the beating. In particular I remember one horrible day when the sons of my masters, who were younger than me, hit me three times with a stick, on the pretext that I had lost one of the flock. I was scared that if I reacted I might kill someone.

Every year we were listed on the religious tax inventory like other goods that the master owned.

Slavery by inheritance means my children are also slaves. My son Ahmed was barely three years old when a niece of the master got married. They took Ahmed away from me to work in her service. They thought he could do little jobs like make the fires. They like to enslave the children early so that they grow up understanding their place.

Ahmed belonged to the family so there was nothing I could do. I was so sad. I spent 50 days pleading with them to give my son back, but they refused. I was so shocked; I worried so much I could not sleep.

Finally I decided I would have to go and get him so I hatched a plan. I told my master that I needed to take Ahmed with my wife Takwalet to her parents' home. I said we would both return the next day, but we never went back. It was hard to persuade them to let me go [to Takwalet's parents' home], but I managed. It was so frightening to leave, thinking they might come after me. Fortunately when I got to GAO there were many people here to help me.

I was nearly unhappy because I had to leave my two brothers in slavery—they are still there and I can't get them out.

Life is not easy now, but at least I am a free man. I am among men who are the same colour as me who consider me as a man. I don't suffer any discrimination here in Gao. I am proud to use my full name these days—before I used the name Iddar but now I use my father's name too.

People respect me—I earn my own money and that brings respect. I start work as a builder every day at 7 AM, and I earn

US$2. But I know that in today's world if you are poor you are not given the same consideration as people who have money.

Sometimes escaped slaves when they come to Gao change their names to become unknown. Perhaps I might change my name, so that if my master comes looking for me he won't be able to find me.

My dream is that I will one day have justice. I have worked since the day I was born but I have never been paid. I am more than 35 years old now. I want compensation for that. If I got some money I could build myself a house in Gao and live in peace. I could go and get my brothers and we could all be together as a family."

Islamic customs and traditions have had a dominant impact in forming the social structure and daily life of the believers, as is evident in people's social code of conduct, and their behaviour inside and outside their households. Islam is not just a religion. It is a dominant social culture based on a religious moral code of conduct that regulates nearly every aspect of its believers' daily behaviour, family affairs, financial and property relations, food consumption, socio-political structure of men and women, education, and religious beliefs. The basis of such social behaviour is the Qur'an's Law (i.e., Suras and Hadiths) which forms its jurisprudence. It institutionalizes customs and traditions down from ancient tribal times. Slavery is one of the most profound institutions whose guidelines and regulations are an integral part of the Qur'an.

In the pre-Islamic world, slaves were taken in tribal raids on nearby Arab tribes, or from wars against Jewish or Christian desert peoples. Arab slaves were also taken in wars between all tribes regardless of their monotheistic or polytheistic religions. In all of the three monotheistic religions, Judaism, Christianity, and Islam, slaves were taken as "war booty," a reward for the desert fighters.

Muslim religious and military leaders always found support in the Qur'an to call a jihad against others. This was partly for booty (gold, food and taxes) but mainly for the purpose of taking female and male slaves. As the Islamic empire expanded, each ruler was able to decide on the amount of war booty needed, all the while justifying his actions based on how he interpreted Islam's theology. More often than not, Islamist leaders found in the Qur'an supporting text for justifying what they wanted to do, and what actions to take to achieve their aims. Their military cries for jihad against their non-Muslim neighbours facilitated their commercial enterprises and filled their households with slaves. The Qur'an allows for Jews and Christians to be forced into slavery if they are captured in war. When the Islamic armies attacked and captured Spain, they took many thousands of slaves back to Arabia. Men and women were sold, but the special booty was in the form of thousands of virgins as slaves. Young slave boys became *Janissaries* who were trained to form part of the Islamic army. This abduction of young boys was most evident in Greece where the "Greek" Janissaries were sent back to fight against the Greek liberation forces during their 400 hundred years of resistance until 1821, when Greece became an independent nation.

People in the western world are not very familiar with the historical extent of slavery in the Muslim world. The consequences were immoral and terrible, and lasted for many centuries. The Islamic Holy Book promoted and regulated the taking of slaves as the spoils of war. From the day that the "prophet" Muhammad led his tribal Bedouins to rob, murder, rape, and conquer the black Africans in the name of his God, Muslims have continued to enslave others.

Muslims enslaved black Africans long before any slave ships sailed from the waters of the Ivory Coast for the slave markets of the Americas. In fact, Muslims took males and females, boys and girls and made them slaves all over the North African continent, Spain, and in other countries. When the time came, slave cargo ships were loaded with black African slaves. Quite often, a Muslim slave-broker had the slave cargo all ready to depart. American, Spanish, Portuguese, and English enslavers rarely had to go to the African interior to capture black Africans. The slaves were already waiting in Liberia and the Ivory Coast, on behalf of a Muslim ruler or Muslim slave-broker. When those ships were filled up, black African slaves were shipped to Damascus, Medina, Mecca or anywhere else in the Middle East to be enslaved by tribal Arabs or other black Muslims as slaves. According to Ibn Warraq:

"Arabs were deeply involved in the vast network of slave trading—they scoured the slave markets of China, India, and Southeast Asia. There were Turkish slaves from Central Asia, slaves from the Byzantine Empire (Greece), white slaves from Central and East Europe, and black slaves from West and East Africa. Every city in the Islamic world had its slave market."

Muhammad was a warlord and an active enslaver. Let us confirm this claim.

In **Qur'an 33: 50**, it is stated: *"Prophet, We have made lawful to you the wives to whom you have granted dowries and the slave girls whom God has given you as booty."* It is simply criminal for tribal Muslims to claim that their slave-booty in war was God's gift to Muhammad.

Qur'an 23:50: *"...except with their wives and slave girls, for those are lawful to them..."*

Qur'an 16: 75: *Allah sets forth a parable [to consider] a slave, the property of another [who] has no power over anything, and one whom we have granted from Ourselves a goodly sustenance so he spends from it secretly and openly, are the two alike?*

[All] praise is due to Allah!

The repugnant practice of slavery is an immoral code of conduct directed against human dignity. The religious text of the Qur'an explicitly and implicitly condones slavery. It shows that Muhammad took numerous slaves, mostly women and children, as spoils of war. Some of the women Muhammad kept as female slaves; he also kept some as concubines. This name was hardly a consolation to the enslaved young women. Whether slavery is practiced under the absolute power of an enslaver, or by a "benevolent" enslaver who practices a "light" form of slavery called bondage, it is hardly a consolation to the victims of slavery. Slavery under whatever name, religious or secular justification, is still an unjust and immoral code of conduct.

Muslims believe that God himself is the author of the Qur'an and that he wrote each Sura himself and had the angel Gabriel (the same angel from the Jewish Old Testament) delivers the words to the illiterate Muhammad. Therefore, the Suras that propagate and regulate slavery are simply the written "Word of God." A God who propagates human misery, women's abuse, rape and slavery cannot hide his immorality under the glamour of the architecturally impressive religious Mosques.

It is historically confirmed that the Suras were written or recorded by Muhammad's close tribal bandits—some 300 of them—called al-sahabah. These Suras, in fact, were recorded by them on parchment, bark, animal skins and shoulder-bone blades, and were written after Muhammad's death. Like the Hadiths, Muhammad's "sayings"—some 6000 of them—were oral transmissions from tribal leaders who claimed that they "witnessed" or "heard" or someone told them about a given issue that Muhammad had talked about. Faced with a problem of the volume of the Hadith, leading Muslim intellectuals placed all of these into two piles: the "real" and the false Hadiths.

According to Ibn Warraq, in his book *Why I Am Not A Muslim*, any prominent Muslim who wanted to infuse a personal agenda onto a Hadith (that "menstruation makes women dirty") just needed to say that "I heard the Prophet Muhammad saying..." or "I know someone who heard Muhammad saying..." This would be added onto the multiple Hadiths Muslim believers would obey and follow. In **Hadith-Bukhari 4. 654**, Narrated Umar, r.a.:

"I heard the Prophet saying, 'Do not exaggerate in praising me as the Christians praised the son of Mary, for I am only a slave. So, call me the Slave of Allah and his Apostle.'"

Indeed the reader may have noticed that the term "slave" has multiple meanings in the Muslim religious texts. It may be interpreted as "obeying," "loyal," "passive," "submissive," "strong-believer," "I'm your to...," "You are mine to...," and "You are commanded to..." etc. The term "slave" or "slavery" is an integral philosophical, religious, and ideological part of the Muslim way of life. It is a view of one's relationship to his religious and secular beliefs. The frequent use of the term of "slave," along with the institution of slavery, has re-enforced this immoral code of conduct of accepting slavery as God's will. In fact, the very term Islam means for believers "to surrender" or "submit to God."

What a religion ! !

Islamic apologists spread gross lies that Islam is intolerant towards the enslavement of human beings. They propagate the myth that the Islamic religion eradicated the institution of slavery. I believe that Islam is not simply a religion which requires its believers to simply believe. Islam requires real submission, which is in the form of multiple sets of governing laws that establish social, political, economic, property and sexual rights.

Islam is a patriarchal hierarchy in which Muslim believers submit to God (Allah), to men, and women submit to the inequality of property rights. The patriarchal Qur'an says that men are superior to women; Muslim men are taught that women are intellectually inferior. They are taught that they have the right to treat women as sex slaves and submit homosexuals to death. Islam is a religious idealism—a set of delusional ideas—imposed upon real humans. Its consequences are not the "destruction" of other ideas, but the material destruction of human life.

The Islamic ideology advocates the concept of submissiveness (as slavery) on multiple social levels: in girls and boys, and in men and women of all races. In Darfur, today, African men and women live a submissive lifestyle, and forced to be subservient toward the theology of Islam.

Like most religious believers, Muslims—even devout ones—have only a superficial understanding of their religion. Like Jews and Christians, most Muslims never made the choice to be Muslims. As with other religions, they were indoctrinated as children, not knowing that submissiveness (as it is advocated in Islam) is a violation of the freedom to choose. Submissiveness and slavery, therefore, mean one and the same thing in all Islamic social relations.

Sexual submissiveness is quite evident in many Hadiths. Whole chapters of the Hadiths are dedicated to dealing with Muslims having taken female slaves and having sex with them. A Hadith taken from Ibn Sa'ds "Tabaqat" clearly describes how Muhammad had sexual acts with slaves that were just captured as war booty. One was Mariyah, a Coptic slave, and her sister Sirin Muhammad. Mohammad kept Mariyah because she was extremely pretty, with a white complexion and curly hair.

The Islamic historian Ibn Qayyim al-Jawziyya in his book *Zad al Ma'ad* (p. 160) writes that "Muhammad had mainly male and female slaves. He used to buy and sell them, but he purchased more than he sold. He once sold one black slave in exchange for another." It is safe to assume that there were many Muslim enslavers, and here are real stories by which we can confirm this **Book 010 # 3901**

"There came a slave and pledged allegiance to Allah (may peace be upon him) on migration; he (the Holy Prophet) did not know that he was a slave. Then there came his master and demanded him back, whereupon Allah's Apostle (may peace be upon him) said: Sell him to me. And he bought him for two black slaves, and he did not afterwards take allegiance from anyone until he had asked him whether he was a slave or a free man."

In this short story, Muhammad bought a slave by trading two black slaves, which is quite a profit. Aside from that profitable exchange, it establishes the fact that Muhammad "the enslaver" owned and traded in African slaves. It appears that the illiterate Muhammad was a shrewd slave trader.

It is obvious from the above passage that Muhammad the "enslaver" was not told of the true status of the slave, and he was conned into liberating him. Because of this embarrassment, Muhammad made sure that he would not be conned ever again. In the future, Muhammad would ask for the true status of a man, free or slave, before accepting his allegiance.

Captured women—as war booty—were given away or used as bargaining favours to Muhammad's men; these women were then traded or sold to others. In Sirat Rasulallah, Muhammad ordered the massacre of 800 Jewish villagers and took their women and children as slaves. He kept the pretty Jewish girl Rayhana for his sex-slave, and gave the rest away to his tribal followers. In the **Hadith Bukari 47: 743**, Muhammad's dealings with slaves is revealed as harsh:

"The Prophet sent for a woman from the emigrants and she had a slave who was a carpenter. The Prophet said to her "Order your slave to prepare the wood (fire wood) for the pulpit". So, she ordered her slave who went and cut the wood from the tamarisk and prepared the pulpit for the Prophet. When he finished the pulpit, the woman informed the Prophet that it had been finished. The Prophet asked her to send that pulpit to him, so they brought it. The Prophet lifted it and placed it at the place in which you see it now."

Ibn Qayyim al-Jawziyya also states that:

"Muhammad had a number of black slaves. One of them was named 'Mahran.' Muhammad forced him to do more labour than the average man. Whenever Muhammad went on a trip and he, or his people, got tired of carrying their stuff, he made Mahran carry it. Mahran said, "Even if I were already carrying the load of 6 or 7 donkeys while we were on a journey, anyone who felt weak would throw his clothes or his shield or his sword on me so I would carry that, a heavy load."

Indeed some Muslim apologists claim that Islam treated its slaves fairly, and that slaves across the Atlantic were treated badly. Whether some slaves were treated "well" or "poorly" is not the point. It is irrelevant if the slave is in a harem, used as a bargaining tool, for hard labour, or as a housemaid. Slavery is essentially about a lack of freedom, the splitting of families, and the selling of human beings.

Muslims were allowed to have sex at any time with female slaves (Sura 4:3, 4:29' 33:49). Slaves were helpless before their masters—they had no legal rights (Sura 16:77). A Muslim enslaver could kill his slave(s), with no fear of being punished by law (Ref. 2:178).

Slaves could not choose their own marriage mate (Ib n Hazm, vol. 6, part 9). A slave could be forced to marry whomever their enslaver wanted (Malik ibn Anas, vol. 2, p. 155). In the thriving Coptic culture, Jews and Christians were made to pay taxes and thus avoid becoming slaves. This style of extortion of tax-money from non-Muslims affected several cultures from the Sinai desert all the way to Spain. Later, the warrior tribe of Turkomans were used to capture land and extort taxes for their Muslim Caliphs and Sultans and to kidnap young boys to be used for the Janissary army, and young girls to be used as sex slaves.

Muslim tribal warriors took slaves from every land they conquered, but many of the slaves were Muslims themselves from the African continent. They were the ones that were forced to do the harshest labour. According to Robert Payne's book on *The History of Islam* (p.185): "There was a famous black slave uprising in Iraq where thousands of black slaves revolted and killed tens of thousands of Arabs in the city of Basra…Their uprising and drive for freedom lasted for nearly 11 years."

The reader may wish to further investigate the perpetual existence of slavery in Islam in Allan Fisher's *Slavery and Muslim Society in Africa* (1961), or C.E. Bosworth's *The Islamic Dynasties,* where he writes that "…the use of this [African] labour enabled the Arabs to live on the conquered land as a renter class and to exploit some of the economic potential of the rich Fertile Crescent."

The Islamic religion and Muhammad in particular have to be criticized for their immoral codes of sexual conduct which includes the killing, raping, enslaving, and abusing of slaves. Women, and in particular, young virgin girls, were used as sex slaves. Such young girls were called "concubines" or "wives" of much older men. Those men can be easily accused of practicing paedophilia under the guise of religion. Sexual relations with pre-pubescent girls is an example set by

Muhammad for his sex-starved followers. The **Qur'an 65:4** states:

"Such of your women as have passed the age of monthly courses, for them the prescribed period [of pregnancy], if ye have any doubts, is three months, and for those [girls] who have no courses [it is the same three months.]"

Under Islamic law pregnant slave women or prepubescent girls were not allowed to be sold. So the rule concerning divorce for their paedophile "husband" was to observe for three months (to make sure they were not pregnant) before evicting or selling them to another slaver. In **Bukhari vol. 7, 62: 17** Muhammad entices his tribal fighters to "marry" young girls for sexual pleasure:

"...Allah's Apostle said to me, 'Have you got married O Jabir?' I replied, 'Yes.' 'He asked' What, a virgin or a matron?' I replied, Not a virgin but a matron. 'He said, 'Why did you not marry a young girl so that you might play with her and she with you?'

Have no doubt that Muhammad, based on his own sexual experiences, and followed his own advice of "marrying" prepubescent girls. As previously mentioned, Muhammad married and had sex with Aisha when she was only 9 years old. In search for the historical Muhammad, we must analyze the Qur'an's for an exposition of his paedophiliac act:

Sahih Bukhari 9: 140; Narrated by "Aisha"

Allah's apostle said to me, *"You were shown to me twice (in my dreams) before I married you. I saw an angel carrying you in a silken piece of cloth, and I said to him, 'uncover' (her),' and behold, it was you. I said (to myself), "If this is from Allah, then It must happen."*

Muhammad had a sexual fantasy about the child Aisha before asking for her from her guardian.

Sahih Bukhan, vol. 5, book 58, number 234: Narrated by Aisha

"the Prophet...[married] me when I was a girl of six [years old]. We went to Medina and stayed at the home of Bani-al-Harith bin Khazraj. Then I got ill and my hair fell down. Later on my hair grew [again] and my mother, Um Ruman, came to me while I was playing in a swing with some of my girl friends. She caught me by the hand and made me stand at the door of the house. I was breathless then, and when breathing alright, she took some water and rubbed my face and head with it. Then she took me into the house. There in the house I saw some Ansari woman who said, "Best wishes and Allah's blessing and a good luck." Then she entrusted me to them and they prepared me [for the marriage]. Unexpectedly Allah's Apostle came to me in the forenoon and my mother handed me over to him, and at that time I was of 9 years of age."

It should be noted that Muhammad was 50 at the time.

Grand Mufti Abu Abdullah Muhammad al-Shemary

Reference # 1809 issued on 3/8/1421 (Islamic Calendar)

"As for the Prophet, peace and prayer of Allah be upon him, thighing his fiancée Aisha. She was six years of age and he could not have intercourse with her due to her small age. That is why [the Prophet] peace and prayer of Allah be upon him placed his [penis] member between her thighs and massage it softly, as the Apostle of [God] had control of his [penis] member not like other believers."

This is Muhammad's paedophiliac instructions to the Islamic men of today:

Bukhari 4: 232; Narrated by Aisha

"The Prophet and I [Aisha] used to take a bath from a single [bathtub] while we were young. During the menses [her period], he use to order me to put on an izar [a skirt] and use to fondle me. While in itikaf, he used to bring his head near me and I would wash it while I used to be in my periods [menses]."

The paedophile Muhammad was 55 years old, young Aisha was 14. When she was 9, she brought her dolls to Muhammad's house for play, and he would repeatedly fondle the little girl in the tub while taking baths with her. By the time Muhammad died, Aisha was just a teenager. Muhammad's obsession when he was in bed with this little girl is stated in Bukhari 47: 755 where "[...Muhammad said] ...the Divine inspirations do not come to me on any of the beds [wives] except that of Aisha."

CONTEMPORARY ISLAMIC PAEDOPHILIA, SLAVERY AND BESTIALITY

The Iranian Supreme Leader Ayatollah Khomeini died in 1989 at the age of 86. While Muhammad established an appalling precedent for slavery and the sexual abuse of young slave girls, it was Khomeini of Iran who continued with the primitive and immoral religious traditions of Islam. In his book *Tahrirolvasyleh*, fourth vol. Iran, 1990, he reinforces:

Qur'an 65: 4:

"A man can marry a girl younger than 9 years of age, even if the girl is still a baby being breastfed. A man, however is prohibited from having intercourse with a girl younger than 9, other sexual acts such as foreplay, rubbing, kissing and sodomy are allowed. A man having intercourse with a girl younger than 9 years of age has not committed a crime, but only an infraction, if the girl is not permanently damaged. If the girl, however, is permanently damaged, the man must provide for her all her life. But this girl will not count as one of the man's 4 permanent wives. He also is not permitted to marry the girl's sister."

In Ayatollah Khomeini's words:

"A man can have sexual pleasure from a child as young as a baby. However he should not penetrate, sodomising the child is okay. If the man penetrates and damages the child then he should be responsible for her subsistence all her life..."

"...It is better for a girl to marry in such a time when she would begin menstruation at her husband's house rather than her father's home. Any father marrying his daughter so young will have a permanent place in heaven."

Concerning bestiality:

"A man can have sex with animals such as sheep, cows, camels and so on. However he should kill the animal after he has his orgasm. He should not sell the meat to the people in his own village, however selling the meat to the next door village should be fine."

What a religion!!

"If one commits the act of sodomy with a cow, a ewe, or a camel, their urine and their excrement become impure and even their milk may no longer be consumed. The animal must then be killed as quickly as possible and burned."

Just how barbaric and primitive Islam really is! Are Muslims really so ignorant as not to know what the Qur'an contains? Is this the divine guidance for religious believers on how to live a moral and righteous life? Just as immoral sexual abuses occurred under Judaism and Christianity, so too, countless human abuses occurred, and still occur, under Islam in the 21st century.

The difference between all major religions is that Judaism and Christianity have lost their power of convincing their believers that slavery and "fornicating with virgins" is God's divine moral code of conduct. Most Muslim fundamentalists believe this out of a long mimetic indoctrination. So long as they believe in "something" (just in case), they can fulfil their religious obligations.

The news world, the Internet, and other methods of mass communication have broadcast the Muslim sexual abuse of children and the continued slave trade in Africa and Arabia in the 21st century. In *The Slave Trade Today*, (1961), Sean O'Callaghan toured most of Africa and Arabia visited and recorded in a number of slave markets with young boys for Muslim paedophile clients. For example, in the African country of Djibouti, O'Callaghan writes:

"Ten boys were ranged in a circle on the [display platform for slaves], their buttocks towards us. They were all naked, and I saw with horror that five had been castrated. The [slave-broker] said that usually 10% of the boys are castrated, being

purchased by Saudi. [paedophiles], or by Yemenis, who own harems, as guards."

Some years ago, like O'Callaghan, I was passing through Yemen (then called Aden) and by chance I witnessed a group of enslaved boys in chains who were being transported to a slave market. As much as I wanted to investigate the destination of those unfortunate children, the political violence in the region did not allow me to stay much longer.

O'Callaghan continues,

"Why had the girl-slaves accepted their fate without a murmur, and the boys howled and cried? [the slave-broker reply] "Simple...we tell the girls from a very early age—7 or 8 that they are made for love, at the age nine we let them practice with each other, and a year later with the boys,"

In Yemen, O'Callaghan writes:

"The Yemeni told me that the girls [young slave-prostitutes] were encouraged to have children, especially by white men (usually sailors). For if the slave girl had a white child, she was given a bonus of 20 pounds when the child was taken from her."

As the reader can see, the baby of a slave girl was itself a slave, and therefore, the sale of a slave was permitted under Muslim law.

"Only one offense was severely punished; attempting to escape from the harem...[private stock of girl]... The wretched girl was stripped and spread eagled in the courtyard..[a customary procedure]...Punishment was administrated by a eunuch..[a harem guard], a huge powerful...[African] who seemed to enjoy his task...70 lashes were given."

It should be noted that a *eunuch* is a man who was once a boy who was castrated to prevent him from having sex with his master's women of the harem. This is an ancient custom. This castration is also legal under Muslim law, which was part of preparing a slave for "service."

In Mecca, Saudi Arabia, O'Callaghan states:

"I was awakened by shouts and screams coming from the courtyard. Rushing to the window I looked down to see a dozen of slaves being herded through a door at the far end of the yard. They were being driven in there like cattle by three hefty guards armed with long lashed whips. Even as I watched, one of the poor wretches, a Sudanese girl with huge breast, received a savage lash across her naked buttocks and let out a shriek of agony...

...As the next slave was let in, a murmur of excitement went up among the buyers and they crowded closer around the rostrum. He was a slender boy of about 12 years old with beautiful classical Arab features. Although much has been written about Arab brotherhood and solidarity, I know that the Arab has no compunction in enslaving his fellows should they fall into his hands.

The boy was naked and tried to cover his privates with his little hands and he ran up the steps of the rostrum....there is an age old saying among the Bedouin [a desert tribe]. " A goat for use [bestiality], a girl for enjoyment [a natural], but a boy for [a paedophiliac] ecstasy. " [...the 12 years old boy was bought and] was claimed by a tall bearded Arab who led him from the rostrum with an arm around his waist."

It is a well-known fact that Muslim enslavers pose as "missionaries" and travel throughout African countries seeking young boys and girls. They tell their parents to let their children travel to the "Holy Places" of Islam to make the

Pilgrimage. Also they suggest the child will be instructed in the Qur'an in its original language (Arabic). Once these children leave their villages, they are made into sex slaves for the vast paedophile population.

Throughout Muslim history, time and time again, it is still from African tribes that Arabic Muslim rulers "collect" sex slaves and sell them to the entire Islamic world: Sudan, Mauritania, Yemen, Saudi Arabia, Djibouti, Ethiopia, Eritrea, Pakistan, Afghanistan, India and Kashmir, sub-Sahara, Niger, and elsewhere. What the Islamic Qur'an has taught its believers (including enslavers) is that slavery is a bounty of Allah. The Islamic religion established an appalling precedent for the immoral code of conduct concerning the abuse of young boys and girls. Unfortunately, this continues to be nurtured by the present-day Muslim believers.

7

THE ART OF RELIGIOUS TRICKERY

"Trickery and treachery are the practices of fools that have not the wits enough to be honest."

Benjamin Franklin

"Religion…comprises a system of wishful illusions together with a disavowal of reality, such as we find in an isolated form nowhere else but in amentia, in a state of blissful hallucinatory confusion."

Sigmund Freud

I was raised in a religious-based culture where *fakirs,* eastern magicians, future-tellers, fortune tellers, magicians, magic-tricksters, healers, and charlatan prophets of all sorts have existed for thousands of years. They are a common cultural phenomenon, in the sense that they are not a curiosity. In the "Old World" societies of Greece, Egypt, Mesopotamia and Jewish cultures, the act of magic is culturally embedded in the social structure—not as an entertainment—but in various religious or mystic cults.

In ancient societies, performing magic was a religious occupation practiced by a select group of gifted men and women on behalf of their cult-temples, priests and priestesses, military and political leaders, rich merchants, etc. Less gifted *fakirs* were plentiful and served the needs of the poor populace who were not enticed to attend some of the highly impressive cult-temples. The Bible's Three Wise Men were actually named *The Three Magists* (the three magicians). Being a magician was a notable profession with social prestige. For the sake of illustrating the effects the Magi had on society, I shall continue with a brief description of ancient daily life and social structure.

In the pre-Christian societies, magnificent temples were built in the name of a god who was empowered to protect his or her believers from perceived or actual threats. The Egyptian gods and goddesses were generally human-shaped deities who behaved like humans and lived among mortals. Deities were not all equal and thus were not worshipped in the same way in the pre-Christian cultures throughout Mesopotamian times.

Particular cult temples and *pharaohs* or *satraps* favoured one god or goddess over others, based on their primary functions. For example, *Anubis* was a funeral god. *Geb* or *Keb* was the god of fertility. *Hothon* was an Egyptian cow-goddess and personification of the Milky Way. *Horus* was the protector Pharaohs and of the youth. Lesser influential gods and goddesses were like today's Christian Saints. There were 12

Olympian gods/goddesses in Greece. The Romans also had 12 gods. The Assyrian and Babylonian gods were also associated with the seasons, climatic changes, the Underworld Ocean, the sky god, mother goddess, midwife of the gods, mother of fate, and the bearer of the skies and earth.

As in many ancient Mediterranean cultures, religion was polytheistic and a great number of followers worshipped and gave great importance to gods whether those gods were simply local or lesser-household deities. Polytheistic religion had an enduring continuity throughout the centuries in the ancient Mediterranean cultures. Such a construct provided certain flexibility to the people's set of beliefs—reflecting the approval, disapproval, and replacement of these gods based on perceived theistic behaviour.

People's daily lives revolved around fertile lands, and lands along the sea or river banks. Most people worked the lands as field hands and farmers, or were labourers, craftsmen, or scribes, while only a select minority of society enjoyed the privileged lifestyle of the nobility. People's central focus in their daily lives was a religion propagated by local cult-temples. Less important cult temples were built for the average people using mud bricks made from chopped straw mixed with mud and baked in the sun. Depending on how wealthy and refined the cult believers were, the inside of the temple would be painted with coloured scenes of everyday life. A simple earth-packed floor would be covered with reed mats, and woven willow sticks or palm rafters made up the ceiling.

Wealth was found in extravagant homes on vast estates on the outskirts of towns. Impressive religious temples were also built and lavishly decorated with statues as the main attraction of the gods and goddesses they worshipped. Around these impressive temples were secluded gardens, courtyards of trees, and water pools with sweet smelling flower blossoms and exotic fish. There were servants who took care of the spacious temple estates. Religious temples of the more dominant cults were built with stone, brick, or marble, enclosing the statues of their chosen gods and goddesses.

In addition to being a primary place of worship and the symbolic home of associated gods and goddesses, temples were also used as major administrative centres that held vast numbers of people and livestock. A large part of their wealth depended on donations from the rich who attended religious ceremonies, and in particular from those who wanted specific favours or cures from the gods. Wealth sometimes came from the spoils of war. Large amounts of gold were needed to support the large number of temple priests, administrators, hired architects, engineers and builders.

Education was expensive and it was usually only the boys who went to school (from around the age of five until they reached their teens). Boys who could not afford to go to school were expected to help their fathers and learn their trade. Ancient societies were basically divided into four classes of citizens. The upper class included the temple priests and priestesses, government officials, generals, and nobles and their families. The middle class included the scribes, skilled craftsmen, engineers, architects, merchants, teachers, artists and professional soldiers. The lower class were these without property (proletarians) who were peasants: mostly farmers, labourers, servants and street cleaners. This lower class was the largest group of all. At the bottom of the scale (holding no citizenship) were the slaves who were foreign captives.

The general educational system and the intelligentsia concentrated on philosophical questions about life, wisdom, medicine, mathematics and knowledge of the Universe. Relatively speaking, there was very little attention paid to mechanical inventions because there was not much public use for them. Agricultural tools remained simple in order to accommodate the horse, mule or bull's physical power. Lifting and pulling of building material was done by methods using human or animal power.

Prisoners of our Ideals

With time mechanical inventions became more advanced due to economic reasons or because of the necessity to produce better weapons of war. In regard to ancient mechanical inventions, there are practically no original sources that describe the technological inventions of the ancient Mediterranean cultures. For example, the Greek architect and engineer Archimedes did not consider it worthwhile to write about his mechanical inventions. The extraordinary works of Heron and Philon are from translations or texts written much later.

A large number of original sources were destroyed on purpose. St. Paul's religious fanaticism led him to pay 25,000 silver coins to Athenians to bring their "magic" books and throw them in a public "book burning" fire. Later, Muslim religious warrior fanatics burned down the famous Alexandria Library with over five hundred thousand manuscripts, books and papyrus filled with ancient knowledge. Today, book burning threats are advocated by religious zealots such as Rev. Terry Jones who, in Sept. 2010, wanted to publically burn the Quar'an.

Ancient mechanical devices like the repeated Catapult of Dionysis, the Planetania of Archimedes, the Antikythea device, gigantic ships (such as those discovered recently in Istanbul), or steam engines show that ancient mechanical inventors were not only "theoretically" oriented but their "theory" and "praxis" were connected. As more technology was invented and developed, some mechanical inventions were directed toward meeting the necessities of temples, and other devices were created for public and private recreation. The inventors of mechanical and instrumental devices serving the temples were naturally in great demand because their technological knowledge was aimed toward fortifying the priestly caste.

Hence, all such mechanical inventions were at the disposal of the temples to create "miracles." This is why the mechanical arts were founded in Greece and Egypt, for there the priest caste was long established and it was also a source of wealth for the inventors. Religious temples, and the temples' mediums that had influence within the politico-military system, were probably the main influences for the rapid development of war machine devices, "magical mechanics," and "mechanical miracles."

The most important goal or duty of any organized group, religious cult, church, political party, or private enterprise, is to perpetuate itself, for otherwise it starts to decline. Temples were political as well as religious enterprises. The site of each temple was chosen for its political or social value. They were, for example, located in a city centre or on the highest part of the city. Temple sites were thus strategically placed in and around the city in order to facilitate religious ritual processions, to show "miracle" performance, as well as to bind together the various neighbourhoods in religious observances. In short, temples were a religious site that said something about the relationship of the priestly caste with the gods—if this relationship was lost, the result would be the caste's intolerable decline.

Ancient societies were incredibly superstitious. Common people were often gripped with fear and angst at the slightest sign of a "bad-omen," unusual or celestial events. The temple's priest-caste and mediums interpreted dreams and observed the flight patterns of birds to determine the best time to start a war. A deep inquiry and a period of logical reasoning accompanied the sacrifice of animals in order to examine their entrails. From these, a temple priest would determine the best course of action for his client to take. At the very least, advice to the nobles on their chances of success could be given.

Other forms of superstition were also believed and practiced by the majority of people. Mediterranean societies were rampant with temple priests, cult deities, astrologers, soothsayers, magicians, tricksters, charlatans, oracles, prophets, long-established heroes, mystery cults, and arcane religious philosophies. In fact, it is not an exaggeration to say that there was no end to the holy sites, temples, shrines and sacred groves.

The common people in the Mediterranean world were illiterate, superstitious, and easily swayed by new religious proclamations. They were simple people who could not think for themselves, and who remained for the rest of their lives with much less sophisticated intellectual cognitive abilities. My point is not to be arrogant, but to state the facts as I know them. Common people were bombarded by advertisements of astrological claims, religious and mystical predictions, and ritualism of all sorts which people could barely understand and would rarely question.

On the other hand, we must ask what the relationship was of ancient science to society. The short answer is that the ancient Greek, Roman, and Egyptian sciences may be considered a social failure! This means that the socio-political conditions needed to ensure the broad recognition and continuous growth of architectural and engineering science did not exist for the benefit of society as a whole. The implementation of some aspects of scientific theoretical inquiries and experimentation was a social failure due to uncoordinated efforts.

No serious or systematic attempts to explore the practical applications of architecture and mechanical engineering were made. The scientific theoretical inquiries and practical applications were restricted to individual scientists at the experimental level. Such experiments were encouraged and financially supported by the priest caste and the militarist nobility for their own exclusive benefit.

Science failed to become a real force in the life of society. In this sense, leading and lesser influential mechanical engineers placed their theoretical and practical science at the disposal of the existing privileged minority. Science thus evolved as a leisure activity, as an entertainment, or as a subject of philosophical contemplation rather than as a means of transforming the material conditions of society.

When we look at the causes of the social paralysis of ancient scientific evolution, it is obvious that it was not due to the failure of any individual scientist. There was no lack of individual scientific talent, nor was there a lack of individual genius in inventing new or improved mechanical inventions. The failure lay within the culture that approached science only to the extent that the mechanical engineers and architects will regarded as the possessors of purely philosophical knowledge. Knowledge for the sake of knowledge was in and of itself primarily an academic concern. This means that the concept of science did not carry within itself the conviction to transform the conditions of the majority of the people (building of better houses, roads, irrigation systems, food storage and preservation, etc). Science did not bear fruit for the general improvement in the material conditions of life, nor did it advance the general emancipation of society from the shackles of cultural religiosity and from primitive superstition. In fact, mechanical engineering was dominated by the priest caste to advance their scientifically-induced and mechanically-activated illusionary tricks to fool their donors and their followers.

Science was positioned to serve the priest caste and the privileged military nobility who were the ones who made an effort to reward the mechanical inventors for their services. This bondage can be identified in its similarities with the painters of the Renaissance who were at the disposal of the Catholic Church and the privileged nobility to paint ecclesiastical themes. They were the only ones who could generously support the artist's talents and their imagination.

In both cases, it was a matter of economic dependency–on the part of the artists or inventors–but with great social consequences. Both created visually spectacular images that supported religious trickery, and both exhibited a disinterested devotion to the truth. They were available to serve the commercialization of the religious institutions. The mutual support and practicality of science and art upon life, and life upon the support and practicality of science/art was not a basic element in their social awareness. Science and art were for the study of the few, at the offering of the privileged few, and for the deception of the very many.

In old Mediterranean societies, magicians, magic trickery, and superstition were well established because they had existed for thousands of years. Although contemporary and ancient magicians incorporated in their acts a large degree of showmanship, ancient practitioners of magic acts were not used to entertain the public. Magic trickery was used as a means of persuasion, as a means of deception, and to inspire awe. For example, in the ancient world of Greece, Egypt, and Mesopotamia, magicians, mystics and temple priests seemed to be able to impress their disciples by turning water into blood or by making frogs appear from nowhere (much more on this later). While it is common knowledge today that all magic is nothing more than the clever art of trickery, people in ancient times believed that there existed genuine magic or sorcery empowered by mysterious forces. Magicians were the *People of the Secret.* It was a common belief that witches could use their power to wreak havoc on the laws of nature and make the impossible happen. Mediums would claim that they could communicate with the dead or elevate (fly) into the heavens simply by uttering some magical word. Common people not able to cope with the difficulties of daily life flocked into temples seeking advice. They were also fascinated by magic and believed that it could be used to make the impossible come true.

Competition amongst magicians was great. So was that between various mystic schools, temples, and occults beliefs. The priestly caste of notable temples used spectacular performances to convince their disciples that they had the only "divine" power to gratify any desires people. Magicians were respected but were also greatly feared. This sentiment is evident even today in the heavily directed religious societies like the "Old World" ones. I remember as a child passing in front of a magician's house with my mother and hearing the sounds of drums beating. She exhibited terrifying fear and told me that the magician was practicing "black magic" at that moment. The mimetic effect of my mother's statement stayed in my mind for a long time.

The fact is that ancient peoples, as well as today's religious people, were conditioned to believe in superstitions of all sorts. It was in the best interest of the priest caste and of the occultists to perpetuate whatever they were peddling in order to stay in business. They competed against each other in a polytheistic industry for believer-clients. Religiosity was present in every aspect of daily life, and people were bombarded with many fear-inducing predictions and threats of God's wrath. Latin America and most countries in the Caribbean today are under a similar style of religiosity—a mixture of superstitious religion and primitive ritual beliefs and acts. In ancient Mediterranean regions, mystics, prophets, and occultists travelled from village to village and town to town spreading mystical messages that villagers believed but didn't understand. As they departed or died off, splinter groups formed, all more or less believing in the same messages (but slightly diversified to include localized bizarre beliefs and rituals). There were the Nazarenes in Palestine, the Mandaen in Egypt, the Nazoraeans of Judaic extraction, the Essenes, the Ebionites, 1st century Hasidim, the Teacher of Righteousness, and many others.

Mystic schools in both Greece and Egypt, the Mediterranean and Middle Eastern regions appeared to have a well-established set of mystic schools and temples. The ancient Greek and Egyptian societies were noted for their large and diversified occultists and refined schools of mysticism, as opposed to the rough peasantry style of mystic lore of the Coptic occult. Competition was widespread in both Hellenistic and Egyptian polytheistic circles and traditions. Wealthy temples and cults retained their religious and mystical reputation and character by delivering spectacular sermons.

By the time the new cult of Christianity appeared, a historical coincidence was in place. On the one hand, societies were dominated by multiple levels of religiosity, mysticism and superstition. The workings of the natural world were not understood, and there was a lack of education. On the other hand, there was a concentration of military power in the hands of an oligarchy that dictated belief in their favoured deities. Added to this base of power and influence was the employment of mechanical technology to re-enforce the delusion of religiosity.

Heron of Alexandria was a mathematician, physicist and mechanical engineer (m*echanicos)* who lived from 10 - 70 AD. According to Heron's writings, it is safe to assume that he taught at the Museum of Alexandria. He wrote in Greek on the measurement of geometric figures and invented many devices operated by water, steam, or compressed air, including a fountain and a fire engine. Heron invented the world's first steam engine and crafted handy gizmos like a self-trimming oil lamp. His clever inventions were particularly notable for their incorporation of auto-regulating feedback control systems that form the bedrock of bubernetics (like today's toilet with its own floating mechanism). Heron's passion was with mechanical novelties: pneumatic devices, automata, and magic-theatrics—including the staged temple mystery rite of flames where thunder crashed and a miniature female Baccahantes whirled madly around the temple's god on a pulley-driven turntable. These mechanical inventions would eventually become tools of the trade for the religious priest caste in order to fool the common people.

Heron's mechanical models consisted of:

- ❖ Vending coin-machine dispensing "holy water" to the attendees of temples.

- ❖ Temple doors that opened automatically by lighting a fire.
- ❖ The sound of trumpets produced when opening the doors of a temple.
- ❖ Trumpets that sounded by flowing water in temples.
- ❖ Dispenser of "purified water" used by worshippers to sprinkle themselves.
- ❖ A self-trimming oil lamp in temples.
- ❖ Statue figure producing a trumpet sound using compressed air.
- ❖ The shrine of a bird made to turn and sing when temple worshippers turned a wheel.

When Heron's "religious" devices were put into action they created awe and fear in the worshippers' simple minds, and strengthened their belief in God's mystical power. Moreover, these delusional beliefs were mimetically passed on to their families, their villages, their towns and cities, and eventually to their whole ethnic nation. The workings of these mechanical "religious" devices were written down and were learned by other "prophets," "mystics," and "magicians" who included them in their theatrical and mystic acts. The propagation of delusional beliefs was an economic enterprise of temples, mystics and occult organizations small and large, wealthy and soon-to-be wealthy. In his book *Mechaniki Syntaxis*, Heron describes the workings of the following inventions that were adopted by Temple priests to reinforce their religious sermons.

The vending coin machine was an upright cylindrical unit. It contained "holy water" that was available to worshippers for a price. A worshipper inserted a coin through an opening located on the top of the machine. When the coin entered the opening, it fell upon a small plate which was connected to a horizontal pipe. The coin's mass would press down the plate causing the horizontal pipe to rise, thus releasing "holy water" into the worshipper's cup. The tilting of the coin's plate would have caused the coin to fall off, thus letting the horizontal pipe back into its original shut position, until the next worshiper used the device.

This vending machine was a money-making instrument for the temple's priests. But the damage that was inflicted was more than the worshipper's loss of their coins. The most damaging aspect in the dispensing of "holy water" was the implantation of a fraudulent belief in the minds of the worshippers about the "holiness" of the temple and of the water. This fraudulent belief is still perpetuated by the Catholic Church by placing a "holy water" container (next to the donation box) by the church's entrance. Believers dip their fingers in the "holy water" before crossing themselves.

A dispenser of purified water was placed by the temple doors of some Egyptian temples. Worshippers who entered were required to turn a wheel that sprinkled them with "purified holy water." Sprinkled with this water, a worshipper's body was also "purified" of all sins. Water flowed through a pipe that revolved so that as its position passed the exit hole, it would shut off the flow of "purified water." This was another ritual that gave an awe of "holiness" to the temple.

The trumpet-sounding device consisted of a statue of a human standing on a square pedestal blowing into a trumpet. An air tube extended upward into the body of the statue in the direction of the trumpet's sound valve in the figure's mouth. Air was trapped in the interior of the square pedestal. When water was poured into the pedestal, the air would be forced out through the air pipe's sound valve and into the trumpet's mouthpiece, producing the sound of a trumpet. Depending on how wealthy the temples were, one or a series of trumpet statutes would be constructed in order to provide an impressive sound system that would enhance any ritualistic religious performance. Worshippers would enter the temple with the sense of its overpowering and dominating force imposed upon them. After all, only "God's" power could make a human figure composed of stone produce trumpet sounds. The secret of using compressed air to create the sound of a trumpet, of course, was not known to the average worshipper.

Automatic temple doors (opening by themselves), allowed the worshippers to enter the temple hall at the beginning of a religious sermon. A ceremony was performed pleading the god(s) to open the temple doors to let the priests in to perform animal sacrifices or other rituals. During the act of this ceremony, a fire was set on a pedestal located next to the main temple doors. As the fire increased its strength, and as the religious ritual became more and more pronounced, the temple doors would open letting the priests and public enter the hall, while the stone trumpets would be sounding the glory of "God's" miraculous power. Such choreography of this religious stage-and-sound show must have left the worshippers with an everlasting mimetic impression that would be transmitted to, and hosted by, other believers. Of course, the public was ignorant of the fact that they were fooled by the "miraculous" automatic opening of the temple doors! This is how it worked.

On a space directly below the floor of the temple's main doors, there was a set of pipes and chains attached by means of a pulley to two suspended metal containers. Chains for lifting or lowering were winched around a pole connected to a cable for opening or shutting the doors. When the fire increased the air temperature in the pedestal, it would expand the hot air in the container's space, driving out the hot water through a tube into a second container, thus increasing its liquid weight and causing it to descend. This descent would pull the chain around the pole connected to the door's hinges, causing the doors to open. When the fire was extinguished, gravity would transfer the cold water back to its original container, causing the doors to shut! Doors were shut when the fraudulent religious theatrics had served its purpose: to once again fool the people.

A thunder-making device was used to announce the presence, exit, or anger of the gods. The thunder sound was created for the purposes or needs of the temple priest, as it could be used to generate fear or perform some other role to control the believers. This device that Heron created for the priest caste was a rectangular wooden box containing a number of shelves and a tin sheet. Clay bells with metal spikes travelled through the length of the rectangular wooden box, bouncing from shelf to shelf, imitating a thunderous sound as it descended. At the end, the ball would forcefully land on the tin sheet creating a tremendous "thunder" sound.

Heron's inventions were a useful tool of the priestly caste of Alexandria. Heron's "religious" devices were not invented with the intention of deceiving unsuspecting worshippers, although that is how the priest caste used them. Heron's intentions meant very little, for the question still remains of how his mechanical inventions were adopted by the temple's priestly class. Who had the mechanical knowledge of the fabrication and installation of these devices in temples other than Heron? How was Heron of Alexandria supporting himself if not from selling his various inventions including those that had nothing to do with the temples? The reader must remember that these inventions, although they may seem very simple to us, especially when compared to today's high-tech gadgetry, were highly effective at the time.

Chemical substances were also widely used for the purpose of demonstrating the priest's healing powers. *Logwood bark* was grated, boiled, and diluted in red wine. When worshippers were given a drink of the mixture of logwood and wine, the next time he or she would urinate, the urine would be red-coloured, resembling human blood. One can imagine the terror and panicked shock of the worshipper. The unsuspecting believer would not recognize the priest as the one who had "doctored" the drink. One can safely assume that the worshipper would immediately seek the priest's help for a cure! The secret to curing the logwood "sickness" was by simply stopping the distribution of the doctored drink to the worshippers, and their urinary system would return urine to its normal colour.

What would be the reason for a priest's duplicity in doctoring and distributing the logwood bark drink to the temple's believers?

First, curing the believer's urinating "blood," it strengthened the priest's power over his flock.

Second, a religious extortion for a large monetary donation could be demanded in the name of a saint or god for "curing the sickness."

Third, the networked message of the "recovered" believer would be treated as a "miracle" by the rest of the community, and it would reinforce the notion that "miracles" are entirely possible.

Fourth, such sickness-curing "miracles" could be performed if the believer prayed to a particular god or saint.

Fifth, the mimetic networking among the rest of the believers concerning the miraculous cure that was performed on behalf of the believer would be worth more than gold.

Worshippers would flock to the temples to witness other "miracles" performed on-demand or as made-to-order miracles. Whether other "miracles" were actually performed is immaterial, for the embedded mimetic belief of one "miracle" in the minds of the naïve and ignorant public would be hosted for the rest of their lives, and then passed on to the next generation. It would form the ideology of a belief system that would spread to other people who would in turn accept the existence of miracles. The term "miracle" would enter their linguistic vocabulary and it would be used at the convenience of those in power. Thus, a culture of religiosity made of all kinds of religious rituals and tricks to fool the people would take hold of societies for many generations to come.

Mimesis is a fundamental human and animal behavioural trait. For example, when a child sees his or her parents doing a particular task, the method of doing such a task would most likely be adopted by the child. Baby animals learn from their mothers' hunting techniques. Some behavioural modifications may occur from time to time, but the fundamental mimesis trait remains intact. It is like saying to a youngster, "You'll first learn to practise it my way, and when you've learned my way, you can change it and practice it your way." This principle applies to daily life among individuals who are learning or experimenting in new social, cultural, economic, and political activities. This is how cognitive knowledge, practical acts, delusions, illusions, or religious behaviour and beliefs are transmitted and hosted in whole or in part, by the next generation.

Worshippers flocked to temples to witness the next "miracle" or the pleadings of another worshipper who was asking for or expecting a personal miracle from God. The temple's theatrical stage-and-sound show would have had such an overwhelming effect on believers that the expectancy of a "miracle" would have been high. *The ritual act of asking for a miracle would have been a form of mimesis adopted by new believers from other believers.* From day to day, from month to month, and from one year to the next, the worshippers' ritual of asking for a miracle would be a "normal" or rational act. The spreading and accepting of such a notion of the "asking for a miracle" ritual by worshippers would have been a profitable venture for the religious hierarchy of the various temples. The successful ones would have been looked upon as an inspiring example for the upcoming religious preachers of less influential temples.

Competition amongst various priests would have forced them to present the most impressive stage-and-sound performances, the most impressive magical trickery, and the most highly declared apocalyptic predictions. Such practices were shared by most priests for centuries, and were most effective between

350 BC and 150 AD due to the adoption of mechanical inventions that served the priest caste to fool the people.

An example of inspiring religious success was there for all mystico-religious castes to see, and imitate the organized religion of Judaism. Its structural and cultural hierarchy, its internal order, its dominant social and political power, its historical foundation, its economic wealth, its holy book of the Old Testament, its documented customs and rituals, its religious prohibitions of consuming certain foods, dress codes, family structure, and the social base of men and women were all focal and served as a beacon for other cults to imitate. Magical trickery was viewed as a means to an end. Indeed, it was an effective short-cut for achieving religious goals.

The idea that there was a spiritual world somewhere above the sky, and that it was possible to make contact with that spiritual world was propagated by many peripheral religious occults. The idea of priests and mediums being able to communicate, at will, with the spirit world of god(s), evil forces, and ancestors had been around in various forms for many centuries. Séances, mediums, and priests were part of people's daily lives. Some occult practices were just peripheral while others became full-blown religious institutions with regular services, customs, rules, and regulations. Every deceptive means was adopted and practised as a matter of survival against competing occults.

The goal was to spread their influence amongst the ignorant populace. Priests, mediums, magicians, and charlatans were viewed as having bodily contact with the spirits and being a moral compass about how one's actions would influence where one's spirit would be sent at death. Temples (churches) became the central focus in people's attention as the only source of knowledge of how the natural world worked and the relationship of man to it. Priests were more than willing to provide "answers" for any physical or spiritual questions.

Magical trickery today is experienced as entertainment and its history extends back centuries. Though it is largely un-researched territory, magic once belonged to the dominion of the temple priests in Greek, Roman, Egyptian or Mayan societies.

Though magic is trickery, it leaves the audience with a sense of other worldliness in which the magicians in temples have been able to use a "divine power," to create a feat that to the eye seems impossible in its dimensions. It is this trickery that channels the audience's concentration, implying that there is more to this world than has previously met their eyes.

One important role of the temple priest was to tell myths, and often those myths were "supernatural" in themselves. The Mayan priest's trick of the talking decapitated skull that makes prophesies is one example. The weeping statue of the Christians' Virgin Mary is another. Both are central features of their religion's creation myth. Their ancient riddle is so simple to unravel; mix it with a pinch of "history," a splash of "archaeology," a heavy dose of theology, and a first-person "evidence" or testimony. As it was then–and today–the priests watched the meek give money and devotion to an idea of the religion's choice, not of their own. In short, many ancient and contemporary religious tricks share components in common with mythology such as a return from the dead or a person in a coffin sawn in half. They mimic the resurrection of the Egyptian god Orisis, or Jesus Christ. Today, Tibetan homeopathic "doctors" perform surgery using their fingers to remove "evil" spirits from one's body. When the surgery is done, no visible scares are evident. Such is their "miraculous" surgical performance.

HERON'S MECHANICAL DEVICES

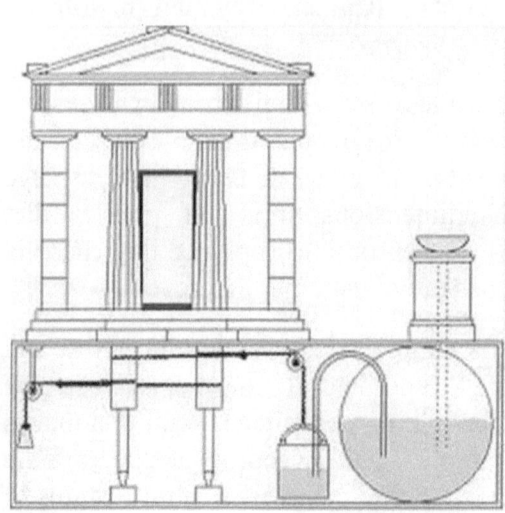

This first image depicts a mechanical means of opening temple doors. A fire on the alter heats the tube attached to an air-tight leather bag from which a weight hangs. A chain is attached across a pulley to the ropes around the poles or hinges, so that they open or shut the doors. When the fire is hot, it expands the air inside the bag to raise it up with the weight. The doors open. As the fire dies down, the air gets cold and the weight descends, this tightens the ropes and closes the doors. This simple mechanical principle fooled people into believing that the temple priest had a supernatural power.

A Trumpet Figure:

A sound is created by compressed air passing through a tube into the figure's trumpet. When water is poured into the space inside the pedestal, air is forced out, passing out through the mouthpiece which produces the sound of the trumpet.

Holy Water Dispenser:

Temple worshippers were required to drink the blessed "holy water"–for a price–by placing a coin in the water-dispenser. When the coin was dropped through the mouth, it fell on a metal plate. Its weight lowered the beam which raised the lid so that water could flow. When the coin fell off, the lid would descend and close the water opening...until the next time. Worshippers were truly fooled in believing that they were receiving holy water.

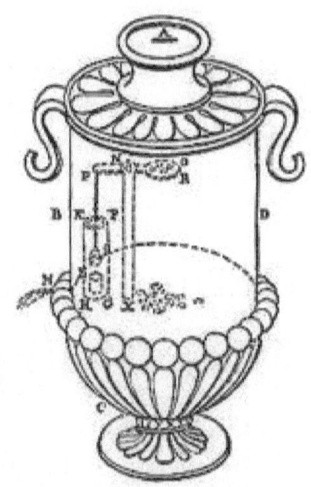

THE SHROUD OF TURIN

Today, people continue to fall for such lies. Logical fallacies and semantic trickery are the very essence of the Christian belief.

During the mid 1360s, Catholic followers flocked to Lirey, France, to catch a rare glimpse of what was believed by many to be the sacred burial cloth of Jesus. The knight Geoffroy de Charny owned the linen cloth, which he proudly exhibited at the local church, Our Lady of Lirey.

Although the Shroud was accepted as genuine by believers, Pierre d'Arcis, the Bishop of Troyes, and Bishop Henri de Posters were highly sceptical of its origins and validity. Both Bishops had reason to believe that the Shroud was a fake, for it had been exhibited for profit by the Geoffroy clan for many years. Thousands of pilgrims congregated to view the cloth, and Geoffroy's clan assured them that the Shroud was indeed the genuine burial garment of Jesus.

WEEPING VIRGIN MARY'S STATUE

Growing up in a southern European culture, I witnessed charlatans exploiting simple-minded people with the old religious trick of the weeping Virgin Mary. Of course, there is nothing miraculous about the weeping of a statue. Let's see how the "miracle" of a weeping statue is done. Many religious statues are made of plaster—a brittle porous material which tends to soak up liquids like a sponge. A ready-made statue is painted and glazed outside, which effectively turns it into a liquid-proof vessel. This means that any liquid on its inside cavity would not pass through its outside liquid-proof surface.

A $1/8^{th}$ of an inch hole on top of the head is drilled. Two very thin small slits are made just beneath the eyes—each just inside into the eye-lid. Using a cake decorating syringe the trickster fills the statute's cavity with Logwood bark natural red dye to saturate the inside of the statue, leaving it immersed overnight. When the statue is exposed to candle heat, the red dye would expand slowly, seeping from the eyes, and that is enough to make the "miracle" of a weeping Virgin Mary.

Today, the meek still donate their hard-earned money, and religious tricksters, "healers" of all sorts and outright liars continue to enrich themselves.

8

IDEALISM IN ADVERTISING

"**Consumerism** is an infectious disease that causes its victims to buy recklessly."

Flo Wineriter

"The only reason a great many American families don't own an elephant is that they have never been offered an elephant for a dollar down and easy payments."

MAD Magazine

One common form of commercial advertising is when a person, a company, a multinational corporation, a product brand, a musical group, a joke, or an altered or original image is promoted on TV, the internet, in newsprint, and on billboards. Great popularity is created this way, and the message itself is transmitted and hosted by consumers. This is considered a commercial meme.

Advertising, a form of transmitting information, is developed by professionals for the purpose of creating "buzz" for the products and services of their corporate clients. It introduces a concept-meme to the general public in order to generate demand or an inflated self-image, to build a system of belief which can be altered or maintained when purchasing a certain product.

A system of belief is a metaphorical iconic image that is used to beautify or distort the utilitarian or practical use of a product, the reality of a concept, a person's background, and historical myth and so on. For example, products like deodorants, clothing fashions, sport utility vehicles, and Viagra are metaphorically connected to sex, success, self-esteem, or delusional images of one's worth. Concepts like religion and idealism serve to distort reality. The ideology of economics serves as a system of belief.

Knowing that the general public places their personal ideas as a primary directional force, and the material reality secondary, advertisers influence consumers by introducing a meme-image, a fetish, a vanity, a trend, an "ideal," that is regarded by people as reality. This is their main selling point, not the utilitarian value of the product itself. Since advertisers do not control the purchasing power of consumers, they are instead capitalizing on human weaknesses like fear, doubt, euphoria, frivolity, wishful thinking—a slew of mental images—all to entice the self-conscious and low self-esteem people to purchase a "solution" by buying into the product-image. Economics as a system of beliefs works at its best when we witness the increased amount of impulse purchases made by the ever debt-drowning public. Marketing techniques and consumer trends are used to transmit influential and self-replicating memes to enhance the effects they have on the public's collective mind.

To create an impression of spontaneous and enthusiastic word of mouth, advertisers hire actors, actresses, and stage managers to create visual and emotion-induced scenes of "friends," "family," "community," "friendly financial advisors," "trusted mortgage-brokers," etc., all to focus idealistic-meme concepts into the consumer's mind. The delusion of "mind over matter" is applied to its fullest extent. This concept is the ideological base of idealism and consumerism which is embedded in the mind of the public. It is regarded as a virtue and a faith that embodies economics as a system of belief, not as a means of earning living necessities.

Idealist memes like "mind over matter" are the kinds of metaphors that affect the human mind like viruses. As such, one who has hosted memes can transmit them to another person who then tell the next person, and then another, with the high probability of it being passed along. Whether an idealist-embedded meme virus influences the host's behaviour is seen by its success or failure to be hosted. Failure would simply mean the extinguishing of the meme from the human mind. The life span of a meme, therefore, depends on the acceptance or rejection of a meme by its host mind or group of minds. In the case of advertising, the whole process is not directed to inform the consumer about the utility of the product itself, as this is the manufacturer's domain. The purpose of advertising is to direct a persuasion-induced meme towards the consumer. This is done with a metaphoric descriptive form "attached" to the item, such as fear, shame, a wish, or an idealised situation.

Persuasion is a mental process based on selective information (or the lack of it) provided by the propagator. It is not to inform but to direct with the aim of popularising a type of purchasing behaviour. Spoken or written words and images are mimetic tools that the advertisers have at their disposal to influence and induce, by delusion or illusion, the consumer into consuming more and more.

Advertising is an integral part of consumerism as a system of belief that propagates the metaphoric consumption of "happiness," "feeling good," images of "self-independence," and "satisfaction" while we participate in an orgy of consumption. Under the system of belief that "we can have it all," we are living beyond our means, we are mortgaging our precious lives by attempting to consume as much as the limits of our credit cards permit. Advertising is a meme virus of rampant consumerism, a mass hysteria of "monkey see monkey do" which is aimed at persuading us to host a meme system of beliefs.

Idealism is based on the mental gravitational leaning toward the importance of the ideal, or the emotions regarding material reality, external social conditions, reason, and rationality. Irrational impulses, beliefs, and blind faith have no use for experimentation and investigation. Idealists regard these things as only the primary propulsive force for a prescribed response. It is very pronounced in the meek who believe in the "power" of the mind where a set of ideas or ideals are far more convincing than reality itself.

Imagery or wishful thinking, therefore, is patterned to induce mimetic emotional needs, inferiority or superiority impulses, perceived benefits, temporary relief of anxiety, a good feeling, delusional hope—a circuit of desires—all to entice humans to purchase a "solution" and consume even more. To do this, corporations and mass advertisers are armed with mimetic tools and rely on the meek's weaknesses to implant upon our collective mind the ideology of economics as a system of beliefs. Advertising is a predatory process where the dialectical relationship between necessity, benefit, and utilitarian products or services is deliberately distorted. For example, the "Marlboro Man" is a case in point where the association and benefits of smoking for healthy outdoor activities is distorted. I suppose that there are smokers who never questioned the dialectical relationship between smoking and health.

An equal distortion of material reality is the idealist meme slogan of "savings" and "spending money." Huge advertising amounts are spent and sophisticated mimetic tools are employed to convince consumers of the metaphoric delusion of "The More You Spend, the More You Save." To some, the absurdity of this slogan is evident; to most, however, it is not. This is not about semantics, because the physical act of spending money and the physical act of saving money are unrelated. Why must you spend money, in order to "save" money? Where is the dialectical relationship between the concepts of "The More You Spend" and "The More You Save?" There is none, for the relationship "exists" only in the delusion of mind over matter or the ideal over physical reality. Basic home economics demonstrates there is a dialectical relationship between saving and **not** spending money. The dialectical contradiction of spending and saving are such that when you do **not** spend, you **do** save.

The New School of Social Research in NY teaches students that:

"Advertising is a profoundly subversive force in American life. It is intellectual and moral pollution. It trivializes, manipulates, is insincere and vulgarizes."

Ogilvy, *On Advertising*, 1983, states:

"Advertising is not the noblest creation of man's mind, as so many of its advocates would like the public to think"

Ogilvy holds that some

"...economists, ever eager to snatch the scourge from the hand of God, hold that advertising tempts people to squander money

on things they don't need. Who are these elitists to decide what you need? Do you need a dishwasher? Do you need a deodorant? Do you need a trip to Rome? ***I feel no qualms of considering about persuading that you do...that buying things...whether you need them or not"***

Consumerism and the advertising industry need persons who cooperate submissively, similarly or sameness, and in large numbers. They require people who want to consume ever more and beyond their means, and whose style, tastes, and wants are standardized in accordance to corporate design, and who can be easily motivated and influenced. It needs persons with an over-inflated self-esteem, those who feel free, independent, and self-absorbed, not subjected to common civility, authority or social principles.

Yet, the so called "rebel without a cause" is the same person who willingly submits to corporate advertising memes that command him or her to fit into a sterile and meaningless consumerist social order without friction, and who can be directed and guided by images, trends, and metaphorical and cliché slogans. They must be enticed to be "on the go" without direction. Sameness is the order of the day! I was once invited to an *avant-garde* fashion designers gathering, in Toronto. To my dismay, as I entered the reception hall, I noticed that all these high fashion gurus were all dressed in black. So much for individualism! Would anyone dare to stand up?

Consumerist technology has socially isolated humans from one another and from our natural world. We have lost our social ability to communicate without using high-tech items, and we have been transformed into automatons, limiting our socialisation skills to emails, using Blackberries and smart phones, experiencing life by being politically correct, seeking a steady job and a steady mortgage. Each of us stays close to the rest of the herd, not daring to be spontaneous and not daring to be different in our consumerist habits. We willingly submit to corporate rules and policies, while "living" in a metaphorical world of similarity or sameness in styles of thought, actions, and even feelings. We stay close to the herd by essentially relating to it as strangers behind "electronic social masks," while each of us remains utterly isolated in our metaphoric virtual-reality.

Our deep sense of insecurity and social anxiety cannot overcome our aloneness no matter how much electronic time we spend, how much we believe in consumerism as a system of belief, and how many messages we post on Facebook or MySpace or Twitter day in and day out. We cannot overcome our social despair by following a pop-psychologist's New Age beliefs, by the routine of the repetitive amusement of video games, or by continuing to remain with poor skills in cultivating social relationships. We cannot distinguish humans from automatons. Passive consumption of electronic sounds and sights, instant messaging, and "surfing the net" are mimetic habits which lead us to consume "happiness" and "have fun" as an object of consumerist but not humanist satisfaction.

The above brief description is similar to the notion of a smoothly functioning corporate functionary who is cooperative, behaves correctly, a team player but somewhat independent, an upcoming climber who is ambitious and aggressive. Wall Street floor traders who thought that the world belonged to them found out in 2008 that their style of economics as a system of belief had collapsed under the weight of external reality. It also applies to those who devote their lives to the obedient consumption of goods, who do not attain happiness and very often suffer from severe delusional conflicts in their desire to satisfy every instinctual and impulsive need.

Herd mimesis occurs far more frequently within consumerist societies where it is aggressively pushed that "getting ahead" in a "dog eat dog" world is a way of life. Such a style of life does not place an emphasis on savings but on spending, on living a "dream," on predatory financial success, on the validation of "everything goes," and in the desire to have more and more. We are witnessing a regression to secular idol worship of technological consumerism, of economics as a system of beliefs, and a gradual transformation of the social character of the human to one fitting the structure of a mindless machine. Such a person views his life as a financial investment in which his return must make the highest profit. His life is counted as a fair bargain and exchange. In a market of fair exchange, praises and offerings are also made in hopes of making another human of the opposite sex a fair exchange partner.

Idealism concerns the deliberate distortion of material reality for the direct benefit of those who propagate it, whether in religion or in advertising. People's beliefs are a fertile framework wherein advertisers plant these ideals. Idealism is the standard and directional force of beliefs in people's daily lives. Our western culture goes along with everything the advertisers and their psychologists promote as "fact claims" and "truth" with regards to beliefs as being equal to reality.

For example, idealism in advertising is a concept which holds that the only truth is a person's beliefs and not the reality of the product's usefulness. In other words, the reality of the product is based on the dialectical opposites between what the advertisers propagate (ideas), and the practical utilitarian benefits the product will have for the consumer. It is not an exaggeration to state that advertising equals deception and theft. Its deception lies in its distortion of the product's properties, the metaphorical benefits it has versus the reality of the usefulness it has for the consumer. Here are some of the most common examples of metaphorical advertising distortions aimed to influence the consumer's mind.

Buy One Get One Free:

Such idealist advertising entices consumers to think that more is better. The profit margin is simply double as this "special" sale is offered while still keeping the desired profit margin. The aim of this false advertising is simply to get more money out of you. "Buy 3 items for $6" distorts the fact that you can still buy only 1 item for $2. The aim here is to entice you to spend more under any pretence or distortion of reality, knowing that the absurdity of the belief of "mind over matter" is as effective as ever.

Introductory Offer:

This is an offer for a limited time. After this period the price will change with a much higher profit margin for the product or service provider. The "hook" here is to entice you to think that you are getting an item or service cheaper, not realising that the "hook" is in your long-term legal commitment—after the limited time is expired—with a higher profit margin for the product or service offered by the company. The aim is to get more money out of you based on the long-term nature of your legal obligation. Guided by the primacy of their beliefs over reality, consumers lean towards the "ideal" rather than what is real.

Going Out of Business:

Most stores advertise a sale with no intention of going out of business, for they simply re-open their store with an "Under New Management" sign. Other stores advertise a "Going Out **for** Business" sale, with the hope that the small word "for" will pass unnoticed. The aim in both cases is to sell out items that do not sell well, and/or cannot be returned to the original supplier, and also to entice you to think that "going out of business" means cheaper prices. The profit margin, however, is not reduced since it has been increased before it is reduced. Deception is a false advertising technique only made possible when or if you think or believe in the image of the "sale" price scheme.

Political Advertising:

Commonly known as attack ads, they are basically a smear campaign against an opponent. These ads often make nasty statements about the opponent's public behaviour, godless morality, sex habits, or lack of "goodness" in his or her "ideals," thus creating a smear campaign of "character assassination."

Convenient Payments:

This is the most extraordinary surrender of individual control and power that is ever given away to business. The advertising of "convenience" is a widespread and popular "hook" to catch the consumer's belief in the concept. The metaphoric concept of "convenience" is propagated by businesses, and it has far wider implications than its image of convenience shows. It is simply an epitome of an "ideal" system of beliefs which is a fundamental distortion of your economic reality and your practical control over your money.

Let's look at the problem a little more closely. First, as a willing consumer you are giving the power and authority to a corporation to withdraw fixed or variable bill payments through your private bank account. This is simply a loss of independence in conducting your own activities as you see fit and in accordance with unforeseen circumstances. Second, the corporation can add hidden charges to your bill and have such added changes added to your overall bill amount without you ever being aware of it. It does not need additional permission from you to do this, because it already has it from the start. Third, when the corporation needs or wants to have additional capital for an investment—under a business-client agreement (read the fine print)—it can make "adjustments" or "corrections" to your account balance by withdrawing more in addition to the regular monthly withdrawals. Think for a moment of a hypothetical number of 100,000 corporate clients whose accounts are violated by $200 each, $200 x 100,000 = $20,000,000 in raised interest free. Small repayments of the "adjustment" or "corrections" funds begin three months from the withdrawal day. Who are those corporations that practice "adjustments"? They are insurance corporations for vehicles, houses, lives, health and so on. There are other corporations who "nickel and dime you to death" for services that are highly questionable.

Inflated Price Comparison:

Retailers raise the prices of items, and then offer them for a lower "sale" price, which falsely indicates to most consumers that they are giving you a "deal."

Advertising's delusions form a metaphorical environment of economics as a system of beliefs. They aim to promote the ideology of consumerism, making the purchase and consumption of goods life's primary objective. This is a validation of the delusional belief that everything is for sale, to be bought, consumed, and owned by everyone. One must remember that advertising is not merely a means to let the consumer know about making a wise decision on a given product or service. It is a means to entice a false emotional "need," "desire," "must have," "I'm a Shopaholic" and "keeping up with the Joneses," all in a deliberate attempt to sell us an emotion, a "good feeling" rather than the product itself. Although the sale of a product is the main objective, advertisers know that the selling of an emotion–a metaphoric image–by any delusional means, has created a culture of client loyalty, a "trade name" of lifetime client following. The psychology behind advertising and its economy as a system of belief is, for all intents and purposes, no different than the religiosity of the Catholic Church's system of beliefs. In both cases, the main objective is to propagate a client/believer devotion based on temporary satisfaction, a good feeling, and a group identity that serves the institution's purpose rather than actual human needs.

A recurring charge against the advertising industry over the last few decades has been its recruitment as a propagator of consumerism. In this capacity, its role was held to serve not the understanding of product quality but the exclusion of lines of thoughts that are hostile to consumerist economics. Advertising propagates economics as a system of belief that is held to be the primary purpose of human existence.

The justification for such a philosophical claim is an attempt to diffuse the conflict between individual corporate interests and the public good. This view of economics as a system of belief is not confined only to those social thinkers who oppose excessive consumerism, environmentalists, and climate scientists. This is also an affirmed view of socially-minded capitalists who regard the plentiful number of small businesses—without political power—as being a fundamental social base. These small proprietors maintain a balance of normal profits and relative optimal resource allocation. In other words, the current economic theory of corporate elitism is not politically and socially neutral; it is designed to avert people's eyes from reality.

The social and political role of economics as a system of beliefs has profound practical consequences, in that it has indoctrinated human beings to ignore or unlearn the fundamentals of household economics. It allows no room for dialectical balance (means versus expenses or wage level versus the cost of living). To help exclude from consideration what is now commonplace knowledge of the powerful role of corporate/philosophical advertising, the industry has employed many slick methods to outwit the consumer. It promotes a new way of "knowing," a slew of perception theories, animated things and metaphorical social bonds of "brand loyalty," all to maintain the maximum role of corporate advertising in the social-cultural life of human beings.

Mass media, politicians, social educators, and the public at large all sense what the concept of economics as a system of beliefs has ignored or denied. Corporations are large but few; however they wield great power over the law, political parties, and the supporters of small business associations. In short, corporate economics and their advertising agents propagate a faith-based religiosity as an "ideal" that has not been structurally beneficial for achieving a healthy lifestyle. As an ideal, it is a closed system of beliefs, defending its own idealism.

Dialectically analyzing the above and indeed concluding that this has occurred, we may also conclude that our western societies are governed and function under a corporate sovereignty. The systematic propagation of the advertising system of beliefs (i.e., consumerism) is a strategy of persuasion and assumptions aimed at the socially and intellectually vulnerable. Like the goal of religious institutions with their believers, the need to control or manage consumer behaviour arises from the social conditions of consumerism, sophisticated advertisements, large advertising budgets, and a long-term focus on consumer targets to manipulate a vulnerable and submissive public. This leads, in turn, to the need to continuously influence the general public by means of advertising and by controlling all possible economic parameters—cost, price, styles and trends—within which the corporations operate.

A certain part of the possibility for uncontrolled consumer behaviour rests subjectively on the individual's economic practices. Advertising may not be accountable for drastic life changes of the uncontrolled individual consumer, but it would be idiotic to presume it has only a superficial impact. Individual consumers are persuaded to make life changes by the advertisers who invest large amounts of money and time to design effective input that entices changes in the purchasing behaviour of the consumers at large. Few may resist such changes but the economic system of beliefs still remains a powerful process by which the individual follows metaphorical mimesis propagated by the advertisers.

It is not my purpose here to argue that individuals just follow advertisers' propagations blindly or without having a choice of what products they are willing to purchase or reject. This I have done elsewhere. But in the large-scale consumer goods industries, there is massive advertising meant to persuade the consumer to purchase goods that are selected, designed, and produced with a view to what lends itself vulnerable to coercive persuasion. One cannot dismiss the role of advertising, for its role is so vast, obstructive and extensive. It is an integral part of the idealist system of belief that propagates the delusion of "mind over matter."

This persuasive advertising effort has increased with the current complex multimedia technology and systems of mass info-transmission like the various sections of the Internet, Facebook, and MySpace and so on. Accordingly, it requires a determined individual to conclude that the taste, style, and easy credit that is expressed in mass advertising originates with what the producer wants to sell. He or she must make the appropriate decisions for a healthy level of consumption. What the determined consumer deems to be a desirable lifestyle may be substantially different this year or the next, and this may conflict with what the corporate marketers advocate.

The more serious problem an individual faces has to do with the consumerist system of belief that clouds the utility of the product by the aesthetics that surrounds it. For example, there is not much that can be said about the utility of a given product. A toothbrush is a toothbrush that does little more than clean teeth. (whether it is manual or battery-operated, or whether its handle is curved or straight). The system of belief, therefore, is not about the product itself, but about the illusion of the aesthetics.

A vehicle is a utility product which is a reliable means of travel between point A and point B. The advertised aesthetic features are the idealist base used to convince consumers that the extra cost is worth it. This is an attempt to hook the human psyche rather than just relating to a physical means of travel. The appeals to the psyche involve the ideology of economics as a system of belief (over and beyond what consumers are persuaded to buy). This includes the "ideal" of social distinction that is associated or invented with on enticing image of sexual fulfilment connected with a particular car style, cologne or perfume, hairstyle, or mouthwash. This is a systematic injection of delusional imagery which all biological, environmental, and scientific reality would reject as the plain fallacy of "mind over matter."

One of the most vulnerable areas of life is one's health care. Health care is not a philosophical issue or an alternative point of view. It is a real material reality that needs the utmost dialectical analysis for the sole purpose of providing human physical and mental benefit. Modern western medicine is almost completely consumerist drug oriented. This simply means that the consumption of medicinal drugs is the fundamental base of corporate existence and not the cure or prevention of illness. The direction, therefore, of the corporate business of western medicine, and major medical schools that are funded by large corporate grants and donations, results in strongly advocated drug "solutions" that generate huge profits. No pharmaceutical corporations will finance studies and research whose venture into commercial business would diminish their "bottom line." Huge amounts of money are invested in advertising to promote a drug "solution" rather than the actual prevention or cure of sickness.

Drug advertising makes up the majority of the advertising in most medical journals. Medical schools offer courses about what drugs to give to persons for what illness. Family physicians (whether caring, intelligent, honest or dishonest, community-oriented or elitist) are basically indoctrinated within a very limited approach to health care. Here, I am not propagating alternative health care, be it chiropractic, homeopathy, acupuncture, or osteopathy simply because I know next to nothing about these subjects. What I have identified, however, is that medical studies supported by pharmaceutical corporations almost never address the actual cause of a health problem with the focal aim of solving it. In short, studies are never conducted to determine how to prevent cancer, juvenile and adult diabetes, or heart conditions but only *how to control* these illnesses with drugs and other non-effective techniques.

Pharmaceutical corporations and associated non-profit foundations have launched successful advertising and PR similar to cultural religiosity, wherein they demonstrate the faith they have in discovering effective drugs. Their idealism lies within their metaphoric moralising of their "ideals" of the "truth," "effectiveness," and "honest concern" for the health of the general public. The familiar idealist mimetic image of the doctor as the "kindly," knowledgeable, "caring professional" is primarily the result of many years of these slick types of advertising campaigns. Please keep in mind that I am not at all suggesting that doctors are not honest professionals. This advertising campaign is psychologically sophisticated and is based on the fact that people do listen to their doctor's advice, thus drugs that are pushed by the medical profession would be purchased by the general public.

Deception—in whatever form—is equal to idealism's distortion of reality. Idealism is the most effective deception of all. One can only hope that idealism will remain a deception identifiable by all humans. One can be sceptical about a world full of politicians, priests, corporations, advertisers, secular idealists, and pop-psychologists, for there is much evidence that the bulk of the deception is coming from them. As long as I care to remember, idealism, religion, and advertising, like all false promises, hint at the power of suggestion. As in religion, advertising has all too often supported an immaculate deception of its idealistic "mind over matter."

Few will doubt the enormous stress advertising has placed on parents of children who are affected by the process of persuasion and the delusion so created between an item and happiness. Children's obesity caused by consuming "junk-food" has developed at an alarming state. Most people agree that school children and young adults are susceptible to advertising persuasion. My point is that if "junk food" is firmly established as the cause of obesity, where is the "happiness" so displayed in the TV and in newsprint? If advertising has firmly established that "junk food" is the cause of obese children's happiness, all parents should be both attentive and responsive to the junk food industry on their children's behalf.

But my purpose here is not to be cynical, as that can be easily done. I am looking at the problems of society as a whole. While we are aware of the causes of children's obesity and advocate "healthy living" for them, are we willing to legally challenge the junk food industry in the same manner society has combated the cigarette producing conglomerates? How far are you willing to be deluded against all dialectical reasoning that shows the obese child's happiness cannot negate the material reality of that child's poor health?

Corporate advertising spreads delusions (idealism) as a system of beliefs to get people to believe and have trust (faith) in that which they would otherwise reject out of hand. This is in connection with personal behaviour, the products people purchase, the way they observe their external reality and their position in it. Propagating "false facts" (idealism) is a method of inventing a non-existent problem. Advertisers then introduce a product or service to "solve" that very problem.

One must remember that society's popular ideas and beliefs are championed by those who are most likely to profit and benefit from them, whose goals may include religious, commercial, or ideological commitments. Their exercise of power results not in harmony between the individual and the economic institutions, but in discontent. Such personal discontent is harmonized by means of idealist-persuasion, but not for the dialectical materialists who are not persuaded and who sense what is actually happening. The discontent is sharply at odds with the propagated economics as a system of beliefs, which is also at odds with social reality.

Tension and discontent is what the individual consumer feels in the grip of large impersonal corporate forces—corporate rules, regulations, and policies—against which he or she feels helpless. The achievement of happiness through a more excessive consumption of goods has never happened. This resulting discontent could not occur in a society in which the consumer or individual has the power to pursue purposes of his or her own, other than the consumption of goods as life's primary purpose. This is different from what is propagated by the corporate advertising industry.

Personal tensions increase when material reality shows advertising to be false. But far from recognising the problem, consumers react by intensifying the idealist fervour of their beliefs of achieving happiness through excessive consumption. This is a system of belief in which "happiness" through consumption happens where there is no proof. Consumer driven belief in "happiness," through consumption can't all be true; therefore, don't believe everything you think.

But this is not all. Contributing to the conflict between what is propagated in advertising and what the material consequences of such claims are, advertising makes people its faithful servants by using images and myths that attempt to conceal those consequences. However, people's financial consequences cannot be concealed when they add to personal and family frustrations and conflicts.

Where do people turn their attention to in order to solve their problem of a lack of happiness and the problem of their economic consequences? Dialectical materialism would state: *people who are idealists would look inwards instead of outwards to solve their frustration and tension.* Thus, an inward solution would include religious beliefs, psychological "help," self-help therapy, expressing their innermost feelings and thoughts to friends and families, wishful thinking, seeking alternative mental solutions, and so on. This is peculiarly the most common approach problems solving in a society in which idealism is the dominant ideology that has taught us that "Mind (ideas, emotions, delusions) Over (power, idealised-solutions ove) "Matter" (reality, fact, evidence, science and real conditions) is the "correct" way to achieve personal or social solutions. ***Theirs is not to reason why, theirs is to believe and to satisfy.*** It reflects not life's living necessities, but the sterility of idealist mental delusions.

Finally, none will doubt that this short article leaves many important questions without dialectical answers. There is, notably, the question as to the idealist theory that here was briefly implied. This is because idealism is not a single topic with a narrow scope that reflects only the role of large corporate advertising in the excessive consumption of goods. Religious institutions, public education, psychology, and the professions that are interested in maintaining secular idealism are also unwilling to surrender their reputations on the altar of established social dogma.

One must ask if there is a trade-off between increased consumption based on credit on the one hand, and increased living standards beyond our fiscal means. I can only ask the reader to answer what this means with regard to the social perception of the behaviour of youth. A lack of social awareness does not allow today's youth to acknowledge that secular and religious idealism are impregnating ideas of old and new forms of thought. It has happened at various historical times when one or the other did not fulfil its ideological repetition as social propagator. Such repetition is done through the secular ritual of delusion, as in "my out of body experience" (religious resurrection) or "it's the thought that counts" (believing is your guide), or "I was born to shop" (shopping is life's purpose), or "the more you spend the more you save" (metaphorical achievement), etc.

Such idealism bypasses certain formidable difficulties by affirming the notion that only the believer of "feeling good" has the insight into that faith experience. Although logically constructed, coherent, and grammatically correct, such beliefs hide their delusion in statements of "my reality," "your reality," "the world inside me," "my inner-transcendence," or "my inner-reality," which carry non-investigative definitions. The only requirement religious and secular idealism demands of people for its validity is a faithful belief in the power of mental thought and emotional feelings over external material reality.

We have a social responsibility to teach each other and our children of the physical dangers and mental illness practiced by secular idealism, such as, in advertising.

Secular idealism, based on economics as a belief system, cannot be regarded as an innocent and harmless in its influence in advertising. It is hidden within visual images on TV, Internet and in daily written or spoken language by millions of people in their ordinary lives. Its hidden religiosity is so powerful that it has taken over the way we speak and think, the way we conduct our social affairs, our political and legal relations, our personal relationships, public education, the way corporations conduct their public business in advertising, and how we treat our environment. It has become a pervasive system of thought. People can no longer avoid resisting the delusion of believing in "mind over matter" if we are serious about saving our environment from impending disaster.

BOOK II

QUEST FOR COGNITIVE KNOWLEDGE

9

LANGUAGE USE IN IDEALISM AND MATERIALISM

"Logic is a very elegant tool… and we get a lot mileage out of it… The trouble is…when you apply logic [to life] it won't quite do…because the whole [evolution] of living things is not put together by logic…
So what do [we] use instead?… Metaphor."

Metaphor?

"Yes metaphor. That's how the whole fabric of mental interconnections hold together. Metaphor is right at the bottom of being alive."

Gregory Bateson

"Literal language says what it means directly without any metaphor.
Literal: "My grandfather died."
Metaphorical: "My grandfather crossed-over" or "He went to the big farm in the sky."

by the Author

Before starting this section an important statement must be made. This is written for the educated layperson dealing with the complexities of daily life. With this plain statement, further analysis of the origins and evolution of language, structure mechanics, syntax and verbal expression and so on, I leave it to the reader to proceed with the quest.

My aim here is to show the reader how words and meaning interact, how correct and incorrect formation of information works. In Genetic Evolution, information is preserved in the genes, and transmitted by Natural Selection. In the linguistic social evolution, information is preserved in the meaning of words, and their formation is transmitted through the linguistic interaction between the speaker and the listener, the writer and the reader. Further variation of linguistic interaction comes from sources such as the Internet, television, and/or other technological transmission of messages. Thus information is preserved in the mimetic memory of the individual host. While there are many facets in the application of linguistic transition, for our purposes, we will divide words/meaning into dialectical opposites, meaning of words with materialist content, and meaning of words with idealist content.

To make it interesting, here is a short story, which could form a stepping-stone for analysis. The main characters are the King, Castle, the Prince, the Shoemaker, Village and the Magician, with props as needed.

In the city state of Drama, a **King** lived in his hill **Castle.** At the bottom of the hill, in the **Village**, lived a well regarded **Shoemaker**, who was commissioned by the King for a pair of **Slippers**. When the King's Slippers were finished, the Shoemaker began the long walk up the hill to deliver them.

As he was doing so, he was confronted by the Prince, a spoiled brat, who demanded the Royal Slippers be handed over to him. After a short confrontation, the Prince stole the Royal Slippers and left the Shoemaker with the responsibility of explaining to the King the fate of the Royal Slippers. Stealing royal property was a capital crime, and the death penalty was mandatory. By royal decree, soldiers were ordered to arrest the Prince and bring him before the King to answer charges of theft. Hearing the bad news, the Prince decided to visit a powerful Magician who lived in the forest and ask for his help, in exchange for a generous fee. The Prince was given a magic herb-juice and was told that drinking it would, by miracle, exchange his Personality (with all Memories, Ideas & Mental Processes) with the Shoemaker's, and the Shoemaker's, with the Prince. The physical appearance of both Prince and Shoemaker would remain intact, including their distinctive style of clothes and mannerisms.

As soon as the Prince drank the magic-juice, there was an instant exchange of personality. At this very moment the Soldiers arrived to arrest him. [For the sake of clarity, **PSP** will stand for **P**rince w/**S**hoemaker's **P**ersonality, **SPP** will stand for **S**hoemaker w/**P**rince's **P**ersonality]. Protesting his innocence, PSP was taken before the King proclaiming that although he looked like the Prince, in fact, he was the Shoemaker, and proceeded to describe his poor shoe shop, his wife and children, including a few gold coins he had secretly hidden at the floor of his house. This was all confirmed to be true, which added to everyone's confusion.

Back at the Castle, both PSP and SPP proclaimed that although they looked like one person, they were, in fact, the other person.. Fearing capital punishment, PSP kept his claim short–I look like the Prince, but I am the Shoemaker. The King was faced with a dreadful dilemma, for in accordance with the law of the land a death sentence had to be carried out for the theft of the Royal Slippers. Who would be put to death, the PSP or the SPP? In the early hours of the morning a death sentence was carried-out…

Before we begin analyzing the linguistic components of our short story, and how that reflects the material reality of the world around us, we must reaffirm how we use memetic tools–ideas in words–as transmitters of messages. Memes are ideas in our mind that are not always of our own original reflection and contemplation. Memes, in one form or another, have been with humans for eons and are expressed in spoken or written words. Language as a memetic tool–idea in words–is intertwined and constantly evolving and changing. Memes, therefore, are part of the social fabric and an important component of human culture, maintaining or altering thought in praxis.

The most significant insight of memes is to know that memes (ideas) do not contain within themselves quantitative or qualitative physical properties. In other words, no ideas or senses, simple or complex, contain mass, space, time, colour, heat, smell, motion or change. These qualitative or quantitative properties are the prerogative of the material world and the reality that exists outside the human mind. In other words, memes are harmless in themselves, unless we permit them, through delusion, ignorance, laziness, carelessness, and blind-faith, to become manipulative. So long as a set of memes–ideas in mind or habits–remain within the confines of our minds, they are harmless, pleasureless, and ineffective. It is the moment that we externalize memes by means of praxis that effects take place.

Words externalize thoughts, and linguistic structures depend upon a cultural context through which those thoughts are transmitted from one mind to another, in the form of memes. Cognitive words and thoughts (dialectics), expressed by language, derive from some materialist experience of human life (i.e., social culture). Conceptual (or metaphorical) words are those that are unrelated to everyday material life, thought and language. Conceptual words need to blend themselves with cognitive meanings and ideas. Otherwise, without cognitive meaning, conceptual words are meaningless, lifeless, i.e., a pure idea of the invisible.

Now let us return to our short story. A word of caution: do not take this seemingly naive story lightly, for there are hidden pitfalls, clouded by a smokescreen of idealism and delusion. By educational training and memetics, imitation derived from past direct or indirect sources, we can easily state that the story itself is understandable. Conclusions, that is, moral and ethical issues, may be raised, some based on personal cultural background, others from objective cognitive experience. Unless the linguistic structure is incoherent, its building blocks are well-founded and meaningful... or are they?

The linguistic building blocks are made of cognitive and conceptual words, all to describe an actual historical or present-day event, and/or an imaginative narrative (as in "Santa Claus is coming to town"). Unless otherwise proven by scientific investigation, "Santa Claus," "Magician," "Magic-Herb," are conceptual words describing something non-existent, yet understandable. Why? The commonality of all three conceptual words is their cognitive/conceptual blend—*bridge-link*–a man (Santa Claus), a person (Magician) and herb (Magical).

If we take the cognitive equation out–man, a person and herb, the conceptual imagination becomes delusion of the real. There is no bodily structure, motion, energy or space in "magic" or "magical" and yet some people believe in its material existence.

Our annual choice for celebrating Santa Claus with gift giving and children's stories is part of our western social culture. It is considered a pleasant children's event, a mimetic tradition, one in which we adults know that we celebrate the imaginary. However, believing in the power of Santa Claus to travel and deliver gifts, in one night, to millions of children, or in the power of the "magician," or a "magic herb", is a delusion. Imagine my own daughter's disappointment when at the age of 6, she came to question the existence of Santa Claus. My point here is that, so long as we know that an image is an image, and that our memetic transference of that image is emotionally or physically harmless in its praxis, we and our children are safe.

But what happens when ignorance and idealism cloud our cognitive conclusions and we put into praxis our delusions? What are the real material consequences when we act on the basis of our delusional beliefs? Conceptual meanings, such as, "Miracles" and "exchange of personality," are blended into cognitive concepts of motion and energy. Motion and energy is induced, not as a real material energy, but as illusions of the fantastic, where the "miracle," "exchange," and "personal traits" are solidified with cognitive meaning. Conceptual words that are not blended with cognitive meaning are pure ideas of the invisible and lifeless.

But what happens when believers in the invisible and lifeless wish to impose their delusional beliefs on the material world of human society? What are the tragic human consequences, when you decide that our short story is actual, that you must inflict the death sentence on someone? Can you identify a conceptual word (blended with cognitive meaning) with delusional beliefs that are imposed (praxis) on reality?

And they warred against the Midianites, as the LORD commanded Moses; and they slew all the males....And the children of Israel took all the women of Midian captives, and their little ones, and took the spoil of all their cattle, and all the flocks and all their goods......Now therefore kill every male amongst the little ones and kill every woman....and all the women children...keep them for yourselves (Numbers 31)

And when the LORD thy God delivered it into thy hands, thou shall smite every male thereof with the edge of the sword... (Deuteronomy 20)

When thou goest forth to war against thine enemies and the LORD thy God hath delivered them into thine hands, (Deuteronomy 21)

Does the above *"children of Israel"* literally mean that young children carried out those murderous atrocities? Do the conceptual words *"Lord thy God"* form a *bridge-link* with a cognitive meaning of "man" that physically acts or commands?

If at the end of our short story, you have contemplated to solve the question of **PSP and SPP** and/or to whom the death sentence must apply, I suggest you investigate historical facts and tragedies of good people turned war criminals. When the gravitational tilt favours ideas in the mind instead of the material consequences, then delusional memes, religious or secular, passed from a propagator to a host, will cause a human tragedy. The Nazi-inspired delusional beliefs of the conceptual "Superior Race" were acted/enforced upon the material reality of the human race. To establish their National Superiority, herd- believers of delusional memes passed death sentences, justified by the conceptual with a cognitive blend of words. Delusional beliefs were externalized (acted upon the external world), to solve a conceptual "problem." The Nazi ideology was imposed on human reality, resulting in the Final Solution and other crimes. ***"Theirs is not to ask why, theirs to follow and satisfy."***

The sum total of all memes, religious or secular, is human culture. Memes are neither "good" nor "bad" (qualitative characteristics that can only be found in the material social life). To blame memes for our actions is to repeat the conceptual meaning of *"The Devil made me do it."* Nor can we blame past generations for transmitting memes **onto** our current culture, by means of custom, habit, dialectics, idealism, religious delusions, music, art, scientific methods of investigation, clichés, architecture etc. For our benefit or not, past generations have transmitted their sum total of all cultural memes, in language and in habits.

Language has made it possible for the human race to describe things of the material natural world, as they are or ought to be. In our quest to change the world, we have used our imagination (mostly based on fear) to believe in other "worlds" that are perfect and bodiless, but which do not exist. We have coined the word "supernatural," a conceptual term to say the least. This single meme, a combination of cognitive meaning (nature) and a conceptual word (super) has been transmitted from one generation to another, from one society to the next, and has spread to religious, spiritual, and secular sectors of our human culture.

We talk about Supernatural Cosmic Forces (the most favoured term of the secular idealist), a poor substitute for the conceptual word "God." Is it possible that believers in the Supernatural are suffering from mass delusion? Is it possible that their religious God did not live up to their expectations? Is it possible that these believers have "exchange personalities" from one all powerful-God to a "Supernatural Cosmic Force" by simply substituting one delusional meme-idea for another? After all, how hard would that be!! We frequently "change our minds" from one conceptual idea (of God) to another idea (of the Supernatural) or from one cognitive idea to another cognitive idea.

But the most striking insight is that this conceptual term *supernatural* contradicts and negates itself, and thus, it is meaningless and lifeless.

"Supernatural" contradicts itself, because the Natural Universe embodies and encompasses all objects, causes and events. Therefore, if an event has occurred, it is not necessarily supernatural, for if it is supernatural, it cannot occur.

Idealist terms, as in "magic," "magician," "miracles," and "exchange of personalities" are entities that were extracted from one or a variety of cognitive modules, such as a physical object, a person, an animal, human traits, an artifact or concept. A physical object, a human or substance would be granted some imaginary power while still being expected to appear and function as usual. In our story, a man, who became powerful only by the injection of the term "magic" is still a man who behaves as men do. The idealist terms "magic," "miracles" and "exchange of personalities," are concepts that are exempt from the laws of nature (birth, aging, dying), from the laws of physics (solids, visible); otherwise the term "magic" plus a man is recognizable as a person (magician).

Anthropomorphic images which are delusional are exempt from the laws of nature. They are "dressed-up" by human mind and desire with all sorts of piecemeal revisions of natural things. Words such as "heaven" and "hell," "souls with wings," "magicians" and "witches," "Satan" and "devil" and how they all act and behave are places and substances of human concepts. With only a few changes to their appearances and standard physical traits, these delusional images become understandable in our ordinary ways of knowing. Any writer therefore can spin ideas, concepts and practices and make them sensible to the human mind.

The Bible, the Qur'an, and our short story, contain delusional images and concepts that expect the reader (or believer) to act upon them. The New Bible, Qur'an and the Old Testament instruct their readers/followers to commit acts of war against the conceptual "others." Delusional images describing the "other" are identified with terms like "God's enemies," "infidels," and so on. In our short story, the reader is expected to act based on a delusional concept and to take physical action (pass a death sentence on PSP or SPP). Under certain political and military situations, delusional mimetic beliefs and concepts are imposed upon the real world in order to make them legitimate. The Nazi's delusional belief of the "The Jewish Problem," imposed upon the real world of humanity and resulting in "The Final Solution" was in essence an attempt to legitimize their beliefs. To the Nazi minions, ***"Theirs was not to ask why, theirs to obey and satisfy."***

Linguistic terms that inspire delusional beliefs are employed by any organization whose agenda is to inspire their clients, followers, believers, to follow a given praxis for the benefit of that agenda. A corporation employs terms and attaches delusional images to its products to entice the public to purchase them. Terms that implant fear, sex appeal, vanity, or overdosing on self-esteem are some of the memetic tools that are forcefully used. Organized religion and idealistic spiritual cults have their own agenda: their products are delusional memetic beliefs of "born-again," "Word of God," "God's Kingdom on earth," rituals, sexual behaviour, food preparation and prohibitions, false sense of security and insecurity etc., all to maintain control over their followers and the growth of their organization.

Language describes all human concepts; whether these are alterations designed to control standard traits of ordinary things, or based on human knowledge that conserves the essence of real social and natural life. Delusional images and beliefs on the whole, written or spoken in any language, for any human culture, for describing any material condition as "moral" or "immoral" are just that–they are delusional and misleading, unrelated to human life and the natural world. Linguistic terms can describe a world of spirits, of people's animistic beliefs and out of body experiences, brought on by an illness or a hallucination, seen as shadows and reflections of a human body, angel, saint, magician or magic herb without having mass, volume and/or continuity in time and space.

The public's demand for instant happiness, instant love, instant wealth, instant recognition, instant success etc., is a secular idealism that amends a natural process of beginning, growth and development. Those useless and even harmful idealist expectations create an opportunity for "experts," "would-be priests," "medical quacks" and "herbal remedies," "financial pyramids" and those with hocus-pocus credibility etc., to exploit the meek and weak. ***"Theirs is not to ask why, theirs is to believe and satisfy."***

Granted, an organized memeplex system such as the religions of Christianity, Judaism and Islam, have endured for millennia and many believers have devoted their lives to them. But it was idealistic-embedded terminology which offered an advantage to perpetuators with metaphoric linguistic skills that transmitted memes. The metaphoric term "believe," for example, is a non-investigative term, yet this mimetic term is very widely transmitted within the religious and idealistic sectors of our society. It has the most embedded gravitational primacy of ideals (beliefs) which form the foundations of personal, religious life and creates an idealist and legal basis of legitimacy *"If you believe it, then it holds to be true."*

Let's examine the moral case of a soldier who is a conscientious objector. A non-violent person may object to inflicting pain or killing another person on the basis of his/her material social pacifism. An atheist's social objection, however, to killing another person based on personal moral grounds, would have no legal grounds to stand on because of the lack of religious beliefs. In turn, a religious soldier's conscientious objections are based upon the religious belief "do not kill" which would form his defense as an objector. Both religious and secular idealists use the term "believe" as a concrete base to argue for or against legal points of law concerning divorce, birth control, sex education, blood transfusions, gay and lesbian marriage, etc. In other cases, believing is the only requirement a person needs to become Christian, Jewish or Muslim, regardless of that person's lifestyle.

I argue that in order for our life experience to acquire a materialist meaning, we must be able to speak about social issues and to express them with *reality-induced* words. Language itself is part of reality, but the cognitive knowledge of reality is not one and the same as knowledge of language.

Hence, in order to acquire a cognitive meaning, we must also understand what we mean when we use reality or idealist induced words. To understand what we mean, words need to be enacted or practiced. Real life's social meaning must be correlated and validated to praxis of that meaning. Validity of reality is a relation of one set of words and the interaction between them and their practicability. Praxis is a must, and the gravitational primacy must be based on real life, whether in education, experience or wisdom. This must be understood and become our cornerstone, because of the mind's inability alone to comprehend the sum total of all social relations in the world around us and how they work. While language in dialectics refers to the theoretical process of knowledge into practice, the word praxis emphasizes the need for a constant cycle of validating the meaning of what can be learned from the external world.

In this sense, praxis is understood as the changing, the transforming–matter in motion–of the natural world and of our life-process. Praxis is objectified in social relations, in human culture, man's dependence on nature, on our fellows and on our societal goals. Life's material process (praxis) is the starting point of cognitive analysis. This comprises the basic process of lifecycle, the relation of language and reality that presupposes that language is constitutive of social reality, and becomes an instrument of change in the external world.

All of our objective experience and understanding of the world around us–the environment of land, water, air and living creatures, must be interpreted. But we cannot interpret those apart from linguistics, for language–whether limited or extensive–depends on how we use it. There can be no such thing as pre-linguistic or extra-linguistic experience or interpretation.

Religious cultists or secular idealists propagate memetics on emotions and feelings, alternative reality etc., which can only be "experienced" outside of linguistic utterance. These claims negate themselves by the fact that unexplainable experience–where language is an obstacle to that experience–is just that, an unclear illusion, a delusion. How can one truly hear what one is saying about the extra-linguistic characteristics of something that presupposes the contrary?

I wish to point out some implications in the relationship between language and the external world, in the firm connection between spoken or written language and objective scientific fact–a connection whose existence makes the reality of the external world irrefutable. My argument here is in regards to the use of language expressing objective materialism and abstract idealism. If abstract idealism is taken broadly, it includes thoughts, perceptions, beliefs, illusions and delusions, obsolete entities, superstitions, and gives a real meaning to symbolic/metaphoric words and conceptual manifestations of the mind. The term "mind" usually refers to the thought process of the intellect: memory, imagination, reason to love and hate or feel fear and joy, and the myriad mental functions that are carried out inside our heads. Those mental manifestations are differentiated from natural or social processes in that mental manifestations unlike natural and social processes do not contain motion, energy, colour, space and shape. Mental subjective/abstract manifestations remain within the confines of the mind/brain, powerless to do anything else, other than be part of an endless circle of perception. The brain is the control center of the central nervous system, responsible for all thought processes, which are the manifestation of billions of neurons.

It is language that makes it possible to externalize "ideas in the mind." Memes are ideas that are spread from one host mind to another through speech, words and phrases, beliefs, gestures, rituals, fantasy, delusion, illusions, reason, rationality and logic. In short, the mind is a playground for memes. Acceptance or rejection of memes cannot be done with pre-linguistic or extra-linguistic exercise.

It is only when we approach reality through scientific knowledge that it expands the limits of language and the horizons of our world. Scientific experiments and confirmations can be described only in natural language. If there were no language, knowledge of right and wrong would not be known, nor true or false, good or bad, or how the Natural Universe works. Written and spoken language makes us understand all of the above, from the most important, to the most trivial issues, from true statements to false claims. Philosopher Thomas Hobbes in 1651 on *Leviathan,* Chapter 5, stated:

"Reason is the pace, Increase of Science, the way: and the Benefit of man-kind, the end. And, on the contrary, Metaphors, and senseless and ambiguous words are like ignes fatui; and reasoning upon them, is wandering amongst innumerable Absurdities; and their end, contention, and sedition, or contempt"

To give importance to their arguments, religious and secular idealists use bogus scientific language and half-understood jargon as in "cosmic energy fields," or "quantum consciousness." This is one of the main causes of human understanding becoming corrupted–it is because of the false meaning of the words in which humans express their thoughts. In other words, ideas in our minds are neither literary nor metaphorical unless we (if needed) qualify them as we speak.

A brief example of an uncorrupted materialist term is *"hardness."* Human brains need convenient internal labels to identify the different parts of a physical object. No one knows if my sensation of hardness matches yours, but both of us can easily agree that the "hardness" that I call hard, is the same as the "hardness" that you call hard, and that, if a physicist measures the object's hardness, it will be found to have similar qualities.

In other words, ideas in our minds are either literary or metaphorical unless we qualify them as we speak. Some "Ivory Tower" (a metaphor) academics, when they speak of scientific and biological issues on genes, natural selection or astronomy present these to the public in a complex, overly technical jargon. These important issues are poorly understood by a lay person, which makes it all too easy to put down a scientific book out of sheer confusion. This point is relevant to those religious persons who have been given idealist explanations of the workings of the natural world. I will explain.

Religion provided its believers with "answers" about human life, the stars, the sun, the seasons, animals and plants, natural wonders etc., by offering fixed and misleading explanations. Through generations, believers have adopted a non-investigative approach in accepting simplified answers. This is laziness and apathy towards scientific cognitive knowledge, which does not entice them to pay much more attention to it. Therefore, for "prisoners of ideals," an overly technical explanation is beyond their reach! To believers, past and present religious "answers" have always been fixed within a closed system of thinking and questioning. Believers are simply kept in the dark due to religious delusional responses; scientist and social thinkers should not do the same by providing overly technical answers." *Theirs is to reason and ask why, theirs is not to just believe and satisfy."*

Language is one of the most important dialectical tools. As a product of human evolution, language describes, prescribes and presents concepts that may be real or false. However, language itself bears no responsibility for the use or misuse of terms that promote delusional memes to our fellow humans. It is up to each of us to teach our brains the reality of the natural world–its balance and unity of opposites–as it is presented by the dialectical linguistic process.

Metaphorical language, written or spoken, projects images or meaning that describe something through the use of unusual comparisons, for effect, interest, poetics, or to present things in a much more "decorative" way. Metaphors, however, are not intended to be interpreted in any real or literal sense.

Yet, in our daily lives we do! Metaphors are used in advertising, or as a means of avoiding true or real situations. For example, instead of saying, "you are making me angry" we are saying "you are driving me out of my skin," or "you are pissing me off." It is also a means of providing "decorative" language in poetry, or as means of providing a *bridge-link* between unrelated things or ideas.

This we understand, but the point is to find ways to tell fact from fiction, or to use metaphors to "confirm" non-literal facts. For example, some years ago, I needed to renew my driver's licence. The government's clerk needed to confirm/verify my identity. She went through a list of questions, starting with my "Christian" name. I replied that, "I don't have a Christian name but my name is Constantine. My point is that our use of daily language is full of metaphors that are used out of memetic-habit. In fact, the idealist system of thought is founded on metaphors with religious and secular idealist meanings that projects different connotations:

- *Jesus Christ!* an expression of frustration
- *For God's sake!* exasperation
- *God's gift to women!* refers to certain men
- *Merry Christmas!* wishes one a happy holiday
- *It is Un-American!* attack on a political foe
- *Bless you!* in reply to someone's sneeze
- *God only knows!* a wondering expression
- *Mother Nature!* as an spiritual experience
- *Damn you!* an abbreviation of God-damn you

- ❖ *Oh my God!* orgasmic cry or praise of God
- ❖ *Take care!* a sign off

Our everyday language is full of fixed metaphors with religious and secular origins. We use them in speech routines such as: *how are you, nice day today, bless you, my out of body experience, my reality, or your reality.* Over time, some of these long-established memetic religious metaphors have become obsolete, clearly losing their original reference. *"Bless you"* was said with the intention to prevent the person from "demonic possession." This is hardly the case today. *Merry Christmas*, for example, is slowly being usurped by *Happy Holidays,* or *Christian name* is dropping out of use as a term for "first name." Whether this reflects a growing secularism, humanism or atheism is hard to tell.

Many times I have listened to myself and others, hearing "theism" embedded in our metaphoric language, idioms or slang. As for myself I have always enjoyed decorating a Christmas tree and I do enjoy architecturally beautiful cathedrals and fine sculpture. But this is not a proof of my religiousness.

Our everyday use of language is full of historically-established fixed terms with religious memes. *Thank god* is another term I often hear as a sign of relief, not in praise of a religious entity. Philosopher Nietzsche's bland statement that *"God is dead"* is not a claim that "God" ever existed, lived his life, and now he's dead. It is a metaphorical expression, in the same way that one talks about Mars or Venus in masculine and feminine ways. Others may describe a valley or a mountain view as a "spiritual experience," but this expression is not a reference to a spiritual belief. A materialist emotional experience need not be a religious experience. We have the richness of this historically cultural memetic vocabulary at our disposal for our daily expressions.

Still, there are some sceptics who ignore metaphorical language because it is completely open to different interpretations due to its vagueness. There are concerns that metaphorical language is very ambiguous when used in communicating cognitive knowledge. Metaphors can "spice" a spoken or written speech to make it interesting, as long as metaphors are not used to validate an argument. For example, the metaphor that *Mother Nature* is good does not validate its quality of "goodness." Saying *God's enemies* are all unbelievers does not mean they should be punished or killed.

In our previously mentioned story of the *King's Slippers,* the whole description contains a metaphoric plot. The story may be interesting because it is "spiced" or "decorated" with metaphors, but dangerous if the story is followed and its metaphors are believed to be true. *Magical power, change of personality (out-of- body experience), magic herb or magician are all* metaphors that are logically constructed, coherent and grammatically correct. Will you then pass a real death sentence to the "Prince" or on the "Shoemaker"? True enough the story allows for manifold interpretations.

The danger lies in taking metaphorical issues literally, believing them to be part of this world, using them as *mental directional forces* and acting upon them. In other words, we need to use dialectical reasoning when evaluating claims. Metaphors or analogies need extra scrutiny to determine their relevance to the argument (i.e., *Matter Over Mind*). It follows that some metaphors should be ignored because on evaluation they are irrelevant. When in doubt, metaphors must not be evaluated at all. They must be ignored rather than blindly acted upon.

Some years ago, I had a lively conversation with a Canadian Jesuit living in Brazil. At one point during our conversation he protested to me that I "should not take the Bible literally because Biblical stories are only religious stories." Unintentionally, the good Jesuit confirmed that anyone who has read the Old and the New Testament can identify that both contain metaphorical stories that are lacking factual and verifiable truths. Whether an event happened would seem very doubtful because much of the language used is metaphorical.

Much of the conflict between literal meaning and religion is the result of the literal interpretation of religious "events." For the Christian Church, asking if an event actually happened in the Bible is not essentially important, for the "deeper meaning" lies in the mythology supported by metaphorical language. So, what is the "deeper meaning" for example, in *"God created man in his own image,"*

Philosopher Ludwig Wittgenstein (1888-1951) states that:

"Mortals, however, believe that the gods are born...have voices and build like [ourselves]. If oxen and horses and lions had hands and could paint and produce works as human beings do, horses would paint the forms of gods like horses, and oxen like oxen, and they all would create them in the image of their own kind. The Ethiopians say their gods are snub-nosed and black, the Thracians say theirs have blue eyes and red hair."

It is noted that it is impossible to talk about any kind of religious metaphors in a non-metaphoric sense. Can a "deeper meaning" be achieved and transmitted by using dialectical language or reality-induced terms instead of metaphors? Can we separate fact from fiction without losing meaning in our casual and cognitive communication, and still use metaphors as non-essential linguistic tools? Do Church, Mosque or Synagogue leaders recognize the delusion of their metaphorical "deeper meaning"?

According to Wittgenstein:

"For when we speak of God and He sees everything and when we kneel and pray to Him, all our terms and actions seem to be part of a great and elaborated allegory which represents Him as a human being of great power whose grace we try to win, etc...etc...Thus in ethical and religious language we seem constantly to be using metaphors. But a metaphor must be a metaphor for something. And if I can describe a fact by means of a metaphor I must also be able to drop the metaphor and to describe the facts without it. Now...as soon as we try to drop the metaphor and simply to state the facts behind it, we find that there are no such facts. And so, what at first seemed to be a metaphor now seems to be nonsense."

Ultimately, it is really the religious believer who is the victim of religious metaphors, *a prisoner of his ideals*. It is largely because a believer's life vision is distorted. He or she feels superior to all of earth's living things, which is a delusion. He/she has accepted the *bridge-link* to bundle facts with fiction.

Back to our *King's Slippers* story. What I am saying about the delusive "obligation" of passing a death sentence on the "Prince" or "Shoemaker" may appear non-consequential because, after all, it is just a metaphorical story. Can you see how the 9/11 hijackers were also horribly deluded by their own religious metaphorical beliefs that "obliged" them to pass a death sentence on those "others" who were found "guilty." Can you see the similarities to the metaphorical delusion of the Nazi "Jewish problem" forming a *bridge-link* to a "Final solution" of death? Were all "obliged" by idealism to pass a death sentence, as were the 9/11 hijackers who were out to kill "Allah's enemies"?

Secular idealists do not realize that they are also *prisoners of their ideals*. For example, followers of consumerist metaphorical advertising believe in a "we can have it all," "buy now pay later" style of life, or on the "American Dream." They believe we can exploit the environment by "drill baby drill" whose consequences were evident in the Mexican Gulf oil disaster of April 2010, or "the bigger the better" or "God helps those who help themselves."

This is all metaphorical language that idealists do not see as being part of a long established belief system whose roots lie in the underlying religiosity of an archaic system of thought. They have accepted that having "a special view of the world" is enough to justify an action, even if it means passing a death sentence on "others."

But have we also recognized that we too are *prisoners of our ideas?* Can present-day devoted Christians and Muslims recognize that the root of their delusions lies in the historical fact that human slavery was practiced by the same religions and their powerful institutions? I would dare invite any of their religious leaders to stand before their "flocks" and explain in detail how human trafficking was regarded as "God's divine order"? Have the African-American offspring of slavery recognized they are also *prisoners of their ideals?* Isn't it strange that they are deluded members of the same institutions that supported and validated the buying and selling of their anscestors?

In our daily language, a metaphor is treated as a sort of "decorative" tool in the business world, especially in advertising. Metaphoric words and themes provide an opportunity to extend their effectiveness, something that requires unusual linguistic skills to influence the consumer in a non-factual form. In the consumerist idealist world, metaphors represent the ornamental power of language that can distort external reality. Looking at the material consequences of the massive personal financial peril of consumers shows the power of language to distort external reality. Looking at the material consequences of the massive personal financial peril of consumers in general, this must convince us that consumerist metaphors do not operate in a void.

We are increasingly dependent on using metaphors for our abstract thinking. Metaphors steer our thoughts as much as by what we say, as by what do not say. I suggest that each one of us should pay close attention to how metaphorical thinking distorts our perception of external reality. It is because "flowery" language—as a rhetorical tool—is so deeply embedded in our daily life and thinking process that most of us do not even recognize it is metaphorical. In short, pervasive metaphorical thinking and language distorts our conceptual system and constructs a delusional virtual reality that embraces our actions in a mind over matter delusion.

It is imperative for us to ask a fundamental set of questions, starting with: can we ever replace metaphors with the literal interpretation of facts?

Not until our legal system drops the metaphorical "spirit of the law" and strengthens the factual "letter" of the law. Not until we adopt a public educational system that teaches our children the fundamental differences between factual and metaphorical language. Not until we are aware that our viewing of the world is mostly through made-to order comparisons. Not until we recognize that our external reality has been disguised by metaphorical thinking and language. Not until we criticize religion, not only as a metaphorical delusion, but as being downright destructive and impossible to understand. Not until we recognize that it is impossible to understand religion because we have nothing to metaphorically compare it with. Not until we recognize that religious metaphors make no sense, for they are neither true nor false, but are literally senseless. Strictly speaking, religious metaphors are not factual statements at all, but just non-sense noises that signify nothing.

The most we can hope for is to remember that the next time we view our loved ones, our social and cultural relationships, or our economic conditions that we are not metaphorically confusing our "metaphorical mask" with our real face. We must, therefore, scrutinize the way the language we use mediates and shapes our perception and understanding or misunderstanding of our natural and social world.

Our dialectical/literal interpretation of our world is shaped by the success of evidence based on science—not by traditional idealist speculative beliefs of the "supernatural" that is riddled with metaphors and imprecision. We must become wary of the dreadful formation of speculative idealism, and we must increasingly ask for reliable proofs and other forms of substantiation. We must practice healthy scepticism and argue that the idealist's metaphors are murky, unproven, and outright untrue and literally devoid of sense. We must replace them with clear literal words.

The heart of any critique of idealism is the contention that *"mind over matter"* is an illusion. Dialectical materialists must do their best to show how incompatible metaphors are with evident truths based on literal sense. It is not a dialectical question whether metaphors are true or false, but that religious metaphors (like spirits), are impossible to understand.

For example, the Islamic metaphorical claim that a suicide martyr would enjoy the favours of 72 virgins in paradise is a non-sensical claim. Because, if the spirit of the suicide-martyr goes to paradise, are the 72 virgins also spirits? Is female virginity a spiritual condition? Or do the male and female "spirits" in paradise only preserve their physical sexual organs in order to perform a sexual act?

You see, all metaphorical thinking and themes are expressions that sound familiar but fail to convey any rational content, for example.

- ❖ *I talk to God:* does this mean if God replies, you probably suffer from schizophrenia?

- ❖ *God exists:* nobody can say whether this is true or false. If "god exists" is nonsense, then the opposite metaphorical proposition is nonsense as well.

- ❖ *I don't know whether God exists:* it is an agnostic proposition that sounds senseless as well.

- ❖ *Too much water under the bridge:* this literarily means too many things have happened between two people. Why don't you say it literally?

The physical world and the literal reality in which we live and learn a language is materialist. The "spiritual world" is a non-physical realm that could not possibly be represented. The misuse of language propagates delusional images of a "spiritual world" that is said to exist "beyond space and time" as spirit over matter.

This image is metaphoric, for it is a delusion that does not acknowledge details of how we can arrive at such a "spiritual world." In the end, metaphorical images are naïve, harmless poetic devices, or destructive terms with deadly human consequences.

Since the unthinkable cannot be thought, since there is nothing to confirm or deny, the existence of the "spiritual world" cannot be literally argued for or against, because it does not exist. This is the natural balance of the dialectical proposition of the "negation of negation" which terminates both sides of the argument. Once this is clear, a great deal of nonsensical chatter will stop and a clear use of literal language will prevail.

10

THE LITERAL BRAIN AND ITS METAPHORICAL "MIND"

"The human brain now holds the key to our future. We have to recall the image of the planet from outer space:

a single entity in which air, water and continents are interconnected."

David Suzuki

"Be master of mind
rather than mastered by mind"

Zen Proverb

It is a commonplace among contemporary social thinkers and biological scientists advancing the understanding of the functions of the human body to make observations of the so called "mind-body." People go about their daily lives forming concepts as ways of knowing, or creating intuitive theories about real things, animated things social bonds, and making comparisons with major kinds of entities in their experience. Some biologists and social thinkers, in their genuine attempt to explain the functions of the human brain, have now adopted literal terms like "hardware" and "software" and use them in a metaphorical way. These terms would have served the educated lay person who knew the *components,* not just the functionality, of such computer parts. At peril of being called a "purist," I would avoid using such terms, and reinstate biological terms in their proper stand.

Let us begin with the general premise that the term "mind" is a metaphorical term, which is an all-inclusive term for the organized connections of neurons within the human brain. The term "mind" is no more than the brain-in-function. Cognitive science progresses by looking at and studying how the brain works and by providing materially-based explanations. Explanations of the "mind" are explanations of the functions of the brain. Dialectical materialism is a cognitive tool that provides an understanding of ourselves and others by **not** reducing us to mere "mental" or "spiritual" entities. In order to confirm the metaphorical meaning of the "mind," let us look at the *components* of the human brain and their functions.

In brief, the human brain, like all physical things (matter), is made of *atoms*, which combine to make structures called *molecules*. As with all living matter, molecules can be large and complex. In short, molecules are connected together to form in gas, liquid or matter. These, then, are some of the brain's *components* and their functions that ensure a sensory and emotional process within it:

- ❖ *Neural pathways* - pathways from the cerebellum to other brain centers, allowing for more complex emotive tasking.
- ❖ *Cerebellum* - connector neurons for complex multitasking throughout the brain.
- ❖ *Corpus callosum* - connects the brain's right and left hemispheres. Sentiments and thoughts that grow from sentiments, cross talk between the right and left hemispheres.
- ❖ *Hormones* - the driving substance in the brain for processing emotions, feelings and act as mood regulators.
- ❖ *Amygdala* - an aggressive response of impulses in choosing to react to a situation.
- ❖ *Cerebral cortex* (neocortex) - processes verbal and spatial strategies. Generally, it transforms emotion into thought.
- ❖ *Brain chemicals* - such as dopamine, serotomin, oxytocin, norepenephine and other brain chemicals transmit emotional responses.
- ❖ *Hippocampus* - memory of emotional experiences, ability to converse about them, emotional processing in the limbic system.
- ❖ *Brain stem* - functions in a crisis situation to act first and think about it later, fight-or-flight responses.

There are a few brain differences between male and female processing pathways. For our purpose, however, we will not be dealing with these differences.

The human brain is a material thinking substance (organic matter) of gas, liquid and solid, with atoms made up of molecules, which functions by its own *energy*. The brain's energy can cause a physical event, such as the interaction between different localities of the brain, using chemical interactions (events) for such processes as memory, speech, cognition, beliefs, feelings etc. Both the substance of the brain and its material events (energy) can be measured and identified.

Science still has a lot of work to do, but certain physical evidence has already been established. A living substance (matter), in order to exist, has to have energy generated by the substance itself. With a natural balance of opposites, *matter vs. energy*. Energy is a material condition of two natural opposites like positive vs. negative, active vs. selective. For example, positive and negative electric energy causes a clash or attraction, (not a balance) between two natural opposites, causing the *event* of a lightning strike. The term "event" is a metaphorical word referring to the literal energy of the lightning strike.

This material energy can be measured, has a temperature and is visual and acoustic. In other words, the material energy is descriptive; the "event" is metaphorically prescriptive. Energy, therefore, is not "pure" because it is connected to physical organic or non-organic matter. Magnetic fields are material energy which, although they are not visual, can still be measured and analyzed for their magnetic weakness or energy-strength.

In the case of the natural opposites of active vs. receptive, both are characteristics of two living bodies called: man and woman. Thus, human relations can be described literally and metaphorically. We can literally describe the chemical interaction between various locations of the brain. For complex multitasking processes, we use basic sounds, the phonemes, and recombine these sounds in word combinations to "mean" something. These "meanings" are fixed only by common convention to identify things or concepts in singular terms.

The meaning of the term "house" is a "short-cut" term for an otherwise complex structure. We can choose to say "The structure that contains ten thousand nails, one thousand 2X4s, eight-hundred 2X6s, 150 pieces of plywood, 2 miles of electrical wire, 24 windows, 12 indoors and 2 outside doors," and so on. Instead, we use the term "house" to mean a structure to live in. The differences between many houses is irrelevant to the general meaning, for the term "house" is metaphorical, applying similarities to dissimilar housing structures. A metaphorical "house" cannot be described literally because "it" does not contain a material description, cannot be measured, cannot be seen and it is meaningless and unidentifiable unless "it" is connected to a specific physical or literal structure.

A literal description of a "house" can include its metaphorical characteristics of beauty. But we do not have two distinct substances, one of the house and one of "beauty," nor can we take away the "beauty" from the "house," for when we attempt to describe the "beauty" we are describing the house *with* its beauty. The beauty is not "pure," for it is not a separate substance but part of the material/physical house.

Does the "beauty" exist, in a literal sense, equally to the material existence of the house? The short answer is no! It is like talking about the human heart and its heart beat. Are these two separate substances, one substance the heart, the other substance the heart beat? They are not, for the heart is a material substance and the heart beat is the heart's energy. The heart beat cannot be separated from the heart, and when we describe a heart beat we are describing the human heart. What is then the result of the brain's energy, if not the metaphorical mind?

Setting this question aside for a moment, let us look at human language. Nobody actually knows whether human language began with a prototypical *literal* and *metaphorical* limited vocabulary before gradually evolving into one with a complex grammatical structure. Whether language's growth was gradual or sudden, it still had to pass through an evolution in which language evolved to its present stage. A social and cultural world in which there is a complex language structure would appear to be much more intellectually advanced than a socio-cultural world in which there is not.

As language evolved and increased its vocabulary horizon, so did the intellectual horizon of our brain's ability to examine our external environment and use it to imagine "virtual worlds" that could only be expressed in metaphorical terms. In fact, these "virtual worlds" were constructed socially by the brain's chemical and structural pathways to allow humans to extend their intellectual horizon of verbal terminology and meaning.

In short, our linguistic intelligence today is far more technologically, socially and culturally advanced than our ancestors. But we still maintain a pattern of thinking, a graph, a map, a metaphoric representation of a series of questions about human purpose on earth, the meaning of life, our socio-cultural behavior and so on.

Our ability to intellectually reconstruct "virtual worlds" with a detailed pattern, description or model has arisen from our ancestor's past pattern of thoughts. We draw on the likeness of our ancestors' ideas that arose from the negative image of the real world. The metaphorical methodology of the "virtual world" depends upon noticing that something can be made to stand for something else and that this may assist our thought or help develop new paths of communication.

Therefore, analogies and metaphorical terms–good or bad–are the human brain's materialization of symbol making in an evolutionary continuum. Symbol-making is a convenient method of communication for expressing possible or literally impossible relationships. A word of warning: the symbolic virtual image can lure us by deception and we may make mistakes by allowing things to stand for unrelated things.

Let us look at the statement that "the mind's power of memory is to recall…" If I was to literally explain "memory" it would be something like this:

"Neurons not only contact other neurons, they also connect with skeletal muscles, at a specialized structure called the neuromuscular junction. There the brain uses acetylcholine–its primary chemical neurotransmitter for memory and attention– to communicate with muscles. Another of the brain's key chemical messengers, dopamine, helps regulate fine motor movement. The role of these neurotransmitters in regulating movement underscores the relation between the body muscles and memory," and so on.

Instead of using a literal explanation of memory, we conveniently included it within the mind's *all-inclusive* metaphorical virtual power. So, now I can claim that "my mind's power of memory is to recall," knowing the metaphor of the "power of the mind" is *unrelated* to my brain's neurotransmitter for memory. The danger lies not with the use of metaphors but with the "virtual power" of the "mind" in a secular or religious idealistic sense.

A delusion takes control of our cognitive knowledge when we *believe* that the brain and the "mind" are two distinct substances, that one is all powerful, all inclusive, as in God's superior mind created the universe. In the secular sense, there is a mind-body *duality* with the "mind" as the primary substance, and the body being secondary. This is the core delusion of mind over matter.

My beliefs, my opinions, my imagination or my delusions of "spiritual-reality" etc, are all thinking processes but they are not *states* or *events*. The "mind" can **not** generate a material state or an event because "it" is not a substance of material opposites. It is a concept or, otherwise stated, the mind is a *metaphorical concept* of a *metaphorical existence* **not** of literal physical existence.

On the other hand, the human brain is a substance in which energy (chemical inter relations) permits the action and reaction of thinking processes. We cannot measure the "mind's" active energy, for if we were to attempt any sort of measurement, we would simply be measuring/recording the brain's movement of neurological activities. We must be careful here, for if we take the metaphorical term "virtual reality" literally and imagine that some God or secular spirit "inside" our brain is causing us to *"experience"* things, it is clearly **no** solution to anything. Regarding the "mind" as a separate substance is a widespread delusion in our secular societies.

The lucrative industry of psychology perpetuates the concept of "mind" by inventing absurd entities far too many to include in this brief analysis. Let us just look at one of these absurdities "out-of-body-experiences." The basic metaphorical "experience" is that "you," as a human being, are not a physical substance but a spirit. Once a person denounces the physical matter as non-existent, then anything delusional is possible. An "out-of-body-experience" refers to an "experience" in which a person's thinking *consciousness* seem to *depart* from the physical body, enabling this spiritually conscious *observation* of the world from a *"spiritual body"* rather than from of the physical body, and by means *other* than of the physical senses.

Let's see now: the "you," the "departure" (resurrection?) the other "spiritual body" and the other "spiritual senses" all form the sum total of a non-physical human being. Therefore, the "I" and the "You" are no more than spirits who happen to live-in a non-primary physical body. This delusion gets more bizarre still, as are the reciprocal delusions of "out-of-body experiences" where one "spirit" operating in a duplicate "spiritual body," travels to a distant location where the first spirit sees the second spirit, and both see (with spiritual eyes?) one another.

We move through a virtual world of "experiences" of our own brain's making. Our constructed models of bodies and spirits are part of the intellectual environment that our philosophical ancestors lived in, no less than the real intellectual concepts we deal with today. Intriguingly, our virtual worlds must also be seen as no less delusive than the ancient *memes* which we have naturally selected. We have pictured a virtual-reality of all powerful "minds" to counterbalance our intellectual poverty, and have selected ancient delusions to survive as companions to virtual worlds constructed inside our heads.

Naturally, as highly developed social beings, our extensive vocabulary contains hundreds if not thousands of new words identifying artifacts and high-tech terms and concepts. Our social thinkers and public education have found the most economical workload by not educating us with real dialectical materialist methods to identify what is *real* from what is not. Yet, thousands upon thousands of "studies" and books have been written as replies to other elitists "concepts" on issues that have minimum beneficial impact on the daily lives of the average person. Philosophers of the "Mind," of "Idealism," of Dualism, of Monism, of Consciousness, of Unconsciousness, of Cross Over to the Unknown World, of a slew of Psychological theories, of theories of deductive and inductive logic, and so on, have done little to improve the perception and lives of "blue collar" men and women.

Can we trace everything that you and I say and feel to a number of molecules in the brain? No, I am **not** saying this! Am I **saying** that human failings are now at an end because we can now analyze neurons? No I am **not**! I am **not** saying that Love, Hope and Passion are a tangle of neurons! What I am saying is that mental processes like Love, Hope, Passion, literal or metaphorical meaning, beliefs and delusions are all products of the brain's material functions, where the metaphorical "mind" rests.

In other words, one can **not** have mental processes without having the brain's neurons function in their designated way to produce the material means to thoughts. One can not take the "mind" out of the brain! The human mind is as weak or strong as the mechanics of the brain's neurons, molecules and chemical reactions.

What I am saying that the only physical existence in the brain are the atoms, aggregates of atoms, and the chemical relations between the sum total of all of the brain's manifestations. The mind "exists" as the by-product of the brain's manifestations not the other way around. As death occurs in the human body/brain, all bodily functions cease to exist. The "mind" does not die because "it" never existed in the first place, other than as a metaphorical concept. In short, the measurable and witness-able physical effects of the brain lead to metaphorical and unwitness-able mental processes.

Scientist philosophers and philosophers of science who study the human brain have come of age, using scanning methods for imaging brain activity in healthy or unhealthy brains, in addition to the developing computational theories of cognition. Dialectical materialists and scientists address new questions about the neurological basis of cognitive processes that are uniquely human, such as speech, thought, conscious memory and sensory connections with the external environment. These steps shows promise of leading to further investigations into how the brain functions are implemented during mental processes.

The challenge is to determine the brain's neurological basis of mental processes, and how these various processes break down when the brain is infected by a neurological disease. Another challenge is to answer a fundamental materialist question: how can immaterial entities, such as thoughts, beliefs, delusions, cognition and memories arise from the brain's biological material and energy? We know that it does, by the results we see, but how?

In addition to being beneficiaries of the brain's complex functioning, people can also be victims, by deceiving themselves into believing that the immaterial mental processes are primary and that the human brain is secondary, forgetting that the mind's functions are **not** purely mental. *Remember this:*

We should refer to the brain's function as "mental processes" and treat the brain's-mind as one inseparable body, not as two distinct entities of body-and-mind.

The mind then is a literary device used to express abstract ideas that come naturally to the brain. It would be bizarre to say that the mind is "pure" immaterial and that the brain is "pure" material with no energy. We know that Matter in Motion exists in nature, for matter cannot exist without its energy. Thus, the mind is the end-product–a metaphorical one– of the brain's neurological energy.

In ordinary conversations we use metaphorical words or arguments when saying, for example, "Have you lost your mind?" We all understand this to mean "Are you a nut-case?" or "Are you cuckoo?" Somewhere between the basic use of metaphors and literal constructions there is a vast inventory of everyday metaphors that express simple or complex concepts. Whether real or delusional, these concepts are "housed" in the brain's hippocampus memory storage.

We continuously borrow from *literal or concrete thoughts* when we stretch our ideas and words to encompass new horizons of metaphorical expressions. We also use metaphors to build new metaphors. This empowers us to construct worlds that never existed by using our imagination along with metaphorical words to construct children's stories, a poem or prose.

The story of *"Snow White and the Seven Dwarfs," is* an illusion using literal terms (persons, the mine, diamonds), and *metaphors* (the imaginary world). All were formulated in the *cerebral cortex* and the brain's *neural pathways*. Most of us would have no difficulty realizing that this story is a harmless illusion, fun for children, culturally creative, and so on.

Parents and social educators may encourage children to allow their minds to imagine things without having to explain to them the fundamental biological processes a "mental story" goes through before it becomes an expressive story. Fair enough, for this is what it is called *naïve idealism*. It is naïve because, as an illusion, it is not destructive. It does not entice human delusions to harm other humans and the environment. Poetry, prose, art, aesthetics and humanist cultural expressions are all harmless examples of naïve idealism. The mind becomes the metaphorical propulsion of imaginary entities.

However, at what point do humans regard the mind as a distinct substance from the brain? At what point do we empower the mind beyond its capabilities? From a biological perspective, we can measure throughout the sensory/emotive processes in the brain's centers. The brain's "power" accommodates only the crucial conduct of emotive electricity and other chemicals that help the brain process emotions into thoughts (cerebral cortex), multitasking (cerebellum) and so on. This brain's "power" is "externalized" only from one center to the next through neural pathways and the bundle of nerves connecting the right and left hemispheres (corpus callosum). Also, this "power" only functions within the limits of the cranial confines and the nervous system of the human body. The brain does not have external power to control biological and botanical life, or to influence the external environment by design. Literally, we cannot add additional power to the human brain other than what natural selection has included, unless, when we are talking of "brain-power" we are referring to *metaphorical power* **not** *to literal power*.

In metaphorical naïve or destructive idealism, every imaginative or delusional belief is mentally possible. So long as the metaphor or delusional expression is grammatically correct and has *a literal or concrete base*, the "story" is understandable, but not provable or disprovable. For example, unicorns, mermaids and superman stories are all grammatically correct, and have a literal *base* (man, horse, horn, woman and fishtail.) But because they are imaginative stories, we can only prove or disprove them metaphorically, **not** literally. Metaphorically, we can add power to the mind, having the ability to change physical appearances at will, add or subtract bodily parts, be armed with magical powers or superhuman strength, cause the resurrection of dead persons, have free floating bodies in the air, cure sick people by the touch of a hand, feed thousands of people with a few fish, have a man walk on water, have out of body experiences, create life after death, kill the factual "other" who does not believe in the same delusional beliefs, and so on.

Moreover, if the human brain does not have the kind of factual power beyond the requirements of biological necessity, what about the "mind"? Is the metaphorical "mind" empowered with capabilities *beyond* the brain's actual neurological manifestation? Biologically, the brain's sensory experiences consist of some of the most complex activities the brain needs to handle in its lifetime. It has "its work cut out" for its entire lifetime. Granted, the cingulated gyrus is a very powerful emotion-processing entity of the limbic system; still this processing does not produce externalized power to be used by design.

The metaphorical "power of the mind" and the "mind" itself, therefore, are both widely acceptable myths. It is a "comfort zone" for the majority of us who are unaware of the brain's workings, its natural restrictions and structural cognitive capabilities. People are caught up in the terrible deception of a metaphorical world of their own design, their personal insecurities, their fear of death, and sincere beliefs in their mental metaphorical "spirit" and immortal "soul" which is consoling to them. False mental beliefs can, in fact, be as consoling as true ones, right up to the point of *disillusionment*.

This applies to the beliefs of naïve-idealism, when a child discovers that dear old Santa Claus or the Tooth Fairy does not realy exists. This also applies to ex-religious believers who "change" to spiritual beliefs because God has disappointed them for failing to prevent a disaster or to fulfill a wishful prayer. As sincere and wholehearted a belief in "life after death" may be, it is no more immune to disillusionment than the belief that praying longer and harder to God will cure sickness. The strange thing is that both religious believers and the Eastern spiritualists who believe in metaphorical reincarnation or life after death can never be ultimately disillusioned. If both believers are so sincere and so convinced that there is a factual life after death or reincarnation, then why then are they so devastated when someone close to them dies? If death is just a stepping stone to life after death or reincarnation they should celebrate, for such a person's temporal life has finally reached eternal life or reincarnation! Or, in the words of Mark Twain:

"I do not fear death. I had been dead for billions and billions of years before I was born, and had not suffered the slightest inconvenience from it."

All of the above metaphorical structural thinking is manifested in the brain's mental process. None of these thoughts could ever materialize because metaphorical description or prescription of life contains **no** living matter and energy, no space, temperature or measurement. The metaphorical power of the brain's mind can only create mentally ready-made things, fixed entities, and "living-dead" entities. A literal or factual description of life's living beings would contain detailed information that always leaves room to be disputed. The mental formulation of the dialectical theory of life's evolutional process could be proved or disproved on the basis of scientific evidence. There are no ready-made entities in the natural world, for all living organisms and structural entities had to have undergone a transformation–matter in motion–which is non-existent in the metaphorical world of the brain's-mind.

In the words of Charles Darwin:

"If it could be demonstrated that any complex organ existed which could not possibly have been formed by numerous successive slight modifications, my theory would absolutely break down. But I can find no such case."

Literal and factual mental concepts are by their very own essence dialectically interconnected to the external reality of the natural and social world. This dialectical factual thinking process is limitless because its terms are mostly literal, factual and concrete, connected to the infinity of the material world. It is this infinity of the material world that makes it possible for the human brain to manifest literal ideas based on physical infinity.

It can be demonstrated that our world is so vast that no human brain-mind could ever be cognitive of the sum total of all the natural, social and cultural relationships of our living world. Million of living organisms, millions of natural or man-made living spaces, millions of botanical diversified plants, millions of social and cultural relations take place daily between humans and their environment. Human language has the potentiality of infinite enlargement, which can only be made possible by syntactic factual innovation which would finally liberate us from the mental restrictions imposed upon us by metaphorical thinking and the metaphorical "mind."

We must be careful here, for I am not advocating the elimination of metaphorical words from our vocabulary. No, I am not! I am advocating that the gravitational lean or directional force must be based on the natural unity of opposites, a rational balance between dialectical factual and metaphorical thinking. This way, no extreme one-sided lean would cause the negation of the other. This process must, of course, lean in favor of the factual external reality: *Matter Over Mind.*

On the other hand, searching for particular examples for a fundamentally metaphorical way to proceed, present-day idealists eagerly seek to fill a gap in our cognitive knowledge. This intellectual gap must not be filled by metaphorical thinking and language, for as science advances; the metaphorical God is under threat of being eliminated. This can eventually happen by mentally replacing one metaphorical God-idea with another metaphor less destructive, where the God-idea would no longer be detrimental and would have nowhere to hide.

It is also essential that naïve or destructive idealists admit their ignorance, even if their ignorance challenges the "fill-up" of their reality gap with their metaphorical beliefs. It is ignorance that drives idealists to their delusional beliefs and their determination to convince "others" of the metaphorical validity of their religious superstitions. The basic deplorable effect of metaphorical religion and non-religious spiritualism is that it mentally trains us to regard "something" as virtuous with no cognitive understanding of it. We are not talking about recognizing ignorance in the sense of confessing a religious fault. It is about educating the mind not to seek out gaps in scientific knowledge and then fill these gaps with metaphorical beliefs and mental delusions until the "hole" is been filled. We are encouraged to leap into metaphorical speculation without even looking to see whether it leads us into a mental-trap or a dead-end pathway charmed with appealing delusions.

There is, then, also a deliberately chosen ignorance about scientific knowledge of the human brain/mind by our secular and religious educational system. Of course, children's education starts at home where parents acculturate their young in whatever teaching ways they personally choose. Parents can choose to indoctrinate their children in an unhealthy dogma and superstition or to educate their children with scientific knowledge. I am **not** advocating here an imposed censorship on parents. I am trying to balance the principle of freedom of speech and the children's fundamental right **not** to have their delicate cognition filled with nonsense. I am neither offering another point of view which can be debated in pros or cons.

The scientific explanation of the workings of the human brain's/mind is **not** a point of view. It is a scientific fact! It is not an exaggeration to say that the fallacy of the "mind" being a separate substance from the brain would disappear as children enter a scientific dialectical educational system. We cannot restrict scientific education so that we can accommodate a "politically correct" attitude to protect one's metaphorical civil right, and let children be guided onto a straight and narrow path of ignorance. In short, children have the right, and the public educators have the duty, to learn and teach the literal truth of the brain's manifestations, and relationship between delusional ideals and cognitive knowledge.

Dialectical education about the workings of the brain is not about teaching children what to think, but how the brain does its thinking. When children having dialectically and rationally been exposed to all known scientific evidence, they grow up and decide that the "mind" is not a separate substance, that the "mind" has no power to influence biological life, that magical-thinking is a delusion, that the term "mind" is a metaphorical not a literal or concrete term, that the thinking process is the sum total of the brain's neurological activity, that the term "supernatural-mind" is self-contradictory, for anything which exists within the Natural Universe is natural.

Of course, these are strong statements that need to be received, with much contemplation to determine if they are nonsense or have a cognitive base. The important point is that it is **not** my *privilege* to decide what we shall teach children, or what the public education system should teach them. But I do strongly criticize the parents and religious propagators who deliberately impose their indoctrination on children before they become adults and are able to decide for themselves.

We must all remember that there is no such thing as children born "Christian" or "Muslim," "Catholic" or "Protestant." As long as children are young, they are vulnerable to whatever indoctrination they are exposed to. It is equally important for us to reflect that one day our children will become parents of the next generation, and they too will impose their dreadful indoctrination upon their children.

Again, a decent humanist reader may become uneasy at my suggestion of restricting the "freedom of speech" of religious propagators. I will gladly accept their criticism if they equally consider whether religion is a mental illness that distorts a child's cognitive functions for the rest of his/her life. Religious *memes* are the most powerful units of cultural inheritance. Religious memes are replicated, copied from parent or educator to children down the generations. They replicate from brain to brain, via indoctrination or any other means. Indoctrinating children under the false principle of "freedom of speech" is no different from promoting unhealthy and highly transfat foods to children under the "freedom" of free enterprise.

In defense of a child's cognitive intellectual health, I suggest that the reader consider placing his/her answer in the child's favor. In all fairness, the parents cannot be blamed for their ignorance, and it may be a bit too harsh to call them stupid or irrational. But they can be blamed for implanting their own beliefs on a child far too young to decide whether "believing" equals reality, whether "believing" and worshipping an invisible entity can justify the atrocities committed under the name of this invisible entity. In searching to maintain a metaphorical freedom of worship, we may want to say that children's cognition must be shaped by their parents in the ways they are, but shall the results be a "creative" mental illness? These issues must come to public attention if we are to create a dialogue among enlightened social thinkers, public educators, humanist parents and secularists to counter the idealist propaganda of *mind over brain* delusion.

From a biological perspective, is there a reduction of feelings and emotions if we allocate them to the brain's *literal* functions instead of the mind's *metaphorical* ones? Brain research has borrowed the popular term "wired" as a companion to the words "brain circuitry," and I am confident that the reader won't think that brain research is reducing feelings and emotions to the level of the 19th century concept of mechanical wiring or mechanical materialism. Granted, the joy of sentiments and emotions grows as much from understanding the brain's wiring as it does from the mystery of metaphorical feelings.

This is not a philosophical rift between *literal* and *metaphorical,* for both take place within the brain. The real rift between them takes place outside of the brain, in the real material world, between healthy and unhealthy relationships. Understanding the wiring and mechanics of the brain can prevent us from a lot of trouble in many walks of life: in family, love, cultural and social relationships.

So, what is happening in the wiring of the brain when we feel emotions? In general, emotions and feelings, as in laughter, sadness, surprise, reactions to a spectacular sunset, death of a dear person, a child's first steps and a million other sensory stimuli are processed through a person's senses to the *limbic system*. The limbic system has two primary tasks: to *process* emotional responses to the external world and to *organize* those sensory responses to our external world. *Thinking* is processed apart from *feelings* and *emotions*. Thinking is handled by the *neocortex* along with speaking, moral reasoning, idealizing, abstracting, and achieving goals and so on. As we learn new cognitive skills, those are also "housed" in the neocortex. However, the human brain is multifaceted and is capable of processing and being many things at the same time.

In exploring basic qualities of the brain, even in these brief few pages, the reader has probably gained a general perspective on the capabilities of the human brain. These capabilities are part of an evolutional process; however, the brain is evolving differently now than it did a few hundred years ago. Differences and similarities between past and present brain processing capabilities lie with the fact that a contemporary human brain is handling emotional, cultural, social, scientific and family situations our ancestors didn't have. During the transition from the agricultural to the industrial age, our brain capacity continued to develop, with the spectrum of brain activity growing to meet new technological, economic and social trends. As social life becomes more complex, the brain becomes more adaptable to external material conditions in order to meet new challenges. These challenges are literal, and therefore, must be dealt with in concrete linguistic terms, building cognitive knowledge, rational thinking and developing more compelling neural pathways. The metaphorical concept of "mind" is restricted to ready-made and fixed images that cause restrictions on our humanist's perspective of the elegance of the brain's reality.

11

METAPHORIC NATURE OF CULTURAL MEMES

"A meme is an imitable behaviour. Religion is a bundle of memes."

Unkown

"The meme for blind faith secures its own perpetuation by the simple unconscious expedient of discouraging rational inquiry."

Richard Dawkings

Genes are an integral part of our evolutionary make-up. Their spreading and replication, unlike memes, are restricted by the small number of offspring a parent can have. Through genetic evolution, humans have passed on their genetic makeup to the following generations. It is not surprising, therefore, that in the last several thousand years, humans genes have remained almost unchanged. Human genes, as genetic replicators, have a well-established and stable genetic structure. This structure serves to support and increase survival and re-productivity of their replicators. This process of gene transition is done mechanically and is not controlled either by the carrier or by the host. This is because natural selection and randomness are responsible for our genetic make-up. That is, genes carry within themselves genetic information that contains both quantitative and qualitative properties. To be tall or short, have curly or straight hair, or have blue or green eyes (and so on) is genetic information that is passed on from a parent to a child.

Memes, however, are ideas, or units of cultural inheritance which include habits, emotions, senses, rational or irrational thoughts, delusional beliefs, religious rituals and customs, advertising slogans and catch phrases, songs, poems, and philosophical concepts, etc., that have survived and have been popularized. Memes, once they are initiated or introduced, are transmitted visually or orally from one person to another through habit, popularity, fashion, books, music, and through reasoning (i.e., factual evidence or faith-based beliefs and wishful thinking). Some memes are popularized and spread while others are short-lived. Depending on the host-mind, memes are accepted or rejected on the basis of the person's cognitive abilities as being extensive or weak, or, because of his or her system of beliefs. It should be noted that memes, unlike genes, do not contain within themselves qualitative or quantitative properties. After all, memes are simple or complex ideas that are reality-based or illusory.

For example, Richard Dawkins's book, *The God Delusion,* has a meme-title which has been widely imitated, transmitted, and read among atheists and humanists. However, such a meme-title has mostly been rejected by theist followers. Such a meme-title is a metaphorical concept and it does not contain nor does it transmit the body of evidence presented in the book itself at the moment it is received and accepted by its reader's curiosity.

For religious persons, on the other hand, this meme-title will be against their convictions and this supersedes their willingness to move towards knowledge and evidence. Such religious convictions are based on "instant" wisdom, blind faith, and trust, which in turn, control memetic acceptance. Religious followers have come to regard faith and a fixed system of beliefs as virtues. To hold fixed beliefs, an idea, or an emotional state as being the only truth will lead to a path of self-delusion. Blind proponents of religion-based memes are responsible for their followers' state of mind, in believing in the invisible and for spreading a passion like "burning ice." A blind believer is influenced by religious memes and also by a yearning to simply believe. ***Theirs is not to reason why; theirs to blindly follow and satisfy.***

Then who controls the transmission of cultural memes? The short answer is that no one has the power to prevent or discourage the spread of memes. Memes are accepted or rejected by a single mind or a group of minds based on people's cognitive capacity to reason, to investigate by scientific evidence, or willingness to follow religious or secular beliefs. In this sense, the question of "who controls the transmission of memes" is inadequate to explain the effects of memes in the human mind unless one looks at the cultural areas where memes are hosted.

Some social thinkers with backgrounds in computing technology associate memes with computer viruses. Proponents of this contemporary interpretation of virus-memes argue that a person is a helpless pawn through which memes can dominate that person's life. They associate the word "viruses" with a bodily infection, a negative concept, which propagates the idea that humans are memetically disease infected organisms. That is simply not true, for memes are not tangible things, such as genes (physical) which contain coded bits of information, where neither the carrier nor the host can have any control over the adaptation process. Unlike memes, a carrier's genes are physical entities which pass from one body to the next in their entirety. On the other hand, the evolution of memes is a cultural and not a physiological phenomenon.

Recently, I read the following about Memetics:

*"Memetics is a neo-Darwinian approach to evolutionary models of cultural information transfer based on the concept of the meme. Starting from a **metaphor** used in the writings of Richard Dawkins, it has since turned into a new era of study, one that looks at the self-implicating units of culture. It has been proposed that just as memes are analogous to genes, memetics is analogous to genetics."*

For the past several years a number of social thinkers have written on the subject of memes and memetics. Ironically, those memetic theories resemble dietary claims (of which most do not work). Writers whose background is in computing technology identify memes as a form of computing-virus affecting our minds, which is similar to the workings of an infected computer. Using the metaphor of a "virus," instead of a material word mimesis (for imitation), distorts and idealises the essential meaning of mimetic cultural transmission. Those with a biological background often associate memes with genes. Genes can limit or express themselves, going from a gene-carrier to its offspring-host from one generation to the next.

Admittedly, the investigation of memetics is a culturally-related subject that has existed under a variety of fields such as: philosophy, language and culture, biology, genetics, and natural selection. My point, however, is that a person or a group of persons in a society have the choice to host or reject a single meme or a set of memes. This hosting process depends very much on the person's cognitive ability, his or her level of education, and his or her idealistic vulnerability to social pressures. With genes or genetic virus transition, a person (host) who is affected by it has no choice whether to reject or accept genetic information. Likewise, a child or an ignorant person has no choice but to accept (host) that which has been propagated to them by a system of beliefs through social or cultural institutions.

Individual choice is expressed by praxis on mental conclusions. It is restricted to a given human culture. Such praxis activates our mental interpretation of the external world, as social and cultural conditions dictate. We have control over our choice of what kind of praxis we are willing to accept in order to change existing social conditions, real or illusionary. We choose an interaction process between materialistic-memes or idealistic-memes or a mix-and- match of both. But the fact that we choose is very much a human cultural activity.

It is through this semblance of memetics that our brains process and that we are able, by our mental ability, to interpret existing cultural conditions. Sometimes we "get it right" and other times we don't. In other words, personal choice is a mental process/conclusion, a perception of our relationship with and about the external world itself. Are our choices and praxis capable of the cognition of real social conditions? Do our ideas and notions of the real world conclude with a correct reflection of reality? Anyone who asserts a gravitational primacy on his or her ideas or senses as a directional force over external reality and material/social conditions follows a school of thought of religious or secular idealism.

Human brains have evolved a built-in faculty for language acquisition as well as conventional understanding of what propagates culture. Brains are not just a means to a mechanical process but have also developed an evolutionary balance of sensory skills. It is with this set of sensory skills (evolved by complicated arrangements of molecules) that humans can securely conclude a dialectical process of theory and praxis.

As much as humans want to comprehend such processes, no one amongst us can fully comprehend the sum total of all human social and cultural relations active in our society. We are not super-intelligent or superior-minds, for such things do not exist. That is, unless we turn to a system of delusional beliefs. Our human brain and mental processes are limited only because of the enormousness of existing external social relationships. Albert Einstein, for example, may have discovered the laws of the universe, but he could not know the social hierarchy of the African gorillas or the structure of the Masonic Society.

My point is that our intelligence and our mental conclusions can be influenced by memetics of all sorts, and our minds have significant limitations. It cannot be all-powerful and omnipotent, which includes a universal knowledge that is unlimited and ever growing. Free will is restricted within our human capacity to act and react, within the limits imposed upon us by our physical surroundings, by our intellect, illusions and delusions, customs, habits, traditions, mimetic preferences (e.g., over this or that style of fashion, music, education, or by random impulses.

It is within those aforementioned natural restrictions of external reality that human thought and praxis have been led to achieve success in art, philosophy, science, and developed cultural and socio-economic advantages. It is also this ability to choose that has led us to incorrectly believe in entities that do not exist instead of investigating ideological manifestations, that has led the human race into the path of destruction and human suffering. We are active agents although at times we behave like automatons–but we are not perfect, not omnipotent, and not all-powerful. We are much smaller than the external world, but we can refine our cognitive dialectical processing of the external world by recognizing the perpetuators of mimesis and delusional memes.

The subject of mimesis and memetics deals with ideas-in-the-mind, confined within the physiology of the human brain. The moment that ideas-in-the-mind are hosted and externalized by praxis, they become memes which are transmitted and affect human culture by an interplay of memetics and human action. Memes influence the cultural relationships of the natural balance of opposites, contradictions and unity of contradictions. Mimesis is also about everyday life processes, an imitation of common thoughts and praxis, how those imitations influence our daily lives, and who or what institution initiates and transmits cultural memes. Particular human attention must be focused on how language transmits dialectical-materialist and idealist thoughts that have an influence or grip over our culture. Natural opposites, contradictions and the unity of contradictions are evident in materialism vs. idealism, in religious idealism and its unity with secular idealism, and in ideas ranging from unity to praxis and dialectical opposites to irrationality. Established cultural memes influence our philosophical models, in one way or another, and have been part of human culture for the last 5,000 years. So, let us not treat mimesis and memetics like a novelty or a new age experience that promotes mental trappings in our brains. True enough, when the human mind is bombarded with some novelty, an existing idea (religious or secular) may alter our understanding of what is possible when we externalize this new idea by praxis. Most popular "new" ideas are recycled ones–like an old wine in a new bottle. New claims of psycho-memetics that claim the gravitational primacy of ideas are a projection and empowerment for the delusion of "mind-over-matter." The old, recycled idealism of metaphysical philosophers have led human culture through religious delusions, wrong social paths, consumerism, and negative environmental consequences.

We need human cognitive intellectual tools and a materialist interpretation of human culture. Also we need to reject idealistic theories that convince us that the whole world is in our brains in mental images, a world inside our minds, while excluding our external material surroundings as being mindless substances that can only be controlled by the power of the mind.

Most memes are trivial or do not carry a motivation for praxis, for these can be a joke, poetry, or simple wishful thinking. Motivation is a process of understanding how and when a praxis or an action should be taken. It is the beginning of a co-operative process between memes (ideas) and praxis, but it's far short of being the primary force for every daily human activity In other words, the simple flow of desires or motivation is not a conversion point for humans to take action. So, do not trust everything you think. We are all motivated to take a given action, but external circumstances may not permit us to take certain actions at certain times. This is simply because the intention or motivation a meme carries is not based on external reality. Therefore, the gravitational primacy of praxis must lean towards material conditions by what it does (and not by our mental intentions or motivations).

In the most general form, if we are to understand memes and how they function, we need to look closely at how natural selection works. Natural selection is in itself the replication of a piece of genetically coded information. It replicates itself with exact copies and, at times, with inexact ones. Memes also replicate exact copies of themselves and, at times, they are culturally modified copies.

In natural selection, a strong gene-replicator multiplies itself at the expense of other weak replicators that are ineffective at making copies of themselves. With cultural-memes, a newcomer would tend to replace a similar or identical meme that is weak and no longer functioning in full force. Fashion styles of a particular type of garment can be replaced by a new style of an identical garment, or secular self-help ideals can be replaced by identical self-help ideals of some new transcendental guru. In both gene and meme processes, this is a brief and simple analysis of how natural selection and meme replication works. They are close analogues.

As time goes on, memes may spread wider or decrease in their acceptance and circulation frequency due to the strength or lack of their information. Their strength or weakness for survival may depend on the consequences and degree of interaction a meme may have with other alternative memes. The alternative memes may exist in books, electronic files, the Internet, advertising, and/or in peoples' brains. Thus, previous memes have strong competition and replicate with much less frequency. As the frequency of replication decreases more and more, this would impact and drive memes out of existence.

When I was a child, I learned how to make homemade kites from an older boy in my neighbourhood. During the process of learning, I would faithfully imitate every hand movement that Jack made to create his beautiful kites. Regardless how hard I tried, I could not reproduce every one of Jack's hand movements. This was of course, impossible. Instead, Jack convinced me that my kites were as good as his, regardless of the fact that my hand movements were different from his. The point is that I replicated as much of Jack's technique as possible and the final product was the meme-kite that I had imitated, not his hand movements.

Regardless of the number of hand-imitations that varied between Jack to me (and from one kite to another), my imitations of making kites were without alteration, for the essence of kite-making passed down unadulterated. To claim otherwise would be illusory, for this is a realist analogy of how genes and memes work. This is due to memes' self-normalising processes whose main purpose is for their adaptation and replication. This may be because they have also a direct appeal–as in my fascination with kites–for some people. Years later, I was teaching a number of kids in South America how to make colourful kites. Every kid was excited by their task of making kites. Some were structured well and some were not. Regardless of their structural variations, each kite flew high enough to get other kids in the village interested of making their own kites. The meme-kite had a direct appeal to these kids and it spread to near villages.

The point is that this gave rise to "meme kite" acting independently and influencing each child participant, regardless of how different these kites were from my own original kite. I might add that no one knew the origins of my kite-making. This brings us to the next important issue: a meme's ability to survive, propagate, and be hosted without having their origins questioned.

There are some suggestions that the origins of religion were not based on a designed effort by some group of influential individuals for their own exclusive benefit. There is a stronger possibility that the spread of religious memes were shaped by humans' direct appeal to mysticism due to a lack of material knowledge. In the case of religious-memes, natural selection provided the human brain with its selectivity and biases for or against one or another kind of ritual or belief. Religious memes ability to survive, therefore, would depend on their adaptation process, guided by people's beliefs and practices. As with the case of the kites, some kids liked them (and continued to build them) while other kids preferred to play soccer instead.

Memes survive by virtue of their widespread adaptation and by their appealing status to basic human psychology. Thus, some religious memes might survive because of the "value" they display. The term value carries no judgement of worthiness. Rather it is applied to their strength for survival. Their strength for survival is maintained because they are organized within and are compatible with other memes. The following is a list of both idealist and religious memes that have a strong survival value among other memes in the meme-pool.

- **After-life** - the belief of your survival after death.

- **Dying for your country** - killing and dying for your country is an honourable cause. Others would follow your example.

- **Reincarnation** - there is an invisible means by which you can defy the laws of biology, birth, decay and death.

- **Miracles** - to save you from sickness, to find a you good job, a wife or husband. If a miracle doesn't happen it is because you did not believe hard enough or did not pray hard enough.

- **Faith** - a non-investigative belief, which is a virtue to be used against knowledge, reason, and rationality. Having faith in God, saints, a political ideology, "my country right or wrong" would be highly rewarded.

- **Belief in God** - a strong meme which is most evident when you express doubt about "Him" but "He" can help you to rediscover your belief when you are "born again" and become submerged into your blind faith.

- Impressive cathedrals, beautiful music, paintings, sculptures, scriptures, rituals and customs, priestly dress code, miracle asking, and prayers are all self-replicating processes of religious memes that are not intended to help believers understand their relationship to the natural world.

- **Kill in the name of God** - the "others" who are heretics, blasphemers, non-believers, apostates, sinners, or immoral must be punished or killed.

- ❖ **Die in the name of God** - as a suicide-bomber you will become a martyr. Your reward will be to have sex with seventy-two virgins. (What it is not clear is whether both the virgins and bomber are spirits having sex and thus both are achieving spiritual orgasm.)

- ❖ **Believe, do not question** - regardless of how weird they may seem, most beliefs, rituals, and ceremonies are meant to be followed. If you begin to question their absurdity and idiocy you may destroy them. Do not question their source of origin or their value.

- ❖ **Opposites attract** - a delusion that leads to the negation of opposites as they clash one another. Attraction is not a unity of opposites.

- ❖ **Mind over Matter** - a core belief of secular and religious memes which advocates that you can make physical changes through thoughts, spirit, or wishful-thinking.

- ❖ **Religious morality** - it is a believer's delusion to imagine that a person without religion has no basis for morality and cannot be good. Yet, the Bible is full of rage, hatred, rape, abuse, killings, and it entices a believer's hatred towards those who do not share the same faith and connected ideals of slavery and paedophilia. In fact, there are "moral" considerations for those and other social topics.

The above is but a short list of secular and religious idealist induced memes with strong survival values which have been circulated to this day. Some of the above memes are alternative memes of similar ideal projection. The afterlife meme, for example, may have introduced the "immortality of the soul" or the meme of "out-of-body experience."

Some of these memes may be different from others (like the structures of kites) but all are within the same idealist or religious meme pool. A group of Catholic religious memes are no "better" than the religious memes advocated by Islam. The initial survival strength of Muslim religious memes was made possible by the fact that believers of the Arabian Peninsula were familiar with the Jewish and Christian system of meme-beliefs and traditions. Adopting those and/or modifying them to fit into the cultural circumstances of pre-Islamic religious beliefs and morality leads to the fact that there are no fundamental differences today from one organized religion to the other.

In much later times, when all three religions became well-organized, sophisticated, and arbitrarily different from other religions in Persia, India, and Syria, there were still mutually compatible memes. The fact that all religions were manipulated by priests, bishops, and ayatollahs (and were intelligently governed) changed very little of the core message the mutual memes they carried. As religions evolve they also adopt and this explains their survival strength and the astonishing speed with which they can take off and overshadow other religious cults.

I don't want to make too much of the power memes carry. But they do provide a fascinating example in how they begin humbly and take root with amazing speed.

There are three religious groups whose mimetic messages were intelligently formulated to provide maximum impact in their appeal to the human psyche. The Seventh Day Adventist Church was formally established in 1863 by Ellen G. White; the Latter day Saints by Joseph Smith in the 1820s who. wrote a completely new bible, the Book of Mormon; and Scientology established in 1953 by L. Ron Hubbard. The speed by which these religions were established is evident by virtue of their memes' survival that appealed to simpletons. Their organized style, sophistication, and elaboration were very well-handled. The social appeal of the memes transmitted was spread as widely as possible. The passion and skill of its leaders and their wealth provided the fundamental means for success similar to that of the early stages of the cult of the Christian Church.

Christianity and Islam, which have spread worldwide, were originally local cults like Mormonism, Scientology, and Seventh Day Adventist; the Jewish religion presumably began similarly. They all advocate an imaginary friend in the sky (if you are obedient) or an angry sky-father if you are a not. Religion fulfills a childhood image of the imagining "friend" phenomenon.

The common link among widespread institutional religions is, at least in part, the intelligently designed messages of their memes. However, their religions were largely shaped by people's psyches in relation to fear, mysticism, faith, and obedience. These were the unifying features of human psychology towards myth and legend. All of these religions made strange prophecies, and their leaders went out of their way to turn their followers against the "others" and to spread the promising triumph of a second coming that would result in an apocalyptic cataclysmic event against the non-believers.

If you are a faithful believer you can look at the "pie in the sky," words coined by the brave Joe Hill in his 1911 song *The Preacher and the Slave:*

> *Long-haired preachers come out every night,*
> *Try to tell you what's wrong and what's right;*
> *But when asked how "bout something to eat"*
> *They will answer in voices so sweet*
>
> *You will eat, by and by,*
> *In that glorious land above the sky;*
> *Work and pray, live on hay,*
> *You'll get pie in the sky when you die*
>
> *And the Salvation Army they play,*
> *And they sing and they clap and they pray,*
> *Till they get all your coin on the drum,*
> *Then they tell you when you're on the bum*

> *Holy Rollers and Jumpers come out*
> *And they holler, they jump and they shout*
> *Give your money to Jesus, they say,*
> *He will cure all diseases today*

My point is to provide you with some general examples of how religions spring up from absurdity to become a powerful memetic that controls the way some people live their lives. I suggest that the meme-Jesus was one of many figures who emerged through history to become a mythological memetic legend. While most cults and their memes died away, the ones above survived and have been honed by systematic propagation and mimetic selection to dominate large geographical areas of the world today.

I now want to turn to the subject of religious taboos which are the most powerful of imposed memes. I want to draw your attention so that taboos can be seen as a by-product of religion. Let's begin by saying that taboos of all sorts are ingrained in societies throughout history and throughout many geographical parts of the world. These meme-taboos are not restricted only to religions but also appear in secular sectors of society as well.

A taboo is a social prohibition relating to a human social activity, attitude, or ritual which is based on social customs or religious sacred ideas or traditions. In secular social sectors we do not break other people's taboos. To break them is considered avoidable, objectionable, and abhorrent by those who feel shame to question them. Most taboos have specific religious associations. For example: working on Friday (for Muslims), working on Saturday (for Seventh Day Adventists), or working on Sunday (a day of rest for devoted Christians). The most notable taboos were put in place to avoid "disrespect" to any religious authority, real or imagined, in the form of moral deviance, dietary restrictions, sexual activities, relationships, marriage, adultery, circumcision, sex reassignment, nudity, offensive language and so on. The most feared meme-taboo for believers was and still is blasphemy and for secularists this translates into their own "political correctness." Blasphemy simply prohibits religious believers from using God's name in vain or from questioning their religious beliefs. The root cause of the meme-taboo of "political-correctness" lies in the social adaptation of religious "blasphemy" minus the religion.

Let me explain. Western societies are noted for their civil rights concerning freedom of speech. We talk about everything that we fancy in daily news, in TV comedy shows, on the Internet, and in our conversations. We can also criticize our politicians, our institutions, our education system, our cost of living and our economy. We have our favoured "talking heads" that analyze everything from fashion to movies, restaurants, to movie star behaviour. Widespread public opinion-polls show new trends, support for one or the other political party, and consumer preferences for goods and services. In short, we practice our freedom of speech as well as we practice our habit of criticising everyone in our society, except religion and religious faith.

For religious believers, silence is obligatory or a self- imposed shame. Blasphemy is a sin! Yet, nearly everyone, including secularists, humanists, and atheists form a protective wall of silence toward religion and religious institutions. This protective wall of silence is not because of our respect, as Richard Dawkins claims, for people's religious beliefs. Lack of extensive public criticism on religion is not out of respect for it, but out of a self-imposed gag of "political-correctness." Richard Dawkins in his book *The God Delusion* (p.20), quotes Douglas Adams's most impressive words–though I do not agree with his notion of "respect"–about societies' lack of criticism on religion:

"Religion...has certain ideas at the heart of it which we call sacred or holy or whatever. What it means is, 'Here is an idea or motion that you're not allowed to say anything bad about;

you're just not. Why not? 'because you're not!' If somebody votes for a party that you don't agree with, you're free to argue about it as much as you like; everybody will have an argument but nobody feels aggrieved by it. If someone thinks taxes should go up or down you are free to have an argument about it. But on the other hand if somebody says 'I mustn't move a light switch on a Saturday', you say, 'I respect that'

Why should it be that it's perfectly legitimate to support the Labour party or the Conservative party, Republicans or Democrats, this model of economics versus that, Macintosh instead of Windows–but to have an opinion about how the Universe began, about who created the Universe...no, that's holy?...We are used to not challenging religious ideas.... Everybody gets absolutely frantic about it because you're not allowed to say these things, Yet when you look at it rationally there is no reason why those ideas shouldn't be as open to debate as any other, except that we have agreed somehow between us that they shouldn't be."

So why should this particular wall of silence matter? By far, atheists and humanists must acknowledge that the "blasphemy-meme" has gotten hold of our ability to criticize religion and organize a legal defence against religious propaganda. We are reluctant to "offend" those who practise their religious "product" of miracles and lies of creation. We atheists are pacifists because we have rejected religious fanaticism and we are humanists because we give privilege to society instead of religion.

Yet we remain prisoners of the blasphemy-meme which we have somehow renamed "political-correctness." We are obedient to this oppressive meme of political-correctness as much as the believers who fear the blasphemy-meme. Is it because atheism is not yet a social cause to be defendant and propagated? Is it because the word "religion" still has a detrimental effect on our senses? Are we atheists becoming conscientious objectors against criticising the religious wars of Northern Ireland, religious pedophilia, the marketing of televangelist lies, the psychological abuse of children attending Sunday-schools, and Muslim fanatics?

A minor legal victory such as reversing a Jehovah's Witness prohibition of giving a blood transfusion to a sick child should give atheists' legal minds the opportunity to extend legal challenges to other pertinent social issues. Has the old philosophical division of Church and State now been reinstated as the division of Church and Society–since the so-called "State" is no other than Society itself? Can humanists and atheist psychologists take the task of identifying victims and evidence of psychological abuse, sufferers due to "religion"? Is public mental health in further danger under religious brainwashing?

If we are to understand how memes work, we must draw attention to the effect religion has on social issues of ethics, morality, and reproductive morals. Public discussions of these controversial issues in the media or in governmental inquiries tend to include religious leaders of all sorts, as if these people were experts in the field of ethics. One area we need to look at is the relationship between freedom of speech and hate speech as it is used by believers and their religious institutions. I am not suggesting that we should place a gag on believers and censor their views.

Freedom of speech, however, is not an absolute right, for when the speech is directed against a particular identifiable group it then becomes hate speech which is against the law. For example, if one prints "Homosexuals are evil" this would not be classified as hate speech. Yet, religious believers and their institutions cannot be legally restricted from expressing such a statement. It is sufficient for believers to declare they believe that "homosexuals are evil" to be legally protected.

Religion, then, is a trump card used by religious bigots to express their hatred. This hatred-meme is most notably spread amongst "born-again" Christians, and it is hosted by Muslims around the world. Christian groups on educational boards, on campuses, and on congressional/parliamentary committees are in privileged and influential positions not often granted to humanists, atheists, moral or ethics philosophers, or family advocators with comparable expertise. Yet, when a religious group claims an equivalent expertise, it does not have to produce evidence since being followers of a religious faith is regarded as being conclusive in and of itself. Thus "hate speech" can bypass the US First Amendment's freedom of speech since it is just seen as Christians practising their constitutional freedom of religion.

This trickery–something with which religious institutions have much expertise–is not beyond the recognition of lawyers and judges. However, both are willing participants in the discrimination against the civil rights of various social, ethnic, and racial groups. Religious beliefs have become a legal justification in favour of discrimination against anyone who is "different" or is the "other."

Our social and secular legal system seems to bow before it. Why? I can understand why religious people fear and obey their faith-driven irrational thoughts and why they become victims of delusional fanaticism. I am not sympathetic towards them, although I admit to feeling sorry for them! But why should we obey religious values when history has proven them to be violent and degrading of humanist concerns. Religion does not hold a monopoly on truth and morality and its memes of superstition and primitive beliefs must be rejected.

If we do not take religious political/legal power seriously and respond appropriately, you and I are contributing to the decline of our human civilisation by increasing social ignorance, racial and ethnic discrimination, bigotry, misogyny, and hatred for all "others" who may be believers or non-believers.

One thing I wish to make clear to my readers. I am not in favour of offending anyone or hurting anyone's feelings just for the sake of proving my arguments. But I am mystified by our disproportionate tolerance of religious propaganda, deception, lies, and anti-human propagation. Religious memes add nothing to the betterment of men; they tend to omit the reality of how our world works; they "create" things that do not exist in the natural world; they offer false salvation from religious criminal guilt feelings; they offer assurance that cannot be supported; and they falsely persuade their followers that religion is the only way.

Deception is at the core of the meme-essence for one's religious existence. We live in secular societies that protect the civil rights of citizens who may be humanists, atheists, or deists. No one disrespects or holds riots against religious beliefs, for the law of the land is there for their defence.

So, what is so unique about religion that secularists have granted it such out-of-balance legal rights and status? Is it because our humanist secularism has taught us to respect others who might be different? Am I going out of my way by saying that religious beliefs insult the intelligence of any rational person? Yet we tolerate these beliefs so gently. In comparison to anything else so insolent, we would not be as tolerant.

Human society emerged over ten thousand years ago and during this time our group size has steadily increased. To maintain group cohesion, human beings transmitted and hosted memes. Humans evolved with a social intelligence based on mimesis of behaviour and the refinement of emotions. But religious superstition and mysticism were well embedded in social thinking and behaviour long before cognitive intelligence developed. This means that from a primitive brain, human beings began to develop a relatively rational intelligence. However, concrete rationality came rather late in human development, and it has only been within the last 200 years that the social conditions emerged for a secular culture based on rationality.

Cultural extremism of intolerance of the "other" still persists today and this is notable among religious groups that are against anyone who does not comply with their belief system. Yet, these same religious groups expect civil and legal rights and protections under the law that are not granted in such a uniquely privileged way to any other rational group. One-sided extremism does not extend tolerance, but one expects special considerations under the meme-religion. In the face of this, humanists, secularists, and atheists must not treat religion with a kind of politeness and gentleness that can be misinterpreted as weakness on our part.

12

MIMESIS: AS SOURCE OF KNOWLEDGE

"Imitation of reality is imitation of the sensory reflection of life on earth."

Unknown

"Beware of false knowledge, it is more dangerous than ignorance."

George Bernard Shaw

Mimesis (Greek for imitation) is a process of cultural imitation or replication of ideas, symbols, custom, traditions, beliefs, practices, delusions, illusions, music or poems. We must be careful here not to confuse the concept of imitation with a representation of reality. Imitation is not closing your eyes in order to "live" in a virtual reality that imitates real life. Nor does imitation allow one to "live" in the blindness of religious faith that creates an imitation world that is irrational and unknowable.

If we are to understand cultural imitation, we need to briefly look at how natural selection works. In 1859, Charles Darwin, set out his theory of evolution by natural selection explaining the adaptation of species. He conceptualized natural selection as the process where those genes or individuals best adapted to their respective environments would be more likely to survive and replicate. Genes are replicates, along with units of cultural replicates (i.e., memes). Mimesis transmits cultural-memes which by definition comprise whatever is copied or imitated from one person to another, one group to another, one generation to another, and from one society to another. The transmissions can be in the form of habits, skills, customs, traditions, spoken or written language, and cultural activities.

Again, memes, like genes, are replicates of a specific amount of information that is imitated by a human host with some variation and selection. This process is called a memeplex or mimetic. A memeplex then is a pool of cultural-memes most of which are good survivors in relation to other memes within the same set of the memeplex. Some religious memes, like faith, belief or immortality, have survived because they have high survival value within an existing memeplex. In short, it has to do with memes fitting in with a mutually compatible memeplex.

Faith, belief, immortality, and martyrdom memes have survived and were propagated because they were hosted and imitated by wishful thinking. They were regarded as virtuous.

The more your wishful thinking defied objective reality, the more piously virtuous you were. Before, we analyzed the effects of religious imitation on our daily life, so how some brief background information on the theory of mimesis will be explored.

The concept of mimesis as "cultural imitation" (i.e., in the sense of re-presentation rather than "copying") is an ancient theoretical principle in the creation of the Arts. The Greek philosophers Plato and Aristotle spoke of mimesis as the re-presentation of nature by humans. The contemporary saying "to reproduce is human" stands for artistic and cultural re-creation as a form that imitates life. According to the Encyclopaedia Britannica:

"The concept of imitation, introduced into the discussion of art by Plato and Aristotle, was fundamental to the 18th century philosophy of art. Imitation is a vague-term, frequently used to cover both representation and expression in the modern sense. The thesis is a common and distinguishing feature of the art..."

Most likely, the concept of mimesis originated in the ancient rituals performed by "priests" in dancing, music, and singing. The term mimesis later came to denote the re-creation or re-presentation of reality in painting, sculpture, and theatrical arts. It also applied to dance, mimicry, and music. Imitation or mimesis signified re-presentation of external reality by expressing it in the visual arts. In the 5th and 6th centuries B.C., the term mimesis began to be applied and included as part of philosophical terminology. It began to signify: *"reproducing the external world in the way nature functions."* This meaning of mimesis encompassed reproduction in arts, weaving (as imitating the spider-web), philosophy, and concepts applicable mainly to *Artisans Crafts*.

Another theory of mimesis which acquired great popularity meant *"reproducing human perception of the appearance of things,"* resulting in reflection upon painting and sculpture. In this, imitating things was conceived as a new concept, thus formulating a new theory of imitation. Imitation is the basic and most important philosophical formation in the history of thinking processes in art, music, dance, painting, sculpture, epic poetry, and dramatic theatre, any re-presentation of "things" as they could or ought to be, with characteristics which are general, typical and essential.

The general dialectical concept of mimesis was expressed as the imitation of *human actions* which included the imitation of human behaviour towards nature as a source of human activities. Thus a human, by skilfully selecting his or her actions, could purposefully seek to "imitate" the actions of life as it is perceived in real or imaginary terms. Our natural world creates similarities (i.e., mimicry). However, the higher capacity for re-producing and adopting (hosting) similarities is intrinsically human. Walter Benjamin, in his work *On the Mimetic Faculty* (1933), stated that the human

"...gift of seeing [similarities] resemblances is nothing other than a rudiment of the powerful compulsion in former times to become and behave like something else. Perhaps there is none of this higher function in which mimetic faculty does not play a decisive role."

Therefore, mimesis can be displayed as a figure of speech, the choice of words we use, cultural activities that are imitated from past legends or current sources, social activities imitated by perceiving those that have been beneficial to a group, imitation of manners in social circles, private lifestyles, and the mode of actions that are the result of in-depth cognitive analysis, superficiality, or wishful thinking. Mimesis is an integral part of human adaptation and exchange of ideas. Mimetic social relations govern our daily lives and our personal contacts with close family members. We explore differences based on the character of the "original," to the point whereby the "new" adaptation may then propagate a new action.

Human mimetic behaviour can be a representation of something idealist, delusional, concrete, real or objective. This is similar to the characteristics of other illusory or objective phenomena. A painter mimes an original from the real world, and produces by mimetic representation a work of art that can be highly aesthetic or inferior. Alternatively, a writer can write something deceptive. Religious activities, where the primary concern is to promote religious idealism, may use the natural human inclination of meme-hosting to its advantage. It may take advantage of believers because human imitation is a natural expression of human faculties—in both empirical and idealized phenomena.

Mimesis therefore relates to social practice, interpersonal relations, and to our relationship with our natural world. It is seen in the way we use spoken and written language, in our system of beliefs, through selective assimilation, in a child's imaginary friends and play, in our customs towards parental and romantic love, and in our civil manners. In dialectical terms, mimesis of real material phenomena embedded in a distorted, repressed and hidden delusion is a manner of non-reconciliation with our natural world. A case in point is organized religion. Religious mimesis constructs a "world" of illusion, appearances, aesthetics, and images in which our existing world is idealized, and no longer in singe, with material reality.

Radical Muslim and Catholic thinkers in the Middle Ages formulated premises that if art is an act of mimesis of nature, let it be concentrated on the *invisible world* which is more perfect than the real one. Artists were made to search the "invisible world" for *traces of eternal beauty*. This was to be achieved through images of symbolism, rather than by re-producing reality. For Muslims in particular, this was interpreted as God's command not to permit any imitation of the external world. This claim underlies the religious advocacy that the existing world is not perfect and nothing is more perfect than the idealization of the spiritual representations of the religious "world." Rejecting the external world as being imperfect became the philosophical and educational basis for regarding the natural world as being unimportant and unworthy of any consideration. As a result, the theory of imitation, as a natural human activity, was restricted and pushed aside.

By the 18th century that concept of mimesis became the fundamental theory in the arts, and the revelation of mimesis and its ideas became an integral part of the social fabric. Various European social thinkers from Italy, England, Germany and the Slav countries used the terms *imitario, imitation, asimilatio, and sive imitary* to further develop the theory of imitation as a human social activity. This kind of interpretation of mimesis did not enter the social fields until the late 18th century, that is, only after it had been accepted in the arts, music, and philosophy.

Various interpretations that validated mimesis were mimetically propagated and hosted (or partly imitated) by German, Italian, and French social advocators. Within this flurry and exchanged of ideas about the role of mimesis in human life, the concept of imitation was replicated and adopted (partially) by religious and secular idealists as well as dialectical materialists. As such, cultural mimesis was not a uniform concept. Various meanings were assigned to it in the visual arts. Distinct meanings were given in the socio-cultural areas of replication and adaptation of ideas, customs, traditions, and how the natural world works. This mimetic relationship was also identified as a tradition passed from father to son, mother to daughter, from a religious follower to newcomers and so on. In the field of the arts, social thinkers tried to overcome in many different ways the obstacles mimesis encountered. High quality descriptions of "good" or "bad" art-imitation, "artistic," "beautiful," "imaginary" as *imitation fantastica* was interpreted more accurately to fit with religious or secular idealism.

On the other hand, dialectical materialist social thinkers interpreted the concept of imitation as part of the natural selection of the laws of nature, rather than in appearances or the perception of them. Philosophers of language thought that mimesis was a far more complicated process than what had begun with words (palabras) and had been replicated in concepts (confetti) and, those in turn, imitated real things and phenomena. Particularly important was the notion that language stressed that mimesis was not a passive human activity. This was first because the natural world had to be "recoded" and be assigned a broader meaning so that it embraced not only imitation of nature but also of *ideas, allegories, and metaphors*. These were separated into two kinds of imitations: the real and the ideal. Two views of imitation–the real that is accurately reproducing the natural world, and the ideal which is preceded by design–scattered and synthesized the elements of perfection about the "other world" of virtual reality.

Philosophy of language introduced a new thesis of mimesis which had greater value and was rich in social consequences. The object of mimesis should not only be known for how the natural world works but, most importantly, to explain who were its best explicators, that is, human beings. This was the greatest revolution in the history of the concept of cultural imitation. It changed the classical imitation theory of the arts into a socio-cultural one. This was a selection from nature, its imitation of natural selection and adaptation. The theory of naturalism and realism was in fact a continuation of the theory of imitation, but with certain differences. It was a theory that was concerned not so much with the imitation of art-to-nature but, like science, explored nature itself.

Biological and scientific social thinkers of the 20th century, such as Richard Dawkins, have re-introduced the concept of mimesis as *memes, memetics and memeplex*, in the sense of being guided by the laws of nature, natural selection, and the natural adaptation of genes and memes. Among contemporary social thinkers, within the process of the imitation of cultural memes, these are transmitted from person to person, from one group to the next, from one generation to another, and from one society to another. It is well known that genes are part of our evolutionary organism's make-up.

However, gene replication, spreading, and adaptation, unlike memes, are restricted to the small number of offspring a parent can have. Genetic evolution and the natural selection of human gene selection are not controlled by either the transmitter or the host (adaptor). It is not surprising, therefore, that in the last few thousand years, human genetic levels have remained almost unchanged. Genes as genetic replicates have a well-established stable structure, almost unchanged, to support and increase survival and re-mimesis of their carriers.

Because genes are an integral part of the human organism, offspring have no choice over the genetic structure which is transmitted to them. Gene transition from one host to the next is simply a mechanical-materialist process. Only natural selection in all its randomness is responsible for our genetic make up. On the other hand, mimesis is transmitted in the form of cultural-memes from an *intended* replicate to the *receptive allowance permitted* by the next host's human mind.

A potential hosted-mind has a clear choice whether to accept or reject an intended explicator's transmitted memes. A religious explicator-transmitted meme may be willingly hosted by a religious believer, but an atheist would have no problem rejecting the same religious meme. It must be noted that memes do not contain within themselves qualitative or quantitative properties. Neither are they an integral part of structural organic matter, for cultural memes are imitations of customs, music, story-telling, emotions, objective or subjective ideas, beliefs, etc. They are simply spread among the populace by a process of hit or miss and not at all as a sort of genetic transmission. In other words, memetics do not have the power, like organic viruses, to affect you physically.

Mimesis refers mainly, though not exclusively, to certain learning situations which occur very early in the lives of children. But the concept of mimesis is also inclusive of a particular explanation of adult modes of behaviour, especially in relation to human habitat. The human child learn early to experience through the senses. One of the first things a child learns is that it depends upon the adults who care for it. Learning experience by the child places its emphasis on a mimesis that moulds the child completely. One must also note the relevant writings of Charles Darwin in his 1877 book *Mind* where—even though the concept of mimesis played no great part in his thinking—he shows great interest in child development, including infant-mimetic learning. Darwin helped to prepare the ground for the study of the interplay between instinct and early imitative-learning.

Instinctively, children learn who their mothers are, and are eventually able to imitate-learn certain acts from her. Religious rituals, like crossing oneself, or praying before going to eat or sleep are some other acts a child imitates without knowing their meaning. Imitative behaviour, including approach and imitative responses developed at only stage of the child's life, become habits instigated by mimesis. Imitation also plays an important part in the child's socialization process with other family adults (grandparents, etc).

There is no doubt that mimesis has implications for human developmental psychology. Mimesis in early life has always been of great interest to all concerned with children's dialectical training, learning, and education. The concept of mimesis deserves now to be further investigated, developed, and refined to take full account of human social behaviour within specific groups and society as a whole.

The individual, by way of his or her mimetic adaptation, is affected by strong memes. The result is that such powerful influences sometimes act against the person's self-interest. For example, since religious memes often transmit as their theme irrational emotions and human frailty, they tend to disturb the balance and rational disposition of the person who is about to blow himself up in the name of his or her religion. The next suicide-bomber would imitate the act regardless of knowing if the end result would be his or her demise. Therefore, balance and rationality are prerequisites for maintaining a state of mind that is not vulnerable to the negative effects of the mimetic processes of self-destruction.

The focus here is on mimesis as a physical behaviour which is an indicator of how something is represented. In this case, the manner and mode of common religious mimetic practices of believers determines how they proceed. The religious unrestrained use of the terms position "good" or "bad," "sinner," "non-believer" or "baby-killer" (abortion), as if they were all equal, should be restricted for the common benefit of humanity.

As a memory device, mimesis can randomly vary and is subject to cultural selection. The criterion of whether an imitation is or is not successful depends on the degree of cultural close assimilation and acceptance by the people who are attracted to its behavioural dynamics. The old saying "monkey see monkey do" is not too far from the truth, for imitation is the stepping-stone leading towards investigation and learning.

Retaining mimesis via memory is a prerequisite for imitation to take place. Retaining mimesis is possible when the imitator host perceives usefulness, real or imaginary benefit, interest or relevance by repeating it through body language, a manner of speaking and task completion.

On a social level, people's mimesis is conveyed in social behaviour that can be qualified as being materialist or idealist. Idealist embedded mimesis propagates, regulates, and dictates imitated practices in accordance to theistic rituals, sexual taboos, moralising women's social restrictions, eating and dress codes, and the imposition of a system of beliefs perpetuated to ensure the continuation of a believers subjugation to organized religion. Typical theistic mimetic propagation focuses on a believer's senses, emotions, and delusions about human death, life after death, out of body "experiences," heaven and hell, God and Satan, miracles, ghosts, excommunication, sins and forgiveness, guilt and the confession of guilt.

Mimesis, therefore, includes a broad range of personal, social, and cultural behaviour and practices that are made available to be accepted or rejected by hosts. In the social arena, human beings imitate one another as children, as young adults, and as adults in consumer trends, points of view, physical behaviour, body mannerisms, and personal conduct set by ritual, customs, or tradition. It should be pointed out that mimesis is not a fixed standard of behaviour as long as when it is imitated it permits room for change.

Allow me to further explain: the beginning of any learning process is based on imitation, which is passed from the teacher to the student. The basic unspoken rule is that *"you learn it my way, and when you learn it my way, you can then change it to your way."* This is unless, of course, the "teaching" is dictated to you or your children by a biblical body. In this case, it does not permit changes, because any fundamental changes would cause the collapse of that religious ideology and organized body.

This is the basis from which idealism functions, whether it is religious or secular, for idealism simply distorts humanist material reality and the "ideal" has nothing to do with material perfection. Its basic premise is the delusion of "mind over matter," which places fixed ideas or images as the directional force in interpreting material relationships between human beings and society. If mimesis does not allow for doubt or change, then it is delusional and against humanist imitation and experimentation.

Materialism recognizes that mimesis is a natural process of copying, representing, or reproducing natural or social conditions. Mimetic behaviour is evident in the animal world as an instinctual learning process passed on from adult animals to their young in the methods of eating, hunting, or defending themselves from predators. On the human side, materialist mimesis stands contrary to the popular misconception that our ideas or emotions are of our own making and that each of us is unique in our pattern of thoughts. It is this system of thought or school of thought that I want to tackle and show just how it influences our daily lives.

In early human societies, such as the tribes around Mesopotamia and further to the East, there was a system of thought based on the worship of many gods (polytheism), as well as the worship of the "spirit" of dead relatives. Every tribe shared or had different gods or tribal customs of worshipping. For some tribes, like those in the Americas, animalist worshipping was predominantly directed to the spirit of the "great bear," or "eagle," or at times to the spirit of a great warrior.

Patterns of worship thoughts were mimetically adopted by youths, and it was the elders who—in order to maintain a cohesive social structure—passed on their social customs and religious rituals as part of their educational system of thought. Such a system of thought became part of the society's learning process on both an educational and a civil level. After a number of consecutive generations, a predominant system beset society's cultural expression in commerce, arts, and governance. This developed into a close similarity of thinking about one's view of the world etc.

The important point to notice is that ideas, morality, and ideological concepts were propagated by those who held hierarchical political power. In other words, the elitists constructed a social structure based on their religious beliefs, on rituals and traditions that would be viewed favourably by the populace and thus would mimetically spread cultural memes among them. Through adopting or imitating secular beliefs, by means of oral tradition, and by formal education for the elitists, a governing agenda perpetuated a system of thought that strongly influenced the average person. Meanwhile, the elitists served their own socio-political governance. The average people may have thought that their ideas or beliefs were of their own making (i.e., original thought) because they were ignorant of the roots of the system of thought which they lived under and through which they were indoctrinated.

Idealism's system of thought and beliefs were passed on beliefs by means of the educational system. Those beliefs were embedded in social relations that were perpetuated on the basis of the same educational system that taught the youth a specific methodology of applied thinking. This thinking process lies in the religious emphasis on the power of beliefs.

Believing and having ideas, feelings, or intuitions was, and still is, very popular as a directional force before taking an action or practice. Believing, then, is regarded as real evidence of the truth to be used for administrating justice or for taking action. A common term today is "I believe that John said...," or "Do you believe that you were in danger...," or "Your Honour, the witness believes that..." which is a common phrase used in the court of law.

Believing or beliefs, therefore, is a by-product of a religious system of thought (idealism) without the inclusion of God. Consecutive generations for the last twenty centuries were governed and educated by organized religious systems of thought where their core essence eventually split to form a secular idealism with a subliminal religiosity. Today the western world's educational system, from elementary to college and university, our mass media, advertisements, entertainment and philosophical thought, are embedded in religious and secular idealism. This means that our societies have adopted and abided by secular idealism in a cohesive system of mimesis that is essentially not distinctive from one religious generation to the next. On the other hand, the three main organized religious institutions have held a system of thought that still remains static (this is compatible with their theistic dogma). Priests and bishops, monks and televangelists, imams and ayatollahs, rabbis, and ecclesiastical bureaucrats hold their privileged socio-political position with moralizing (idealizing) justification.

Of course, there is nothing cynical about trying to advocate a non-scientific system of thought that serves a cultural purpose, for this is a natural progression from the old to a new cultural manifestation as in the arts, poetry, or fictional writing. However, religious and secular idealists from Plato to Bishop Berkeley have not realistically answered questions about the natural evolution of ideas and language and how we have come to think about the way we do things. Questions also need to be answered regarding the existence of the human race, the geological evolution of the natural world (matter) and earth's biological and botanical life (living matter).

Bishop George Berkeley (1685-1753) stands as the founder and most influential perpetuator of the contemporary system of thought called idealism. Berkeley placed a gravitational leaning on ideas in the mind over material existence. His arguments were logically constructed, coherent, and grammatically correct, but such idealistic beliefs hide their delusion in today's secular idealistic views of "my reality' or "your reality" as if the existence of the reality of the external world is a multiple mental choice.

In dialectical materialism, mental thought proceeds from the external concrete reality to the mind's abstraction. Provided it is evidentially correct, it does not get away from a confirmed truth, but comes closer to it. It leaves no room for preconceived ideas that are fixed and are used as mental directional forces to be forced upon the external reality of humanity as a whole. The abstraction of matter, the material laws of nature, and human mimesis are serious scientific investigations. They are correct and not the wishful thinking or absurd abstract manifestations of "talking-heads." They reflect the material reality of society, social changes that need to be done, which, in terms of material reality, are deep, true, and complete.

Dialectical materialism starts from the living perception of this world to the mind's abstract thought. From this, mimetic human behaviour turns back to the reciprocal path of the cognition of objective reality. Dialectical atheists and humanists exalt their concrete knowledge of living matter from nature and human needs and social relations. They consign religious and secular idealism of non-existent entities, superstition and magic, into the theistic recycle bin.

I am a social thinker, and I will not pretend to be a biologist, a botanist, or a scientist. To have a better understanding of such disciplines you may wish to read Richard Dawkin's books. But I am a dialectical materialist with a fundamental understanding that regards matter as primary and mental processes of the brain as secondary. I further contend that the natural world exists independently of my mind, and that it is the material reality of my surroundings that determines my consciousness, and not the other way around.

At birth, humans enter the natural and social world where vast opportunities for experience exist. These are natural forces that affect the human body, the mimesis of social activities, new levels and qualities of sound, periods of solid nourishment, air breathed in by the lungs, new stimulations felt by the human senses, and an extensive range of visual information given to the developing circuits of the brain. Materialists maintain that human brain development depends on how stimulation from the natural world reinforces inner function. Positive or negative emotions, ideas or images, and how experimental thoughts are verified depend—when these thoughts are related to the existing world—on their validity and are not delusional. In short, we humans are equipped with the necessary dialectical tools to properly function in our daily material world, and in *mimetic* adaptation with other humans.

The social behaviour of mimesis is an interpersonal mechanism that promotes social bonding and it perhaps sets the conditions for strangers to form homogeneously as a group. People prefer the company of others who imitate each other. Humans often will make gestures and display the mannerisms of persons they encounter. This social behaviour is mimetic. Both the imitator and the person being imitated are unaware that mimesis is taking place. Persons who are not aware they are being imitated often share an affection and empathy for their imitators. In short, cultural mimesis provides the basis by which human beings ultimately form lasting social and cultural groups. Persons that share each other's social mimesis tend to sense a natural attraction for each other, making conflict less likely and cooperation more likely.

Mimesis, however, is not absolute, nor is it like a virus that affects you whether you are aware or not. Being aware is the best method to change one's mimetic behaviour. Being ignorant of the mimetic process results in blindly maintaining a convenient mimetic behaviour, whether as a religious attitude or in corporate behaviour. To imitate is to behave like another, though most such likenesses may not be imitation but a social choice. The tendency to imitate is normal to human nature. Whether this tendency is necessarily beneficial or not is another question.

Suggestion reinforces mimesis because humans are suggestible beings. Ideas, beliefs, sentiments, and actions are suggestions, thus, they promote in turn social and cultural mimesis. The spread of trends, fashions and conventions, the social inheritance of customs, gestures, and linguistic terms come to us through the avenue of suggestive interaction and mimesis. Religious behaviour is distinctive widespread type of social mimesis.

Religious fundamentalism corrupts civil manners exhibited in all forms of social activity and family life. In this case, mimesis provides a delusional interconnection between the symbolically general "world" and the natural world of everyday life. This means that social mimesis of people's religious beliefs are *intermediary*, stretched between a symbolically produced "world" and the real one. Thus, mimetic learning is the main propagator by which we learn to be anti-social or social and cultural beings. The anti-social is the negative side of religious mimesis that creates a rivalry between its believers' set of beliefs and the positive humanist side of society.

Basically, if a religious fundamentalist wants you to imitate certain behaviours, it creates a rivalry between a humanist and the fundamentalist. This rivalry takes place not because the fundamentalist is a "good" or "bad" person. It takes place because the humanist is free from any religious restriction of fixed beliefs that the fundamentalist wants the other to imitate. In short, the root of the hostility of religious violence is not only a depravity of humanity. It is also due to its mimetic propagation that is intrinsically deprived and violent.

Is religious violence and oppression "good" or "bad"? Long established Biblical mythology would have people believe that religious violence and the oppression against "others" is "good" violence. It is simply a delusion to believe that God's violence is present until there is no more of the "others" "bad" violence. Because Christians and Muslims believe that they are good, their violence and oppression is "justified." Millions of Muslims and Christians around the world imitate this claim without being aware that all violence is imitative, leading to further violence.

We must comprehend that religious culture has a strong influence over its believers. It propagates a system of beliefs that is based on the delusion of mind over matter. This delusion is shared by religious believers of all institutionalized religions where mimesis is also shared among its members as to what their fixed rituals and rules expect of them.

As well, religious culture reinforces the notion to its members not to imitate the behaviour of the "others." That is, after indoctrinating believers in what they must believe and follow, the religious sacred texts and mimetic behaviour forms an invisible "safeguard" perimeter against the "others" whose mimetic influence may possibly spread among religious believers. Rules, prohibitions, and administrative rituals control believers' social behaviour.

For example, the fundamentalist rule that prohibits women from working outside the home, attending school, and leaving their homes without a male escort, if challenged, may change the status quo which would result in a "loss of distinction" of rules, customs, and traditions that are distinctively Islamic. The loss of distinction would set members free from mimesis shared by their cultural group. In turn, this would cause the failure of the institution itself through internal conflict and chaos, soon breaking it apart.

It should be noted that mimesis is at work—through the spreading of memes—in every social and cultural system, every institution, community and national politics, in educational bodies and entertainment gatherings. Equipped with the knowledge of how mimesis functions, religious believers may use this knowledge to seek ways to downplay their fear of the "other" and allow them to be associated with positive humanism.

Dialectics of nature shows that one cannot separate the "idea" of mimesis from its practical implementation (i.e., matter over thought). The delusion of mind-over-matter would demonstrate the ineffectiveness of mimesis as non-committal and non-interventional. The concept of *"thinking"* is not restrained from *"acting"* about reality. Propagation of mimesis without reality becomes irrelevant. The concept of mimesis should translate into a materialist one if it is to become a dialectical guide for social and cultural practice. Otherwise, matter (reality) would not bridge the gap between the mind (thought) and the natural world.

Thus, dialectics of mimesis must overtake the idea in a very empirical sense: a scientific, technical, and materialist process. Otherwise, the "idea" of mimesis would be understood as all "pure" mimesis—an intellectual exercise—removed from the human condition. Because we humans are social beings, we need to be aware that there are different kinds of social mimesis. A young person who enters a sporting activity imitates moves from the other athletes. Religious and personal mannerisms and attitudes, and youth violence (youth gangs) are also mimetically learned attitudes and acts.

What is important, however, is that for human beings, no matter what mimetic activities they are involved in, mimetic attitudes which are mental, are not fixed. This is because one's mimetic mental attitude and (physical) behaviour can change day to day or hour to hour. Thus, no mind over matter! We choose a mimetic cultural act, partially adopt it, or even reject it based on actual or potential positive or negative materialistic consequences.

Memes are an integral part of the social and cultural mimetic process. Religious mimesis and its memes are the most powerful and elaborate meme-complexes in our human environment. They are closely connected with idealism—from primitive superstition to today's "spiritualism"—as a cultural propagation that has evolved over millennia into countless variants and co-evolved in many cultures. The core messages in idealist memes are in religious stories, dogma, metaphorical interpretations, in the belief of the invisible God, and salvation through the mental mimetic-image of "Christ." This is all to enforce the delusion of: mind over matter.

The religious memes throughout pre-Christian history transmitted elaborate forms, mostly as oral stories, through upbringing, and, in some cases, as written texts. The powerful and elaborated myths and superstitions were presented by Temple priests and cultists, future tellers, magicians, and prophets as the truth about how the natural world worked. Variants of these religious memes increased their strength by the high rate of hosting within the population of various cultures. Travelers and trade merchants were the main mimetic carriers who transmitted religious memes that were invented in distant lands. The best priests and prophets gained the most converts, which became the next generation of mimetic hosts who would initiate some of the best religious memes regardless of their ethnic or cultural origins. The most powerful memes in pre-Christian religious cults in Greece, Egypt and Asia Minor (Mesopotamia) were the metaphorical baits of "spiritual salvation," "spiritual fulfilment," personal "happiness," "trade prosperity," and "eternal life." Mechanical and hydraulic trickery was used in both Greek and Egyptian Temples to convince the convert of the power of the Temple gods, and the power of the priests to perform "miracles."

These metaphorical bait-memes were more likely to be reinforced by personal factors such as a sense of identity, a sense of belonging, conformity and a personal and "secure" world view. It is worth noting that cultural mimesis was not fixed and "hellfire" threats were mostly used to change, adopt, or reject previously hosted cultist memes. Such negative mimetic threats were widely used but left the core meme message unchanged (i.e., obedience to the invisible God). Prophet John the Baptist's "hell and fire" memes was one example. Fear was spread in the minds of believers of different sects (the ignorant and superstitious were included). In short, religious mimesis works only on an emotional level, creating a simplistic and satisfying "ideal-world," regardless of its inconsistency with cognitive reasoning.

Thus, religious memes can spread and be imitated by believers regardless of the truth or falsity of their claims. The fact that believers cannot disprove their validity further strengthens the meme's stability. Therefore, Christians must choose between religious delusion and humanity and like the ancient believers, they've chosen delusion ("Ye cannot serve God and Mammon" (Mathew: 6:24)). By the time the cult of Christianity appeared, the *mind over matter* principle was embedded in the cultural religiosity of ancient societies. Necessary delusional characteristics for establishing institutional religions were already set, based on the foundations of centuries old pagan and cultist traditions.

The dialectical analysis of mimesis is the primary tool that can lead us to comprehend concrete aspects of human behaviour. As with all actual means and tools, dialectics is not on absolute but may be the best solution for understanding the social trappings of mind over matter. This is why we educate ourselves with the dialectical system of thought as an analytical instrument. In doing so, humanity will be able to choose an efficient approach to social solutions. It should be related to daily life where an intelligent layperson can avoid the confusion generated by professional "ivory-tower" memeticists.

Any theory of mimesis and memes that it is not understood by everyday persons is irrelevant to material social life. It is entangled in a web of unnecessary complexities of categories and sub-categories of memes and complex cognitive structures that serve other elitists but are alienated from the daily lives of the general public.

At this point, I wish to inform you of my not too secret goal. It is my intention that by now you have a basic understanding of the delusion of mind over matter. I hope that by reading this you have hosted a dialectical meme, and it is my sincere desire that you will talk to your family and friends about the delusion of mind over matter. Furthermore, it is hoped that you are transmitting and further hosting, as well as being protected by, a very strong vaccine against any sort of delusion.

BOOK III

ELEGANCE OF REALITY

13

OBJECTIVE REALITY OF THE MATERIAL WORLD

"Life is not a [mental] problem to be solved, but a [material] reality to be experienced."

Soren Kierkegaard

"Science is not marginal. Like art, it is a universal possession of humanity and scientific knowledge has become a vital part of our species repertory. It comprises what we know of the material world with reasonable certainty."

Edward O. Wilson

People who have the knowledge of how mimesis works gain the ability to train their minds and teach others to protect themselves and their children from delusion-induced memes. Reality induced memes cannot be influenced by religious and secular idealistic dogmas on morality, women, the environment, birth control, the rights of minorities, the use of language, or the natural world and its external reality.

The natural beauty of our material world has long been an interpretative subject of artists through music, paintings, wall tapestries, poetry, books, photography, and in the electronic media. All emphasize the awesomeness of the natural world, its strength, its vastness, and its depth.

Beyond certain common characteristics, humanists, atheists, astronomers, biologists, chemists, birdwatchers, ecological divers, star-gazers, and others share the common conviction that our material word is impressive. Looking through the human eye, from Daintree to the Amazonian Rainforest, from the salmon hatching rivers of Canada to the Arctic and Antarctic poles, from the Sahara to the Kalahari deserts, from Victoria Falls to Niagara Falls, we can capture the wonders of our material world. How lucky we were to be born!

Our cognitive biologists and scientists have begun to study our natural world, first because nature is useful for it provides humanity with the means of nurture. Otherwise, human life and bio-organisms would not have existed. Material nature has its own governing laws of harmonious flow and abrupt motion and change, and a cycle of birth, decay, and death. Millions upon millions of plants and organisms, including the human race, enter this precious lifecycle. How lucky we were to be born!

How the natural universe came about has not always been as clear as what we know today. Ancient philosophers, priests, and kings attempted to interpret the natural cosmos, its planets, stars, and the solar system. This was an enormous task. They lacked advanced instruments and knowledge but they gave interpretations and meaning to myths and legends. Created out of ignorance, fear, superstition, and false perceptions, myths and legends shaped their audience's images of (and beliefs about) the relationship between our natural earth and the natural universe. Those myths and legends perpetuated a system of beliefs that heaven and gods were above us, the world with its lesser-gods (angels) was in the middle, and the kingdom of the underworld with its demons, death and hell was underground. This was the order of things, a set of fixed beliefs, and a way of controlling the "unpredictable." The social order of religious mimetic passed on from one generation to the next for thousands of years.

Animal and human sacrifices were offered to appease the gods at times of natural cycles, or abrupt geological changes and meteorological events. Some gods were replaced by others when they failed to protect people and crops. The natural world came to be regarded as a mindless and hostile place, a place to be feared because natural events contradicted their fixed beliefs. Little did they know that their fixed beliefs were atrophic and lifeless. Fixed beliefs, ignorance, myths, legends, and all sorts of apocalyptic superstitions became powerful mimetic tools used for socio-political and religious control over the populace. Lacking literacy and basic knowledge, the vulnerable followed blindly.

Medieval Christianity continued peddling the same old dogma of fixed beliefs and absurdities. It depicted the natural world as a threatening place. In the idealist realm, this world was not perfect: it had no symmetry, no equal division, and no other perfect elements. Scores of publications and idealist art kept reaffirming the distortions of our material world. There was an overwhelming religious power squared against tiny voices of reason and dialectical evidence that were attempting to be heard.

Historically, others praised the nurturing features of the earth, and embodied it in an anthropomorphic image of a mother. Terms like Mother Nature and Mother Earth are images of female goddesses and are associated with fertility: nature became a personified pagan deity.

"Beneath the clouds lives the Earth-Mother from whom is derived the Water of Life, who at her bosom feeds plants, animal and men." (Algonquin Legend)

In any human society, the political, tribal, religious, and mystical leaders' primary goals have been to influence and control their people. Through a long historical evolution, the religious social fabric of the make-believe system–based on fear of the unknown and superstition– set its grip on the social structure of that society. Gods, magic, demons, evil-eyes, saints for every occasion, invisible and all-powerful forces, celestial myths of good and evil, purgatory and heaven have been employed as mimetic tools to serve the governing leaders. They have controlled the collective mind by recycling old beliefs. Failing this, physical threats and punishment have been used to subdue the unwilling.

Yet, the forces of material reality could not be subdued by metaphorical slogans such as "mind-over-matter." Historically speaking, our cognitive concept of our material universe is still in its infancy, but it has begun its first steps of tearing down delusional beliefs and is attempting to replace them with cognitive knowledge and scientific evidence regarding the functioning of our physical world.

In 1859, Darwin's work on evolutionary biology began to set the record straight. It documented the fact that evolution occurs. It made the direct connection between genes and change, and stated the fact of natural selection. This discovery further contributed to the rapid expansion of biological science and the explanation of the elegance of the natural world.

Are human social relations part of the material world? Is human social behaviour, harmonious or violent, delusional or real, part of its cultural and historical development? Are we a social continuation of countless past generations of mimetic knowledge, some of which has long been extinct. Are others still being hosted by us? Are we still so delusional as to believe that it is our individual consciousness which determines the existence of both the material world and human social relations? Or, is it material surroundings and human culture that determines our social behaviour and mental processes?

Most of our scientific discoveries are accidental, while others are discovered in the process of experimentation. Trial and error is a fundamental material and social process. It concerns dialectical reasoning and its applicable experimentation.

We humans must be proud of our historical development which has always been based on the social process of trial and error. Our collective aims, goals, and instincts for the survival of our species were developed by looking forwards and backwards. Through doubts and hope, by small successes and some large failures, we have advanced the social betterment of man. Above all, we as the human race did it our way! We began our social and scientific learning from the humble beginning of ignorance. We have indeed come a long way, since after all ideas don't come from the void!

At times, we were misguided by our delusional beliefs in or about gods, Satan, Heaven and Hell, demons and ghosts, priests and monks, sacrifices and prayers, myths and legends, and patriotism and nationalism. All of these things are not easily dismissed mimetic adaptations.

Our progression of social successes happened by leaps and bounds. Religious crimes against humanity killed and tortured the best of humanity's social thinkers. But scientific materialism and the laws of nature have kept their concrete reality base strong. Simply put, the idealist delusion could not hide that which is real and replace it with an illusion.

In terms of human history, we must think of all the social and scientific accomplishments we have achieved. These were made possible by individual and collective efforts, without the need for the delusion of God. Look at the vastness of our material world, its physical space, and places you can visit and learn about without the need for the delusion of God.

There is not enough time on Earth to visit, learn and be a part of all of our richly diversified cultural landscapes. But, you can always try. There's no need for the delusion of God. Investigate concrete ways to elevate social ignorance through literacy and scientific education without a need for the delusion of God. Think of all the musical instruments you can learn and teach others to play without the need for the delusion of God. Study the underwater marine world, and what you can do to keep it clean and safe without the need for the delusion of God. Wonder about all the new discoveries that arise from experimentation without the need for the delusion of God. Think of all the above as the beginning of the rest of your life, without the need for the delusion of God.

Now, once we have recognized and confirmed these points, and how our natural world works, then the questions about evolutionary biology and the fundamentals of reality must confirm the following: there is no such thing as a Christian World, a Muslim World, a Jewish World, a Scientific World, a Supernatural World, an Ideal World, or a Sub-terrestrial World. There is rather just the materialist natural world and its materialist reality. What we are trying to do is describe how the world works, and also describe the human experience within it. This affirms the notion that the material world was not created (i.e., that matter was not created). It shows that our species also evolved by natural selection. God had nothing to do with bringing the human race into being.

The fundamental entity of reality is that we, as biological animals, are the products of a long biological stage of evolution. You and I share a biological commonality with the rest of the human species. There might be all sorts of mimetic religious and idealistic "world-views" but we do not live in one or two distinct worlds apart from Earth. There is no mental idealist world which exists apart from the physical material world. In fact, there is just one world. It is the world in which we live and on which we depend for our existence and the propagation of our species. It is this basic commonality that we share. It brings to our attention the thing of the utmost importance: the elimination of the long conflict between the natural world and human culture. In the final analysis, the natural environment is far more powerful and the human species and its culture will, if the battle continues, lose.

Today, more than in any past generation, we talk about real science, so we need to clear away some misconceptions of what science is and what it is not. Let's begin by stating that science–like the existence of the natural universe–is not a philosophical concept or a point of view. Philosophical speculation has no place in natural science. Nor can science advocate the distortion of the reality of things or evidence that is confirmed by known physics and the Darwinian Theory of Evolution. Science is not a monolithic ideology–functioning by mental processes–for science and its application exist only in the external natural world, and it is impartial to philosophical and metaphysical thought.

Materialist scientists are unbiased observers who use investigation and experimentation to confirm a set of scientific facts. It is their goal to obtain knowledge about the workings of the natural world. Science and scientists do not have an ideological hidden agenda nor do they propagate for or against a particular set of opposing ideas. Scientific theories and their great strength lie in leaving room for doubt surrounding their conclusions and the scientific method. It is not a closed system of beliefs that is sterile, fixed, obsolete, and absolute.

Science is science; it is neither "good" nor "bad." It has no meaning, no moral foundation, no ideological purpose, no system of beliefs. Its theories can be proven correct or incorrect. Science can be disputed and rejected based on new scientific evidence or developments. Scientific theories can be corrected by scientists or can be self-correcting–unlike metaphysical claims that leave no room for the believer to doubt or dispute. It is what it is, like life itself, for science is also based on the material laws of motion and change, precisely because natural life and the social world function in accordance with these laws.

Dialectical materialism is the scientific method with which scientists analyze and dispute idealist distortions of external reality that are shown to be improvable and irrational. Scientific materialism is interpreted by the dialectical process by first collecting information about physical processes and/or contradictions of evidence before concluding and preparing to act. True enough, finding and supporting dialectical evidence can be a rather laborious task. But that is by no means a rational reason to abandon applicable evidence and replace it by a variety of tendencies, beliefs and feelings, biases, fear and intuitions, wishful thinking and superstition as a directional force for our personal behaviour and our relationship with our natural world and society. Idealist theoreticians ought to be humble in the face of this dialectical practical wisdom.

Other than the technological advantages and disadvantages, has humanity benefited from scientific knowledge? Since ancient times, humanity's social thinkers have strived to learn about our natural environment. They were not content with religious and metaphysical interpretations about star and planet formations, about nature's harmonious and abrupt events and celestial signs and occurrences. But as time and experimentation went on, scientific knowledge established a method by which humans could separate illusive and delusive perceptions from the only material reality that existed, the external world outside the human mind.

The right or wrong perception of reality by humans–whether as scientists or laymen–is where we must always pay attention. The fundamental fact is that we must realise that some kinds of things have to be established so as to enhance the development of science. In this way, dialectical knowledge can be reliably obtained.

Having said that, one must also remember that scientists–whether ancient or contemporary–are humans and humans can be fallible beings. They can be mistaken in their ideas, propositions, and conclusions. It would be erroneous to think that a scientist is a completely objective person who is free of bias, preconceptions, and beliefs. They persevere towards favoured theories that are actually built into scientific research. Trial and error, repeated experimentation, and field application of scientific propositions quickly demonstrate theories to be scientifically adequate or inadequate. But the fact that science leaves room for scientists to doubt, make mistakes, and take corrective actions is part of being human and not "divine." This is the elegance of material reality which has provided humans with an undisputed field of vast dialectical knowledge that idealism could never be a substitute for.

The elegance of the physical reality of the material world relies on the notion that the natural universe and reality form an unbroken continuum that is eternal and infinite. Nature has no beginning or end. It has no barrier from place for non-material, non-physical, or spiritual types of entities. Life is wholly the product of natural biological and botanical processes and not of human thought. Human thought–consciousness–is the ability to think about things, to imagine, to feel a range of rational or irrational emotions. All of this is within a physical body and not as an entity distinct from the rest of the natural world. This is a natural balance that exists between dialectical material opposites: matter and energy.

The ancient Greek and Roman materialists Democritus, Epicurus, and Lucretius of the 6th, 5th, and 4th centuries B.C.

were the founders and interpreters of what was known as classical materialism. Lucretius' *De Rerum Natura* or The Nature of Things was written in the form of a long poem supporting nature against the gods. In the East, at around 700 B.C., Chinese naturalists began to look at the functions of the natural world in terms of the relationships of opposites (i.e., matter and energy). By the years of 476-221 B.C., the Naturalist School in the Warring States Period was systematically elaborated upon and written about by Tsou Yen, the materialist philosopher of life and well-being, known as the balance between Yin-Yang, which is still very active today.

Out of the long historical development of scientific trial and error, today we can claim a victory over the religious and secular idealist schools of thought. However, I want to emphasize that this victory is not one of mere intellectualism over the delusional forces of idealism. Scientific materialism is not a mere intellectual thought, for it is scientific human discovery based on how nature really functions in terms of the relationship of opposites: The Law of Opposites. Material reality shows a number of familiar relations of opposites we all are aware of:

- ❖ Darkness/Light
- ❖ Ideal/Reality
- ❖ Masculine/Feminine
- ❖ Problem/Solution
- ❖ Rest/Activity
- ❖ Quantity/Quality
- ❖ West/East
- ❖ Theory/Practice
- ❖ North/South

- Number/Letter
- Earth/Sky
- Idealism/Materialism
- Right/Left
- Planned/Spontaneous
- Flat/Round
- Matter/Energy
- Question/Answer
- Water/Fire
- Child/Adult
- Below/Above
- Education/Ignorance

This brief example demonstrates that the relationship between the interdependence of opposites is a continuum of matter and energy, and their reference can only be spoken of within a constantly changing balance, never in static states. No material relationship exists without its opposite, no matter without energy, no day without night, no love without hate. They all constantly transform one another. The elegance of reality lies within its definition:

"the state of things, conditions and circumstances, as they actually exist, whether or not reality is visually observable or comprehensible by the human mind."

Personal experiences, real or delusional, "those which appear," curiosity, inquiry, delusions, illusions, dreams, "magic thinking," spirituality, "my" consciousness, perceptions, and emotions of all sorts are mental phenomena but not material reality. Yet, psychologists, secular philosophers, and religious idealists have "created" a slew of theories surrounding phenomenalism which, when put together, do not go beyond what appear to be the manifestations of mental consciousness. All tend to avoid "that which exists independently of the human mind" (i.e., external reality). These disciplines treat external reality as a philosophical construct, a method developed to justify the "world of ideas" as propagated by religious institutions secular idealists who promote the "marketing of delusions" for profit, cultists, and all manner of self-help pop-psychologists. Do they know that the world exists independently of the human perception of it, like the sun, the moon, the solar system? Do they know that all those social things, conditions and circumstances change and undergo continuous transformation from one form to another? Do they know that these things are not just mere perceptions but are real? No they don't. This is because they truly believe that individual beliefs are the only reality. For idealists, perception is reality. It is a concept that includes a wide variety of other ideological and theoretical concepts dealing with "philosophical-realism," "ideals," "romanticism," "beliefs," "attitudes towards reality" (e.g., "Your reality is not my reality" or "My reality is different from your reality"), and so on. In the world's six billion people, with everyone's potentially "different reality," just how many "realities" are there?

Reality is such that our knowledge of it can be reached by a dialectical process that goes beyond metaphysical "appearances" of what is real. This is because dialectical materialism is practical knowledge tested within the reality of the existing world. Again, reality is not an academic mental exercise or a philosophical concept that can be dogmatically presented to support a desired social or political goal. This statement should be sufficient for refusing to enter into the field of confusion and sterility that leads us to the sheer failure of understanding situations in our daily lives and the decisions we need to make to better our social environment.

I take my stand that we have wholly failed to talk about reality as an understandable thing, of what is certain and real. I mean that, by various bouts of trial and error, natural objective thought allows us to comprehend reality. Mental appearances are a "virtual reality" of our brains' ability to create an image of a unitary body called the external material world.

Accepting as a fundamental fact that the reality of the external world is a single whole, we can now briefly state something about the evolution of life itself. All life developed from that very first cell of primary living matter. It was born in the sea some 4 billion years ago. Hundreds of millions of years later, life moved from a single cell into a cluster of cells. These clusters began to transform themselves through cell differentiation into organic complexity. This organic complexity split into two basic forms of life, plant life and animal life. Both life forms were deeply interdependent, for each was a source of life to the other–much as it is today. The laws of the natural world governed biological and botanical development by chance and by accident and not through the use of the "mind." In short, nature did not plan to design its own future in accordance with an immaterial entity or an out-of-body "spiritual-thing." In other words, life's development contained within itself all the necessary complexity both in body and energy to adapt to its specific environment. Both plant and animal life began to live in their unique land and sea environments, always changing and adapting but still very much interdependent.

Fascinating stuff!!

Perhaps no more than approximately two million years ago, this biological life process finally evolved into our own early and recognizable human ancestors. This biological life called *home sapiens* was not developed outside of nature's biological

DNA. Scientific evidence today confirms that humans are not only kin to apes, but also to the botanical life of cabbages. In other words, human beings were not created in the image of the "design-mind" of a deity. In fact, we are part of earth's emerging biological and botanical life force that is sharing the only common environment we've ever known with every other living thing. Biological life is an integral part of the natural universe, not a creation of some theistic "divine" mind. Life is life, with all of its own complexities which does not include the invented worlds that do not exist. Since it has biological birth, biological growth and biological death, it is with this finality that all of life's complexities end. Recognizing this biological process, the external reality of living life should guide us also to live in harmony with our living environment, and make living life not a sterile confusion of virtual reality about the meaning of life, but done in harmony with the environmental elegance of external material reality. For no delusion, images, dreams, wishful and magic thinking, religious and secular idealism, nor lies and distortions of promoted virtual reality, no metaphorical themes, and no wrongful perceptions can ever replace the real vastness and beauty of reality's natural complexions and its myriad fascinating life forms.

Simply put, virtual reality in the human mind is so limited in scope that it can never be able to hold the sum total of all life's complexities. And it is because of such a natural limitation that those who live in a virtual world also live in a limited horizon of human life. For to live a full life, we humans must focus our attention on external material reality, and thus externalizing our focus and becoming an inclusive part with the vastness of the natural world of the living matter over mind.

Placing the external reality as "first things first" and our thinking process as secondary–whether these are concepts, emotions, feelings, daily decisions or ideas–it is humans who must constantly make complex choices. Life in general does not have a singular survival instinct goal. Human genetics, however, is undoubtedly crucial to human behaviour which is, in turn, tied to our survival goal. Humans must make decisions that require conscious choices and planning. Living in social settings much larger than any other single species on earth, our primate DNA and our instincts or chemical imperatives are not much help without the principal dialectical process of first things first. This is a fundamental principle of setting personal or social priorities based on the reality of external conditions.

For example, how many of us want to do everything at once instead of prioritizing tasks based on their real necessity? Sometimes we can't even decide what to do next. This happens when we have conflicting priorities. Why do we want to do everything at once? It is because we place our ideas in mind as directional forces for our behaviour (mind over matter) instead of facing the external reality of first things first to drive a dialectical process of setting priorities.

For example, in a large social setting, many public projects (like parks) are based on social planning that meets financial requirements. If a financial requirement is done as a first things first priority, the public project will proceed. Financial requirements are the physical conditions of external reality; social planning (park design) is a set of ideas organized in accordance with that external reality (i.e., matter over mind). At other times, we misjudge what the external reality of first things first priority is, even if we know what we want. For example, to save energy in our homes, it will not do any good to paint the interior walls or change the interior décor. It will not accomplish the prioritized goal of saving energy. In this case, identifying the external reality of the problem is the first things first priority, otherwise all the wall painting and décor changes will not reach the desired goal. Insulating walls, windows, and doors is also an external first things first priority that must be implemented or else the process of saving energy will not move forward.

In far more complex situations, there may be several problems blocking the forward motion of progress. However, identifying and resolving external priorities on the basis of *First Things First* will allow secondary and tertiary external priorities to be addressed in their proper order. To meet this challenge, external reality demonstrates that ideas or theoretical concepts or external reality are opposites not just in appearances but in their essence. Therefore, to unite or negate opposites, is a dialectical thinking process in which mental concepts must be flexible enough to unite with external reality's motion of change.

For example, the 2008 housing economic disaster in the U.S.A. resulted in countless foreclosures. Many people lost their homes. Most of those losses were due to "wishful thinking" (non-flexible ideas) that appeared to be a superficial balance between opposites (i.e., income vs. expenditures). When external reality changed (matter in motion) it meant that monthly mortgage payments increased (changed), the latter negating the former. People's own versions of "reality" or "virtual reality" were a set of fixed ideas that were placed as directional forces for their actions instead of investigating the external realities of their financial conditions vs. their financial commitments. Thus, one opposite negated the other.

A unity of opposites would have been a dialectical balance between mental thought–to buy a house–with the external reality of change–the financial ability to pay changed monthly mortgage payments. Had the ideas been flexible–that payments could not be secured–based on a balance of their financial evidence, people's choices would have perhaps led them to less expensive housing. The point is that external reality is not a philosophical concept that can be qualified as a "good" or "bad" reality. External reality is what it is, with its own governing laws of motion of change. Personal appearances of "virtual reality" of "my reality" or "your reality," is a delusion and, as such, can be viewed qualitatively as "my reality is good" or "your reality is bad." Placing "my reality" as a directional force of my behaviour would, in most cases, be negated by external reality (i.e., matter over mind).

It is now time to briefly explore the social and natural world we live in. I don't mean to say that both worlds are cut off from one another, but I use both terms as points of reference. The "social" may include man's social structures while the "natural" may include both constructive and destructive human acts as well as things that are or were in their original state of nature.

Perhaps no more than one hundred thousand years ago, natural selection reflected man's ability to create sounds and symbols (words), develop primitive tools, and brought about a thinking process to convey abstract ideas. All these combined to make us uniquely human, Homo sapiens. What set Homo sapiens and further human evolution apart from the rest of the animal species was not our ability to think and sound out symbols. It was our distinctly human ability to create hand tools. However primitive these tools were to begin with, they encouraged humans to create and control new environments for growing food and constructing shelters thus guarding against climatic changes.

The use of tools set the material conditions for humans to think in relation to their external reality, and gave them new ways to better their physical conditions in spite of the harsh environment and hostile enemies (both human and animal). Some tools became weapons and other tools were for fishing, hunting, agriculture, or had structural and defensive uses. This ability to generate a food supply and manage the conservation of it led to the formation of social groups for common support and protection. The earliest evidence of social grouping is found in Mesopotamia, which was established some ten thousand years ago. Anthropological excavations show housing, streets, water-cisterns, common food storage tanks, gathering halls and areas, all based on some governing social order. Up to this historical time, no animal creature and no human social group could dominate the world, as those early humans later sought to do as they began to spread across the African continent and Asia.

The development of the western world, in fact, had a humble primitive beginning and the concept of the "dominance" of the world was based on primitive religious beliefs and superstitions about the world. The natural leaders of the hunting and gathering era, who had been selected based on their best hunting abilities, were long gone. They re-created themselves into a social caste of "magicians" and promoters of priestly delusions in order to maintain socio-political control over the populous.

Still, the social life of human inhabitants was essentially practical. All religion-promoted mysteries led to the ideology of mysticism for interpreting the world. Practices of animal sacrifices and rituals of giving praise to gods gave meaning to the world around them. Religion then was used to keep the populace on a leash by the early temple priests who invented gods in order for the populace to gain solace in their beliefs. It had something to do with the "fairness" of their labour-slave status. Generation after generation, the natural human instinct of mimesis of religious fallacies and metaphorical attempts at understanding life became an integral part of human essence that was transmitted to and hosted by other ethnic cultures.

Due to people's general lack of education and ignorance, religion became attractive because it provided a powerful antidote against the ineluctable features of life, namely the people's "dreadful, brutish and short" life span. Religiosity became a cultural system of belief that "explained" and "educated" young and old about the "other" world, that it was far better than this one on earth. It contained no sickness, death or suffering, and all people had to do was simply believe "it" existed, obey, and comply without question to what the priests decided. In short, religiosity became a cultural social institution with a political power base. It became economically strong and politically astute–as was the case with the Romans and Jewish power sharing in Palestine some two thousand years ago.

For the next several centuries, institutionalised cultural religiosity dominated the practices and education for peoples in Jewish, Christian and Muslim societies. People were taught to look inwards instead of outwards for solutions to economic and social problems. Personal virtual reality, including "sins" committed, "immoral" behaviour, and "God's punishment," were the causes of natural disasters, sickness, poverty, and social unrest. The list can go on, but the point is that, in general terms, people's feet were on the ground but their heads were in the clouds. By the 1800s, nearly every European country had its revolts against poverty and social injustices, yet groups and fringe political parties like the Christian-Socialists insisted that their followers look "inwards" to solve their problems to become better Christians: adopt better behaviour, similar to that of today's "born-again" Christians.

There was slow development and progression of the sciences. The lonely rational voices of the early dialectical materialists were dimly heard due to the overwhelmingly powerful influence of religious institutions. Simultaneously, the long-ingrained ideology of looking "inwards" resulted in a widespread delusional belief of multiple existing "realities," something for everyone! The religiosity of idealism (without god) in practice and thought remains to this day the dominant ideology of the world's cultural societies. This is far more so than in the past because the marketing of "ideas," "feelings," and "wishful thinking" has become a very profitable enterprise.

Metaphorically speaking, the world has long been divided into two opposites: idealism's personal reality and materialism's external reality. For secular idealists, the consequences of human activities on Earth was of no importance because the environment was "mindless" and thus of no value other than what could be extracted from it. For religious idealists, the Earth was not worth being concerned with because God's heaven is the "real" place where all true believers would live in eternity.

But Earth and its external reality are fighting back against the old biblical call of man's purpose being to be fruitful and multiply (Genesis 1:28), to subdue the earth and have dominion over all living things. Overpopulation, a destructive consumerist economic system, over-fishing by the fishmeal industry to supply us with precious proteins for home gardening and pet food, chemical and mining pollution, over-harvesting of forests, the overuse of pesticides in agro-industries, and river and lake water pollution are the results of not regarding Earth as the only home we have.

Some years ago I visited the southern part of Chile–which reminds me so much of the Canadian landscape–when I noticed that children were wearing wide-brimmed hats and dark sun-glasses to protect themselves from ozone's ultraviolet radiation. This radiation was caused by industrial air pollution which opened a "hole" in the ozone layer over Southern Chile. I am inviting those who wish to "have it all" to take a look at that external reality!

External reality encompasses complete ecological living organisms and non-living things that function as natural systems. This includes vegetation, rocks, animals, micro-organisms, the soil and the atmosphere. The built environment also comprises the natural environment and it includes structures that are strongly associated with human activities. In this case, a geographical area is regarded as natural with a human impact on it that it is kept under control. Society is a built environment that encompasses ecological living and non-living things. Human beings and domesticated animals are living organisms, while buildings, roads, traffic lights, cars, trains, and buses are non-living things. This human ecosystem encompasses a relationship between humans and their environment. At the present time, there are few areas on earth that exist in isolation from human contact, although some swaths of wilderness still exist without any form of human impact.

Does progress require the conquest of nature? To answer this question we must provide an analysis of ecological development. This is the fundamental basis that underlies human existence. It is necessary to produce and reproduce the material requirements of life. Production as a means of subsistence does not get carried out in the abstract. Human beings collectively work on nature by the material means of production. This includes using tools, instruments, technology, landscaping, and raw materials. By applying human knowledge (ideas) and abilities, we can use these means of production.

Human beings can be distinguished from animals by consciousness, or anything else you'd like. But external reality confirms a distinction from animals as soon as humans begin to produce their own food products. It is an activity which is conditioned by the social organization in which we live. By producing their own food and other products, human beings are directly contributing to their actual material life.

As individuals, humans also express their socio-political conditions of life: what they are, how they produce things, the skills they acquire for their work, and how they consume. These practical acts are not philosophical concepts. They are practical material economic processes. They are carried out as matter-in-motion (which is primary), and through the use of thought (ideas) about economic abstractions (which is secondary). This means that the economic processes form the material-social base of society from which concepts and ideas derive and rest upon. All evidence of external reality confirms this practical applicability of *First Things First* as in: *matter over mind.*

What happens, then, when we do the reverse and place economic abstractions (ideas) as a directional force of our consumerist base ideals especially as they are related to economic development and basic consumption of necessities? An idealist economic abstraction is a mental concept of "we can have it all" so long as we can pay for it or borrow the money to purchase things whether we need them or not, or whether we are environmentally destructive in the process. This mental delusion of present day consumerism has even distorted the original message of the "American Dream," for it is not a dream to "have it all." The term, historically speaking, was first coined by the author J.T. Adams in his 1931 book *The Epic of America* where he states:

"The American Dream is that dream of a land in which life should be better and richer and fuller for everyone, with opportunity for each according to [his/her] ability...It is not a dream of motor cars and high wages merely, but a dream of social order in which each man and each woman shall be able to attain to the fullest statue of which they are innately capable and be recognized by others for what they are, regardless of the fortuitous circumstances of birth or position."

My central point is that ideas can be bastardised from their original intended meaning to become merely a slogan for anyone who propagates the pursuit of "happiness" by means of environmentally destructive consumerism. But material life and its external reality cannot be distorted, for the reality of material life is what it is. This idealist "American Dream" functions in the present economy as a system of beliefs to convince people to dedicate their lives to the pursuit of bigger cars, unaffordable yet fancy houses, high-tech gadgets, and 500 channel TV, in return for having less time to enjoy these things because now they have to work longer hours to pay for this "prosperity."

I want to finish this article by stating that the reality of the material world is infinite in terms of measuring it with the span of human life. Enjoying and taking care of the only home we will ever know is our duty for the survival of our species, our environment, all large and small animals living in their ecosystems, and, above all, the awesome beauty of earth's landscape. Its rivers and forests, wetlands, deserts, diversity of human cultures, exhibition of human love, compassion, hatred, violence, art, science, and the amazing opportunity to travel and explore the colours of flowers must make us think how lucky we are to have been born! You may wish to consider the following gifts that external reality and the material world can offer to you:

- Catch a fish with your bare hands
- Run with the bulls in Spain
- Witness a volcano erupting
- Ride the world's highest roller coaster
- Visit the Taj Mahal
- Make out on the beach
- Laugh until your cheeks hurt
- Visit the lost city of Machu Picchu in Peru
- Skinny dip at noon
- Run a marathon
- Stand on the Great Wall of China
- Bungee jump
- Travel far, far away in a hot air balloon
- Conquer your worst fear
- Spend a week by yourself away from all forms of civilization
- Learn another language
- Learn to play a musical instrument

Prisoners of our Ideals

- Fly a glider plane in the Grand Canyon
- Remember a moments wish that was worth a lifetime experience
- See the Aurora Borealis
- Give a homeless person $ 100
- Get a sexy tattoo on your_____
- Take a chance and leave a job you hate
- Spend the holidays volunteering in a soup kitchen
- Reach 100 years of age
- Plant a tree
- Take a flying safari over Skeleton Coast, Namibia

Take all of the above as a starting point for the rest of your life!

14

SCIENTIFIC MATERIALISM

Materialism…states that the world is, by its very nature, composed of matter, and everything that exists comes into being on the basis of [physical] causes.

This is important because:

[Scientific] materialism teaches that matter is objective reality, existing outside of and independent of ideas, emotions, feelings and beliefs…and that while much of the physical world might not have been discovered, there is no unknown sphere that lies outside of the Natural Universe of the material world.

Author

Scientific (dialectic) materialism is a term that was coined by the social philosopher Georgi V. Plekhanov (1857-1918). Its basic premise is that the external world is the only reality and everything in this world, including ideas, emotions, feelings, perceptions, and experiences implanted by the senses (e.g., hearing, seeing, touching, etc), can be explained in their truest sense by evidence, experimentation, cognitive knowledge, and rationality. All of this opposes idealism. Cognitive knowledge regards ideas in the mind as nothing else than the physical (material) world reflected by the human mind and translated into "forms of thought" of personal situations like love, happiness, success, the environment, art, culture, friendships, working or studying. These are all social external concepts that humans perceive rightly or wrongly.

Nature is a proof of dialectics (scientific evidence) and it must also be said for science and biology that dialectics has furnished this proof with very rich material. Nature works dialectically, as was proven by Darwin. He found that all plants, animals, and humans are products of a process of evolution occurring through millions of years. This intelligent conclusion was arrived at by dialectics (Greek for dialogue), which is a form of reasoning that leads to the truth via the exchange of literal arguments as a correct representation of the natural universe. Its evolution, the development of humankind, and the reflection of evolution in the minds of humans can therefore only be obtained by the method of dialectics.

Daily life and human cultural activities convince us that the natural world exists independently of our mental processes, sensations, and desires. This existence is objectively of a material nature. The recognition of the existence of the natural world, apart from and independent of our mind and mental processes, is fundamentally formed by scientific knowledge. It follows that matter is what we must regard in nature as primary and dialectical (scientific) knowledge of it, is a product of matter.

Dialectical concepts are to be regarded as images of cultural, social and natural things and phenomena. Dialectical (scientific) knowledge proves that the natural world is not a complex of ready-made objects, but a complex of biological processes–of the general laws of matter in motion, the development of nature, of human society, and dialectical thought. The natural world contains an infinite number of natural objects—plants and animals—and social and cultural phenomena that we call concepts. Phenomena are "things and their relations," matter-in-motion that we name in order to identify them. A little reflection, however, will make it easier to understand why this is so.

Let us consider how many flowers there are in the natural world. Of all the millions of varieties of flowers, we identify them with the term "flower" and we use it to identify a rose, a tulip, or a lilac. Identifying "flowers" is no different than identifying objects, plants, animals, or cultural or social conditions. On a more personal level, let's say I am sitting in my favourite chair, reading my favourite book, sitting in front of my computer, or holding a pen in my hand to write a love letter under an antique lamp. I can use a single word to identify the book, computer, chair, and lamp, for all those "things." In dialectical logic the relationship between my person and those "things" is called concepts.

The question is: how are such concepts formed? The things called roses and lilacs, chairs and lamps are all different from one another, yet they have something in common. It is what they have in common that identifies them within the general concepts of "flowers" or "furniture." This identifying concept does not include specific features that make one flower different from the next or one lamp different from the other; it only speaks of their commonality. What is important to note is that some abstract concepts of "things" embrace a wider circle of objects or phenomena than that of a concept of the single "thing"—a chair or a flower. A concept may identify a specific "thing" while other concepts are quite extencive.

Dialectics (scientific investigation) studies the concepts of a wide range of material objects and phenomena that are related to the real and extant world: matter is a dialectical concept (i.e., dialectical materialism). It is important for one to acknowledge what the common and essential properties or similarities of things are. First and foremost, one should be able to identify the concept that all things are of a material nature and exist objectively apart from human cognitive knowledge. In fact, all material objects and phenomena have this common foundation. This, however, is not the sole property that is common to all material objects in the natural world, for objects share yet another important property.

When, for example, you take a shower, you have the sensation of hot/warm water washing your body. When you are walking through a park, you see the various shapes and colours of trees and plants, and the sounds of bird songs. As such, those things and phenomena possess the property of acting on our sense organs and evoking related sensations.

It is clear that the most general properties of objects and phenomena give us a definition of the concept of matter. Matter is a dialectical concept denoting the objective reality which is given to humans by their sensations. Matter is that which, acting upon our sense organs, produces sensations. Matter is also the objective reality given to us during sensation. Matter is that which surrounds us, everything that exists objectively—the boundless external and material world—by acting on our sense organs and producing sensations.

Dialectical concepts (scientific investigations) refute all religions and the beliefs in God, precludes all divine intervention, and make nonsense of the religious idealism concerning the creation of the natural universe, our Earth, the stars and planets, our solar system, plants and animals, and the human species. Christianity, Judaism, and Islam yield delusional beliefs in maintaining that God created the natural world "out of nothing." Contemporary scientific evidence has firmly established that, in the natural world, nothing arises out of nothing and nothing disappears without a trace.

The scientific conclusion is that the conservation of mass is the conservation of matter. Matter never came into existence, for it has always existed and will always exist. The natural world is eternal and it was not created by anybody. The scientific thesis concerning the eternity of matter radically disputes religious beliefs about the creation of the world.

This dialectical conclusion of the eternity of matter often evokes questioning from religious believers. They tend to ask, "How is it possible that matter has always existed?"–when in our lifetime we see that everything has a beginning, undergoes decay, and then dies. This question can be answered dialectically (i.e., using a scientific argument to test a theory), by way of example using the law of the conservation of matter. This law states that matter can be changed or transformed but cannot be made to disappear.

Take water as an example. Its liquid state can undergo evaporation when you boil it, and the liquid will become solid when you freeze it. By extension, lake and river water evaporates to become clouds and will in time turn back into its liquid state in the form of rain. Another example: when you burn a log of wood, it will be transformed into ash. This means that while matter has been transformed to another state, it is still matter. Whatever transformation water and wood undertake, as matter they are eternal and thus cannot disappear into nothing. This explains the dialectical concept of the law of conservation of matter.

Since matter is the basis and source of all the phenomena of nature, there cannot be any false phenomena, which are not susceptible to being investigated by the sense organs, physical evidence, or other scientific means. This also means that there is no reality regarding religious miracles, sins, heaven, hell, spirits, and angels; there is no room for divine providence, or religious and secular idealism. Why are angels, spirits, or ghosts not detectable by our sense organs, physical apparatuses, or anything else for that matter? Why is the effect of their "actions" not observable? Is there anything in human society that is attributed to the work or act of angels? There is not, because there is no God, angels, or any other world that exists.

The Catholic Church, Protestant evangelists, televangelists, Muslims, Hebrews, or cultists are unable to refute this dialectical conclusion. That is why the dialectical concept of matter (scientific materialism) is so hateful to the religious idealists and the Church in particular. One can argue that idealism was inherently variable throughout historical times and between societies, wherever social and cultural efforts were made to pursue stability for religious or secular beliefs. This is because their followers were not completely willing to accept idealism's social, religious, and cultural shaping. Thus aside from old established organized religious sects like Protestants, Evangelists, Mormons, Catholics, Orthodox, Southern Baptists, Seventh Day Adventists and Jehovah's Witnessess, secular idealists (not of any known religious sect) have appeared to entice the meek to follow them. These days there are a slew of them such as: the Church of Oprah, Eckhart, Satan Worship, Feng Shui, Shamanism, Eckankar, the Church of Scientology, Sun Myung Moon's, and Moses David Berg's just to name a few.

Scientific materialism and its thinkers opposed the numerous claims set forth by idealists. Dialectical interpretation is based on the simple premise that human, social, and cultural life is a response to life's practical challenges, earthly problems, and existence. On the other hand, religious and secular idealists have "beautified" the concept of idealism to mean something "good" and "high minded." It is their attempt to entice the meek and inspire them to be idealistic with their thoughts and behaviour. What would happen to them if they abandon their "ideals" and "sell out"? Would "they" turn out to become unforgiving materialists and atheists? It is a dialectical materialist propagation to scientifically expose the fallacies of idealism that deny cognitive knowledge and Darwinian principles in human-based behaviour.

Still, materiality rather than spirituality is fundamental to reality, which forms the dialectical-scientific concept of social structure, language, law, politics, visual arts, biological science, etc. This is because materialists regard ideas and concepts as the results of life's material conditions. Society evolves and develops based on the matter-in-motion of trial and error, within acceptable limits; otherwise it stagnates and ceases to exist. Idealists on the other hand, regard dialectical materialism as too simplistic as it does not consider the "good spiritual influence" that religion has on society.

Materialists are all for society's intellectual and cultural influence upon its members, but they tend to be against any claims of cultural values that religious and secular idealists may have to offer. For scientific materialists, when praxis (or reality) does not correspond to its related thought (ideas in mind), or thought (ideas in mind) does not correspond to its related praxis (or reality), then delusion or illusion takes control of the human mind and it clouds the *elegance of reality*.

As the term itself signifies, scientific materialism is a school of thought that regards physical matter and its relationships (matter-in-motion) as the only reality in the world. It investigates, experiments, and explains cosmological events from the conditions and motion of matter, and thus refuses the idealist notions of creation, the existence of God, saints, heaven in the sky, etc. These are ideas in the mind and they are delusional because they are not related to scientific evidence. The fundamental premise of scientific materialism is the recognition of the external world, the existence of matter and its physical relationship to the outside world (existing independent of our mind). Moreover, the human brain is an organ of thought, and thought is a function (mind) of the brain.

Our thinking process, however real, relative, imaginary, delusional, or confused it may be, is still a product of the material bodily organ called the brain.

In the geological sphere, the natural universe forms an unbroken material continuum that is eternal and infinite; nature has no beginning or end but evolves in perpetual transformation. This is an eternal, self-generating material fact without any barrier from a non-material, non-physical, or invisible supernatural being. Earth's natural foundational being and all that it contains was and still is a material being, and its natural geological substance underlies all the visible, measurable and verifiable phenomena.

Scientific materialism has always maintained that life itself is wholly the product of biological processes. This claim champions Darwinian Theory included in the *Origin of Species* that states that materialism could justify the theory scientifically. Scientific materialism has been implicitly atheistic, and has viewed its atheism basically as its necessary premise, not as a philosophical end in itself. Superstition, spiritual and supernatural gods, religious moralizers, ghosts, life after death, and immortal souls are not regarded or even imagined to exist in such a scientific materialist premise.

How does scientific materialism regard emotions, sensations, images, and perceptions? The short answer is that these concepts are only complicated forms of matter in motion. They are physical manifestations of physical features. Their functions are entities of a material body—the human brain—and are culturally determined or reinforced. Delusional beliefs, magic thinking, wishful thinking, superstitions, and beliefs in imaginary symbols and their references are still physical manifestations of a material body, the human brain. They do not exist outside the human brain, however complicated and appealing they may appear to be, nor do they have an "existence" per se because they are substantially nothing and thus can generate nothing.

Scientific materialism maintains that human behaviour comes from the human brain. Among other developments of the human neural system, there is the ability to imagine, to mentally construct sensor patterns, recollect them at will, and use them as if they were real. Conscious thought, an awareness of identity, an ability to imagine and fantasize (to create mental experiences of a real or imaginary scene), to imagine that one is in control and thus imagine a solution, is a brain function based on real or imaginary sensory memories. Intelligent thought—scientific materialist methodology—is a far more demanding process than philosophical speculation.

Scientific materialism is rooted in the ancient world of the artisans of Greece, Rome, Egypt, Persia, India, and Mesopotamia where their quest was to invent and build dependable structures and products. Repeated experiments provided the learning and application of provable knowledge. The rejection and restructuring of experimental results that could not be proven at the time aided in developing provable knowledge. The ancient engineer, the architect, the stone mason, the irrigation builder, the inventors of mechanical devices (*Mekanikos*), and the ship builder were born and revered by both the religious temples and Legionary Armies from the beginning. This intellectual thought process was then, and still is, not as entertaining as art, music, sports, popular trends, pulp fiction, and lifestyle philosophy.

Above all, scientific materialism is not easy or fun. It requires a measurable and provable intellectual basis, thereby utterly destroying a lot of popular illusions. It allows the secular materialist access to beautiful and imaginative thought representing our natural world and our real human aspirations as they are or as they can be transformed for the betterment of man. Knowledge preparation produces real, measurable results in educating children and in promoting and protecting our social and natural environments. Idealism's delusional imagination and conjecture on a intangible basis, such as it now exists in religious and secular theism, is diametrically opposed to scientific materialism, and thus can only breed mental distortions about our real world.

How then does scientific materialism relate to our daily personal life? It is important to remember that *nothing comes from nothing, for if there were nothing, nothing could come into existence.* In our daily activities we encounter problems and solutions that need to be dealt with. We learn about the workings of the natural world by training and education. We also deal with nature in accordance with how nature itself has an effect upon us. For example, when we leave our home on a rainy day, we either wear a raincoat or carry an umbrella to avoid getting wet. Our reactive behaviour is naturally instinctive in order to protect ourselves from the forces of nature. Countless times during our lives we have behaved instinctively because our behaviour is determined entirely by reaction, conflict resolution, and co-ordination or co-operation with natural events.

Moreover, our intelligence or memory is not separate from our sensory motor or instinct mechanisms. Nature's rain is related to climatic conditions which are governed by the material laws of the material nature. These laws of nature are both predictable and, at times, are unpredictable as it relates to our daily lives. A sudden rain storm would be an unpredictable natural event which would lead us to a different reactive behaviour from the first case. In both cases, a well-trained and educated person would view natural rain through objective reasoning. This is a materialist conclusion derived from the materialist climatic conditions that causes rain.

In short, rain, snow, wind, heat, and freezing climatic conditions cause us to adopt different reactive behaviours to overcome the challenges. This, of course, is valid unless a person is disillusioned and behaves according to his or her beliefs rather than reacting to external material conditions. Not surprisingly, a man who believes that he is naturally intelligent and then acts intelligently at all times cannot be wrong. He believes that logic and reason alone will always result in a coherent behavioural action.

However, he does not recognize that his intelligence is able to produce divergent answers for the same questions related to instinctive behaviour. In the case of rain, his behavioural instinct fit a particular problem and his reaction was correct. But since he depends on his reactive instinct (ideas in his mind) as well as on his intuition or imagination, his finalized decision is based on the virtue of his intelligence alone.

For example, he may look up at the sky and conclude that because it's been raining for days and because there are only a few clouds, it will not rain today. His argument is logical and reasonable but the material laws of nature do not act in accordance with man's logical and reasonable conclusions. So, he might get wet because his intelligence was coherent with what he calculated would not happen (i.e., thinking it will not rain).

Was this man wrong in his calculation? Yes he was, but only because of his idealism. Scientific materialism explains that acting idealistically in daily life is the core characteristic of a man who regards his idea(s), intuition, imagination, wishful thinking, intelligence, etc., as standards and a primary directive force when dealing with his external (both social and environmental) material surroundings. It is also because he regards the external world simply as a copy of his imaginary world, intelligence, and sensibility. Consequently, he believes that his ideas, emotions, feelings, and "higher thoughts" are all stamped on the external material reality, which all becomes "immaterial" in nature. Thus, the external material world exists merely in his thinking.

The brilliant success of Darwin's natural science, as written in his *Origin of Species*, gave scientific materialism a powerful confirmation. The study of material (biological) nature confirmed the non-existence of the soul, spirit, and religion's "other world." Various proofs from the natural sciences have been brought forward by 90% of the world's biologists who are atheist scientific materialists. Darwin's theory of evolution has proven that evolution is not a reactive process, nor does it plan ahead. It does not build in excess of the biological requirements, nor does it overstep its universal limits. In short, nature does not function on the basis of design. Natural selection finds that each natural progression is based upon another as its cause. The chain of natural selection can only be broken abruptly by natural causation.

Before we continue further, it is important to declare what scientific materialism is not. It is not, "the path," "the way," "a folk religion," "spiritual," "a belief system," "a philosophical view," "mysticism," "an inner peace," a way to "be in touch with yourself," "theism," "pantheism," "a way of life," a "linguistic metaphor," "symbolism," "a magic-thought," "wishful thinking," "a system of morality," "ethics," a western or eastern cultural propagation, a political ideology, etc. What scientific materialism is can be stated simply. It regards matter as primary and it includes personal, social, cultural, and political relationships because they take place in a physical world. Humans confront these material relationships, co-operate with, maintain, or transform them for their own benefit (or the opposite). Scientific materialism regards thoughts, ideas, images, senses, and feelings as secondary. If humans need to deal with their personal material relationships, as they really are, thoughts, wishful thinking, images, etc., must reflect the external real world first in order to derive appropriate material solutions.

Let us analyze the response of a scientific materialist and the response of an idealist towards an advertisement for a new and shiny car. An idealist's personal needs—in this case, a new car—is thought to originate from him. For the scientific-materialist, this personal need is ultimately "created" at the behest of the automobile industry that supplies them. The manufacturer controls his own prices in the consumer market.

But the firm goes beyond this control, for it designs methods to mentally influence the potential consumer to elicit the appropriate response behaviour. Since the idealist-consumer regards his ideas as being primary, the car company selects and designs cars with the aim of fetching a high price whilst subjecting the consumer to influential (mental) persuasion.

And so it goes in our western societies that the powerful car and advertising companies repeat and reiterate images with wishful thinking clichés in praise of shining car(s), making them the prerequisite for one to achieve "happiness" and thus enticing the idealist-consumer to become attentive to these claims. For the idealist-consumer, the exorbitant possession of goods contributes to his or her sensual-image of "happiness" rather than to his or her physical necessity. Theirs is not to reason why, theirs is but to satisfy. Unlike the scientific materialist, further consequences for the idealist are that he is open to mental persuasion where physical effects alone are involved.

The 2008 World Economic Crash was caused by consumers who did not pay attention to the material relationships between their physical ability to pay upfront for their cars, large houses, credit card purchases, and mortgages/loans. The human misery in 2008 caused by people's loss of their jobs, homes, and possessions resulted in divorces and family abuse. Over-consumption is not merely a point of view or a philosophical ideology. These negative things are real material consequences of decisions that were not analyzed first (matter-in-motion) in order to achieve an appropriate mental conclusion (second) that would be related to external material conditions (i.e. actual affordability).

For the scientific materialist, the external world is not a reflection of his senses. His intelligence is not used as a standard and primary directive force. How then does he achieve what he wants? For him, his personal, economic, or social relations (needs) are material relations. Thus, they are regarded as primary and his wants are physical first and mental second. This means that his material economic condition determines his material ability to pay for his physical needs, a house, a car, a vacation, dental or health care needs, an education for his children, or entertainment.

He is not a prisoner of his thoughts, images, wishful thinking, delusions or intelligence, nor does he regard them (by whatever combination) as standards toward achieving his physical wants or needs. His scientific materialism places him in relative control of his physical life and material relations, and "sex does not sell" for him when he purchases cologne or a shiny new car. The emphasis on the satisfaction of images, feelings, overblown self-esteem, and delusional beliefs of the self are easily avoided. For a lot of material conditions, including the detrimental effects on the environment, the scientific materialist is not a victim of predatory lending and consumption. The idealist stresses the "power" of his ideas, not recognising their ultimate weakness because of the far greater authority of the external material conditions. The subjectivism of his ideas and feelings (interchangeable and in flux with his emotions and wishful desires) are a "mental prison" where the idealist is sentenced to lifelong imprisonment.

One must also ask: does the scientific materialist become inspired by sensual emotions, imagination, and cultural innovation? I say that of course he or she does. These are learned by trial and error on the basis of reactive behaviour, knowledge, and productive material effort. Human creativity is materialist in its essence: whether in science, biology, music, theatre, arts and crafts, social and humanist propagation, preventative health, and environmental protection, etc. Deriving reactive knowledge from these creative materialists' productive efforts is a slow process. This is because the process of knowledge requires the mastery of praxis and the mastery of theory.

For example, if I want to learn the art of environmental protection, I must first know the material conditions of the environment, and also know about various environmental contaminants. Once I have all this theoretical knowledge, I am still by no means competent in the field of environmental protection. After much trial and error (praxis and theory), eventually the results of my reactive knowledge become one with the material protective solution. Within this interactive process, there is the factor of my ultimate humanist concern—a mix of my feelings and emotional attachments for all living things. But these mix and match ideas, emotions, and feelings cannot serve as standards and primary directive forces because they lack the material imprints to be environmentally effective. I say that this holds true for music, preventative health care, carpentry, and for personal, cultural, and socio-economic relations, etc.

Maybe, here lies the answer to the question of why people in our culture are not scientific-materialists and so rarely learn this: they live under the illusion that their ideas and inclinations are original, that they are all "unique" individuals, and that their own thinking just happens to be the "real world" to be followed (this is in spite of their repeated failures, such as becoming victims of the 2008 predatory marketing and the idealism of slick advertisement).

Man is, therefore, also capable of being an absolute idiot, the more usual case since he is not normally trained or educated in the materialist intelligent thought processof provable premise and frequent verification, and willingly considers his imagination and emotional rollercoaster as primary directives for his pursuits. Nor does he recognize that many of his sensual perceptions of external reality are archaic and only partially applicable. He is educated in idealist social interaction on false and self-serving premises and follows his mental manifestations which are rarely (if ever) verified and thereby rarely applicable.

Scientific materialism is in outspoken and adamant opposition to religion. Secular and religious idealists since the age of the Epicurean materialists have reared a mighty attack against the historical development of materialism. But the classical age of scientific materialism began in the 18th century when the natural sciences and atheist humanism made it a powerful factor in refuting idealism. This intellectually materialist triad—science, scientific materialism, and atheist-humanism—recognizes that there exists nothing beyond the natural universe, and all beings, including the human race, are an integral part this natural universe. The idealist term "supernatural" is a contradiction, because if something exists within the infinity of the natural universe, it is natural. Biological science has long confirmed life's natural biological cycle: birth, decay, and death.

The natural environment is what it is, and no more. It has no planning, and no reason, design, meaning or purpose. The end result of Earth's biological evolution or process—including man—appears to be accidental and inventive. Evolution is inventive in the sense that it is governed by abrupt processes squeezed through a filter. In short, mutations are accidents and are, therefore, not controlled by reason or design. Scientific materialism maintains that the natural world cannot be influenced by design, as is claimed by religious idealists.

The process of biological evolution produces life forms—from the single cell to the more complex and advanced organisms—which can survive within the given constraints of nature. Plant and animal life forms—from tomatoes to giant maple trees, from tiny mice to elephants—adapt themselves to meet the fixed requirements of nature. Other life forms adapt to the environment to strengthen themselves and, in the process, they change their physical surroundings.

The most successful of Earth's life forms has been man. Man has challenged his environment by design. This is because man alone is a problem solver, yet produced by evolution pure and simple. As long as the material solutions to man's problems were environmental, he conquered them all, one at a time.

The problems lent themselves to the objective human effort of trial and error. For example, the material solution to agricultural problems resulted in a constant and reliable food supply. The organized efforts of animal husbandry led to the supply of meat, milk, and high protein foods. The use and control of fire for generating heat and cooking was developed. The need for protection from natural climatic conditions, such as, heat, rain, cold, and high winds led to the steady development of reliable shelters using a variety of natural and man-made construction materials. Scientific medicine has developed from man's ignorance of the functions of the human body and superstition practiced by religious charlatans to high tech curative and preventative medicine. Above all, the invention of tools and instruments set man apart from the rest of the animal world—the latter remained in its state of nature; the former mastered and transformed his environment—for good or bad—by the use of his tools.

Biological science has given concrete proof that the cycle of life evolves in the birth, decay and death of the organism. An organism's death naturally ceases its functioning life-energy in its totality.

Religious and secular idealists claim that the "soul" exists in a form of energy (immaterial) that cannot disappear in nature and cannot originate there, and therefore, the "soul" is immortal. This is a core religious philosophical argument to support the delusion of the existence of the "holy spirit." Scientific materialism, however, explains that everything that organisms including man-do in ecosystems, such as, running, breathing, thinking, procreating, reading, and growing, requires energy. In fact, of all the factors that influence how living organisms in the ecosystem function, none is more important than the flow of energy. Organisms conserve and spread energy as they need it, and in the process, living organisms interact with one another and their biological environment.

So, where does this energy come from? The question cannot be answered merely idealistically or philosophically but scientifically. That is, energy flows into the biological world from the sun! Life exists on our planet Earth because photosynthesis makes it possible to capture some of the photo (light) energy from the sun and transform it into chemical energy. All organisms in an ecosystem are chemically active organisms driven by the energy captured in photosynthesis.

Biologists and ecologists have discovered that every organism's life span in an ecosystem is determined by the organism's available source of food energy. Plants in most terrestrial ecosystems have the shortest lifespan. Organisms (man and animals) that consume both plants and flesh have the highest level of energy. Energy as photosynthesis, therefore, originates from the sun, and sustaining life on earth is its natural causation. Biological evidence has shown that the energy of photosynthesis in the human body is equivalent to the nutriment consumed.

The natural laws governing the organism's energy and its conservation are empirical law and not merely philosophical thoughts, for it is deduced from the material world and it is based on the activity of matter in motion. This means that an organism conserves and spends energy derived from photosynthesis in the ecological system. Thus, in the material world where all humans live, motion is an integral energy-force of life. When an organism (a man) ceases to live (by accident, sickness, or natural causes) his body's energy force dies as well. But the photosynthesis energy in the Earth's ecosystem continues to function uninterrupted as millions upon millions of other organisms are born, decay and die. This is not a mere philosophical idealistic non-investigative belief. As long as the sun's energy continues to support life on earth, life on earth as we know it will continue to exist until billions and billions of years from now when the sun's energy ceases to exist. Then life on earth will die also.

Scientific materialism is greatly interested in investigating the material relationships and patterns that occur in both nature and society. It maintains that no single species or form could possibly exist in isolation, that is, without its opposite. It studies human relationships with their surrounding environment. Nature and society are seen in relation to natural occurrences of complimentary or opposing natural and social characteristics. Both combine in a complementary manner and form a system for investigating and explaining relationships of matter in motion in the material world.

The ancient materialists came from the observation of nature and their environment. Some of these observational occurrences included the sky and earth, day and night, water and fire, hot and cold, movement and stillness, and so on. Thus, natural occurrences take place as pairs of opposites on a complimentary or opposing basis (i.e., nature's laws of change). Laws of change are matter in motion. Identifying change in nature and society allows humans to take appropriate steps to meet the challenges. In nature, some things change slowly, like young people growing old, day turning to night, and environmental pollution slowly polluting the air, water, and soil. Abrupt changes can occur, such as an earthquake, the burning down of a house or a serious car accident. Some changes are "happy," others are "scary." Some are both "exciting" and a bit scary, like your first day in a new job, or skydiving for the first time.

In scientific materialism, the investigation and analysis of our natural world contains no mysticism or any need for invisible sky gods, Satan, miracles, delusions, or misguided beliefs that you are "unique" enough to have a personal god who would grant you an afterlife. Our natural universe embodies all the opposites of every atom, every solar system. Scientific materialism is interpreted through its own linguistic tool called dialectics. Dialectics is used as a system of understanding the existing state of things and concepts as they really are in the natural and social world. It is also used to explain how these real things and concepts change. In short, dialectics is a social tool that enables laypersons to deal with the real world—and identify unreal or delusional claims.

Briefly, here are some of the fundamentals of scientific materialism interpreted by dialectics:

Matter in Motion: dialectics acknowledge that all material elements of the universe are subject to the same physical laws. Thus, physical laws of the material universe are applicable to matter and its energy (i.e., matter-in-motion). Newton's physical laws of motion (energy) explicitly state that any process only moves matter forward if a force causes it to move. A dialectical understanding results in a complementary understanding of the entire process of matter-in-motion.

Concepts: Concepts are not things or objects. They are important principles of detailed human understanding of physical, chemical, biological, mathematical, psychological, and political social and personal occurrences. For example: (a) in mathematics: + vs. −, differential and integral; (b) in mechanics: action vs. reaction; (c) in physics: positive vs. negative electricity; (d) in chemistry: combination vs. dissociation of atoms; (e) in social science: materialism vs. idealism; and (f) in the natural world: the laws of nature vs. human life; etc. At all times, we must question what we take for granted, what politicians propagate, religious beliefs and morality, and the false corporate consumerist belief system that claims "happiness" can be achieved by consuming or possessing more and more.

Opposite Occurrences: Opposite occurrences are achieved in the natural world by mutual control that is maintained within certain limits. The change of seasons illustrates this concept. Winter is followed by spring which is followed by summer and fall. Weather changes from cold to hot from winter through autumn. Opposites depend on one another to exist, to have a function and a meaning. Otherwise, it would not make sense to talk about "cold" if there were no opposite "hot" or the meaning of "night" if there were no opposite as "day." In short, natural occurrences happen in pairs, in both complementary and opposing characteristics.

Complementary Opposites: Some concepts such as love vs. hate are mutually controlled and inhibited by each other, which results in a state of dynamic balance (i.e., love contains some hate and hate contains some love), or heat can dispel cold, while cold can reduce heat. Both examples function in a mutually complementary controlled balance. This balance is neither static nor absolute.

Opposing Occurrences or Negation of Negation: Negation is a starting point toward an opposite, (an attraction). There is always some degree of the opposite contained in everything that exists—pure or absolute negation does not exist. For example, opposing occurrences begin when daylight negates the starting point of night, back to the negation of the starting point of day but with something different. Whether daytime or nighttime is longer or shorter depends on the season. As another example, yesterday is negated by the starting point of today, which is negated by tomorrow. Thus every day is different from yesterday. There cannot exist any antagonism with a negation of negation: both processes are always complementary. The process of negation depends upon its opposite in order for both to exist and hold each other in balance and exert mutual control. The process of opposing occurrences allows us to focus on the real essential elements of life's constant changes. Dealing with opposing occurrences is primarily a human dialectical concept because it requires a focus-oriented process to sort out life's myriad changes and the opposing forces which are constantly swirling about us. This natural cycle does not exist in the delusional religious "world" of "heaven" or "hell," for these are dead/fixed/static in relation to any lifecycle or change.

Dialectical vs. Judgmental Thinking: To explain dialectical thinking is to think of the many apparently opposing occurrences a person encounters in his or her daily life. Dialectical thinking sees matter in motion (change) as a vital process of life itself. Therefore, dialectical thinking is flexible and it unites the opposites rather than only being the *"this* **or** *that"* of dichotomous thinking. The unity of opposites is regarded as an alternative: life is both this **and** that. In other words, the fundamental characteristics of dialectical thinking encompass its main emphasis on change. It is based on process and movement. The underlying point is that one should look at *"what it is now and how it changes."*

The opposite to dialectical thinking is judgmental or dichotomous thinking, in which the emphasis is on "all **or** nothing," "black **or** white," "this **or** that," "take it **or** leave it," "my way **or** the highway," "you either love me **or** hate me," etc. This approach leads, metaphorically speaking, to a mental trap or a dead-end in one's own mental pathway. Dialectical thinking is about finding the unity of opposites as a middle path: replacing the "or" with "and." This means that one can express his or her emotions without overreacting (extremes of thought) and control one's emotions without suppressing them.

Dialectical thinking identifies the existing states of nature and society's continued changes and progress. This state takes place through conflict or opposition and, at times, through a smooth or harmonious process of complementary occurrences of opposites. Thus, a person with a dialectical thinking process can identify opposites within people's lives and situations. The easiest thing to identify is that opposites depend on one another. An opposite is not "pure" for it contains within itself a segment of its opposite.

For example, if one is to understand the natural state of "darkness" one must understand its opposite as "light," that light contains some darkness (shade), and that darkness contains some light (light-shade). If I'm to understand the human concept and emotion of "love" I must also understand the emotion and concept of "hate" for each opposite (love and hate) seems to need the other to have a true meaning of what it is, and each one of these concepts and emotions contains some characteristic of its opposite. Thus, opposites occur everywhere in nature's biological processes and everywhere in society's personal and social concepts. Life is about overcoming obstacles, and resolving and smoothly uniting occurring opposites. On the other hand, judgmental or dichotomous thinking is a one-sided way of thinking leading to the distortion of reality and becoming delusional.

No one can claim that dialectical thinking and practice is easy to achieve, for it is not. Perhaps one can begin by considering the ancient Chinese dialectical writing of Taoism. Its Yin-Yang symbol shows not only the interdependence of opposites, but also the unity of opposites.

Unity of Opposites. Dialectics signifies a dialogue between two persons as an interaction of opposites (otherwise it would be referred to as a monologue). This means that if we consider a concept and take it to its one-sided extreme, it actually turns into its opposite. The equivalent of this is to idealize or turn something into a delusion (i.e., opposites attract).

For example, let's take the human concept of love to its extreme. Any notion of love must begin with the concept of human existence, of harmony, that is based on both reason and instinctual emotion. So if one takes his or her love to the extreme, and distorts or idealizes it, that person's "love" becomes so one-sided that one's "love" turns pathologically dependent (a fatal attraction). That person's whole humanist existence depends absolutely on the whims of its opposite, "love." Also, if we take the human concept of "hate" to its extreme, and distort or idealize it, we equally get an unhealthy counter-dependence, a complete monistic dependency on the other person. Throughout history, religious "love of god" wars were taken to their extreme opposite of hating the "other" opposites who did not believe in their concept of extreme "love."

Another example would be the social opposites of "wealth" and "poverty." The unity of opposites is quite evident when one travels through the Third World nations and witnesses the concentration of wealth—free enterprise taken to its extreme—and the extreme widespread poverty. Wealthy people depend on poor people to provide them with more wealth by means of extremely low labour costs. The poor would pathologically (to the extreme) depend on their wealthy opposites to earn their meagre living. One opposite idealizes the concentration of wealth as "freedom," "creative opportunity," "the Protestant work ethic," and the non-wealthy opposite idealizes life by striving to become "happy" like their opposites.

The appreciation of the paradox—negation of negation—is one of the dialectical strengths that makes it superior to formal logic. The paradox of negation of negation seems to say two opposite things. As one negation begins to change to its opposite negation, a process of balance takes hold of both opposites, which may or may not lean towards or away from the other.

For example, a harmonious (not an extreme) negation of a portion of the concentrated wealth would effect its opposite (poverty) to more or less a degree because that portion of the negated-wealth would be passed on and thus decrease poverty. A healthy balance between the two opposites (negation of negation)—wealth vs. poverty—would be much more socially just.

Therefore, the degree of balancing between the negation of a negation lies in the process of negation from each side of the opposites' equation. What unites the opposites, therefore, is the paradox negation of negation, which is contrary to formal logic, which says that A = A, and assumes a static state of A. Something being "to itself" means that despite quantitative change, it remains what it is: there is no qualitative change. "Self-identical" means something totally lacking opposites, contradictions, and vitality. Thus, the concept of "equal to itself" or A = A means that the concept is lacking in contradictions and is therefore abstract or motionless and generally isolated from connections with other things.

Scientific evidence tells us that such an idea is a delusion. A person's life with no opposites or contradictions would be static and lifeless. Since all things are in motion and occupy different places in space/time, "A = A" is impossible. Of course, there is nothing that says you have to live in a static lifestyle where human concepts like love, art, human rights, equality, free choice, personal likes and dislikes etc., will not move forward or change.

What enables the human intellect to handle complex concepts is dialectics (whether instinctively or by the brain's chemical imperatives). This is because humans must constantly make complex choices. While genetics is undoubtedly important, humans must also make decisions that require reactive behaviour, mimesis/planning, and spontaneity. This is not always a conscious choice. The logic of paradox is handled by dialectics with any everyday activity. This is because, unlike nature, human concepts are mostly goal-oriented. Most of nature (e.g., the sun, a star, a planet, an ocean, a plant, an animal etc.) does not appear to have any goal: it just is.

Human concepts, both personal and social, however, depend on what the goal of life's overall process is, which can be both planned and spontaneous. This is a crucial concept, which dialectical thinking makes easy to understand and easy to practice, intellectually, emotionally, and intuitively. For example, if my goal is to live a healthy and active life, I'll need to exercise, eat healthy foods (instead of pre-fabricated ones), and practice moderation. This is a balance of Yin-Yang or the dialectical unity of opposites. If I want good grades as a student, I need to do my homework, and prepare and study for exams. If I want to build my own house, I must plan to start this project by building the foundations first, then the floor and walls.

At the same time, watching what and how other people do things—mimesis—is a natural human learning process. So, if I see people that I know living beyond their means—negation of negation will proceed to destroy their financial well-being. With constant changes and social contradictions taking place about us, our personal well-being will depend on deciding what to do next. Dialectics teaches us that matter in motion is made up of complementary and duelling opposites, and people's needs can be solved when you and I can weave through and clearly identify a given problem (one opposite) and its solution (its opposite). Therefore, take nothing for granted, practice the process of planning and spontaneity, and break the routine of your fixed patterns and beliefs. This means that you can be responsible and playful at the same time (opposites), and this is one facet of the elegance of reality in which dialectics excels.

Conclusion. In this brief presentation of some of the fundamentals of dialectical materialism, I have tried to demonstrate that dialectics is a way of understanding the laws of nature, social concepts, reality, personal concerns, thoughts, and emotions. Its system of thought concerns the unity of scientific materialism and dialectical theory. This brief essay is by no means a comprehensive analysis of dialectics, so I encourage the reader to read further about the subject.

Dialectics is for daily practical life, scientific investigation, humanist psychology, and serves as a refutation of delusions, illusions, idealism, religious fallacies and their dreadful consequences upon humanity. It is a means of escaping from religion. Dialectics is not a fad. It has its origins in the ancient societies of China, India and Greece where social thinkers sought to understand nature as a whole, and saw that everything is in motion, constantly changing, coming into being, and passing away.

The last hurdle to be cleared in the reader's mind is the misunderstanding of the concept of materialism. Do not assume that the meaning of the term refers to man's material interest or his strivings for ever-increasing consumerist gain and luxurious comforts. The ancient philosophers were "naturalists" and held the materialist view that matter in motion is the fundamental constituent of the natural universe. Darwin's *Origin of Species* fortified the concept of scientific materialism beyond the general definition that was held by the ancient Greek, Indian and Chinese naturalists. Dialectics is a system of reasoning which aims to understand things beyond their appearances, but concretely in all their movement, change, and interrelationships with their opposite and contradictory sides in unity. For dialectics, things and concepts can be contradictory not just in appearance but also in their essence. There are various aspects to dialectics because dialectics is a system of thinking in which concepts are flexible and in motion.

In our daily life we act dialectically all the time. It could not be otherwise. To be aware of that is to be aware of the dialectics of our own actions. Dialectics can be understood on the basis of practical and theoretical activity. To comprehend dialectics, a person must have experienced the transformation of one opposite into another (negation of the negation), and have seen and participated in a dialectical sequence of events and felt its logical power and necessity. One must be able to identify the meaning of dialectical words vs. the illusion of the metaphorical meanings of words.

If one is fortunate enough to have read the right books, one can more easily grasp dialectical materialism. One must be careful here: book learning without the necessary act of experiencing will result in knowledge of dialectics that is formal, alienated, immature, and disassociated from practical activity (praxis). This would not be useful for the conduct of daily practical life.

Here I must briefly bring forward the subject of ethics and morality. Dialectical morality involves any concern with human needs, desires, experiences and non-discriminatory relations amongst humans. Analyzing the concept from its general dialectical description, we can see that morality is not a particular set of dogmas or a specific system of beliefs. Instead, dialectical morality and goodness is better described as the materialist perspective on biological life and humanity.

Based on this factor, do humans need to be religious in order to be moral as well as good citizens? Can people be humanists without God? Biblical leaders do not think so. The objective analysis of dialectical moralists is in strong opposition to such a religious claim.

The dialectical concept of morality maintains that it is the result of the growing influence of humanism or atheism permeating society that causes it to retreat from religious ethics and dogma. In fact, millions of humanists and atheists around the world live in harmony with other religious and non-religious members of their society. They have meaningful relationship with their families; they are at peace with themselves and with their natural environment and conduct their affairs with humility and generosity. They are clearly against any violence towards women, children, minorities or persons of other sexual orientations.

Dialectical morality is clearly based on humanity's needs, and maintains moral judgments based on reason and wisdom. Thus, it holds to a more human-centric view of morality, with values that are derived from human experience based on love, kindness and generosity. All are regarded as being good things in segments of our society where no religion is practiced.

On a more personal level, I do not know of any atheist ideological book that advocates against anyone who is a religious believer. Nor do I know of any person or persons who are motivated by atheism and are willing to physically or verbally attack a religious person. Neither are organized atheists or humanists advocates of revenge against religious believers.

Ethical claims under religion are a pure delusion. It thus carries no moral credibility. Past and present ecclesiastical leaders involved in corruption and paedophilia around the world do not project acceptable ethical behaviour, nor does the idea that their claims are humanly-inspired, projecting goodness, societal order, decency, empathy, pity and compassion.

The question, however, still remains whether humans can be good and act in a morally conscious manner without being religious. Can they feel compassion when they see an old homeless person, a suffering animal or an abused child? In short, what gives the urge to help someone who is highly unlikely to reciprocate the helping offer?

Dialectical morality is not just a "good" feeling towards another human being, a victim of natural disaster, an animal, or a sentiment based on the "ideal" of a humanist notion. Taking practical steps to eliminate poverty, unequal treatment of women, the socio-economic inequalities between "have's and have not's," and racism are moral social actions and help maintain cultural order. Eliminating such inequalities is not related to religion. It is a human- based social obligation derived from a real interpretation of human needs. Those needs can be resolved by real human solutions that are not derived from a make believe system.

Dialectically analyzing socio-economic issues of inequality is very much related to moral problems. It is a rationalist approach to conceptual thought and external reality. This approach shows that religious ethical claims of morality have historically been far too narrow and indifferent to moral values originating from within the real social fabric of human society.

Abstract ethics is a core fallacy that is just based faith based on lies:

❖ First, because morality does not come from the void nor does it functions on its own field, that is, as an abstraction of the mind.

❖ Second, because moral attitudes—to be meaningful—are necessarily dependent on the external dialectical world.

❖ Third, just as in the natural world, if morality is taken to abstraction, it is unrelated to humans. When morality is conceived merely as a purely religious-idealistic entity. It is bound to be illusionary and ineffective.

❖ Fourth, morality should not be divorced from the concrete sociality of humanity which must be based on applicability for its related praxis.

❖ Finally, all speculation about the existence of religious ethics in the imaginary "God's Kingdom" must be rejected from the moral sphere of humanity.

Dialectical reasoning of society's moral and cultural development is the base which governs all human activities. It is part of human essence as a ruling rational force that impresses all moral, social and cultural activities in unity with reality and its material nature. In other words, the dialectical interpretation of our biological world involves not only our human existence, but also the social structures which include morality, the kind of morality which is brought from the plane of religious fallacy down to the human realm, thus becoming social, dynamic, organic and natural. This means that morality cannot be detached from the dialectical world, or from its historical and social dimensions of moral universality. It must be applicable to all humans of all ages, ethnicity and racial background.

Humanist morality is created out of the terrestrial natural laws of continuity and change (matter in motion) based on the historical and cultural progression of society. It is also based on the perception that all moral norms and rules are justly regarded as being humanist. This dialectical standpoint is rational, reflective and fundamental, and provides the content of moral conduct. Otherwise, if morality is regarded as being "transcendental," "divine," or "celestial" and ignores its humanist content, it becomes meaningless and ineffective.

Moral terms, such as, "good," "bad," "right" or "wrong" that are rooted in the dialectical world as practical moral principles, are generally accepted in society and recognized as binding duty and relevance to human attitude and behaviour. Its principles on morality are taken as being based upon an elaborate scientific knowledge of the beneficial workings of the human world.

Ethics that are based on delusional beliefs are associated with hypocrisy, ineffective preaching and mere appearance. One cannot understand the content of humanist morality without its relation to its moral practice. Religious piety of ethical relations merely indulges in "moral" reflections which misuse the concept of morality for immoral purposes: financial exploitation of the meek, paedophilia, hatred of "non-believers" and followers of other religions or spiritual sects. Ethics that are based on "divinity" stand in opposition to the real stimulus of life's activity.

Scientific materialism acknowledges that human beings are motivated and re-motivated out of a social-cultural and economic process which is the foundation of all earthly moral concepts. Humanist classification and views thus depend and are formed (matter in motion), out of cultural elaborations, not just, on mere mental perception alone.

Having said this, scientific materialism does not ignore the fact that mental perception also shapes human behaviour in the formulation of a person's moral character. It maintains that a human's personal moral character is thus formulated by external cultural and sensory factors. This is because the moral character and life of a human is an organic growth, not just a set of fixed and sterile arrangements of religious dogmas. It is because of this organic growth, that humanist morality is distinct from one culture to another, changes from one generation to the next, or is rejected and re-adapted, modified or accepted at different historical times.

This means that only humanist and atheist morality, which is based on the beneficial understanding of the social, cultural, historical and dialectical character of human needs and aspirations, is truly human morality. Sensing morality and acting in a moral way will both take place in the context of a humanist social structure. It is simply a delusion to claim that morality is based on divinity and derived from outside the human reality.

In closed religious groups or societies, ethics have always been subordinated to theistic dogmatism and this subordination is the distinguishing mark of the so-called divine "high-level" of morality. The sole purpose of any organizational advocacy of morality is simply to win the minds of the people and thus broaden their base. To those religious institutions, the spreading of their base is the primary focal point, and they are indifferent as to whether the means used for this purpose are cruel lies, hypocrisy or delusional beliefs presented as "divine" eternal truths. Such a religious "ethical" stand is already fixed in its perfection, for there is no organic process of change that includes all temporal human relationships.

Dialectical social thinkers are focused on the concept of morality in order to set the idealist misrepresentation straight. We are very much concerned with its realistic form involving the relationship between human knowledge and external reality, between thinking and being. This question of morality lives in a world divided between idealism and scientific materialism.

The idealists assert the primacy of ethics on the ideal-morality over the materialist nature of real-morality. Idealists ignore the social conditions in which moral men live and maintain this idea active.

The scientific materialists assert the primacy of morality in the principle of matter in motion—natural world and social conditions. They maintain that the objective content of morality must be determined by the external world. Dialectical materialists take into account the physical science of biology as an adequate account of nature, and of ultimate reality. This is dialectical materialist methodology over abstract idealism and religious speculation.

In the sphere of biology, for example, one can see in the animal world a mother caring for its young or a male willing to risk his life to protect the group's females and their young. This is not dictated or inspired by God. Some of us have also witnessed animals like wolves, elephants, chickens or ducks etc., dependent upon each other for protection from common enemies, or joining together to hunt for a common meal. This also is not dictated or inspired by God.

We know about animal socialization, passing time grooming one another, courting between males and females. They are basically behaving in accordance to their natural habits. All are natural instinctive acts without God's revelations. Nor do they involve instinctive inclinations for or against God or knowing or using instincts of "good" or "bad."

I do not mean to suggest that there is an instinct of morality in the natural animal world at large, because there is not! The natural world is neither moral nor immoral. Nature is amoral, that is, without morality. Nature neither acts to "punish" or "reward" humans for their behaviour. In the natural world there are no rewards or punishments.

We benefit when we act in one way; we suffer when we act in another way. When we pollute our environment, then nature responds by reducing or eliminating the quality of life on earth. This is a natural fact, for there is no moralistic quality in natural events. Nature does not act to benefit or "punish" humans for being "destructive" or to hold them morally responsible.

In religious ethics, however, human beings are fundamentally regarded as being immoral, criminal and potentially evil. Based on this premise, humans must be kept from acting criminally by instilling into them fear and threats of punishment and suffering. The "carrot" is a promise of a "divine" reward, not in this life, but in the after-life. This means that the moral practice and reward of a religious person would not endure if there were no after-life, and thus religious ethics is a deliberate lie.

Human dialectical morality is an imitable cultural subject and activity passed on from parents to their children, from group to group, and from society to society. It is related to the biological and cultural phenomena of life's functions of good and bad, as thoughts and practice. It is a dialectical relationship of the whole biological structure of the physical life that was built-up through adaptation and natural selection. It also has to do with geology, biology, astronomy, chemistry and how humans have overcome diseases or found their causes and cures.

Did the Biblical texts ever teach humans about agriculture, mathematics, engineering problems and their solutions? Or how to develop better agricultural crops; or how to drain a wetland or to construct a canal; teach humans the aesthetics of understandable arts, music, or weaving a tapestry; how to build a steam engine, an airplane, a submarine or a phone; and thousands of other things that are indispensible for supporting society, human, vegetable and animal life?

For religious texts to claim God gave everything to humans, is to deny the existence of human adaptation and natural selection. Is it credible to believe that it was God that gave morality to humans?

Does this mean that an atheist mother would have never learned to love her child? Or that men and women would never have loved each other? Or humans would have never learned the moral values of how to practice honesty, respect, loyalty, truthfulness, trust and sincerity?

Dialectical materialism maintains that humans are an integral part of the material life of the natural world.

The American Humanist Organization, in its Manifesto II declares the following:

"We affirm that moral values derive from their humanist experience. Ethics is autonomous and situational needing no theological or ideological sanction. Ethics stem from human need and interest. To deny this distorts the whole basis of life. Human life has meaning because we create and develop our future. Happiness and the creative realization of human needs and desires, individually and in shared enjoyment are continuous themes of humanism. We strive for the good life, here and now. The goal is to pursue life's enrichment despite debasing forces of vulgarization, commercialization and dehumanization.

Reason and intelligence are the most effective instruments that humankind possesses. There is no substitute: neither faith nor passion suffices in itself. The controlled use of the scientific methods, which have transformed the natural and social sciences since the Renaissance must be extended further in the solution of human problems. But reason must be tempered by humanity, since no group has a monopoly of wisdom or virtue. Nor is there any guarantee that all problems can be solved or all questions answered. Yet critical intelligence, infused by a sense of human caring, is the best method that humanity has for solving problems. Reason should be balanced with compassion and empathy and the whole person fulfilled. Thus, we are not advocating the use of scientific intelligence independent of or in opposition to emotion...feeling and love. As science pushes back the boundary of the known, humankind's sense of wonder is continually renewed and, art, poetry, and music find their places along with...ethics."

Some problems with morality are caused by an unequal distribution of national wealth, life changes, opportunities for education and employment. The result is an impoverished moral character of part of society facing economic segregation, pushing individuals into an illegal lifestyle. Deprived social circumstances exacerbate unhealthy and alienating conditions, which weaken social and moral bonds between the economically deprived with the rest of society. In consumerist-driven societies, people strive to "have it all," to have the things that corporate advertising tells them they need and must have. Our wants and needs beyond the basic necessities are then obtained by finding alternative ways of procuring them, from overextending credit-lines, borderline legal acts, to outright crime.

Morality that is not related to external reality of equal rights is regarded as an abstract concept that shifts from one ideal extreme to another. Morality can not be based on a purely ideological abstract system of beliefs, but on socio-cultural characteristics of people's wants and needs regardless of colour, creed, sex, sexual orientation and ethnicity.

Dialectics of morality tells us that any human value we have, if it is one-sided, will surely result in a delusion. This means that we cannot take personal morality and exclude its social opposite, for if we do this and take it as extreme and idealized, it will turn into its unintended opposite. In short, the only moral values which will be truly stable and coherent are those which include their opposites. Social morality is intensely personal (its opposite) at the same time.

To recognize this dialectical unity of opposites frees us (personally) and socially (impersonally) from the "either-or" which can be fixed, dogmatic, idealist, distorted, oppressive and delusive. Personal and social moral values are concerned with ethical opposites that unite humans and the natural environment. Simultaneously, the moral principles governing those relations determine our duties, rights, obligations and responsibilities with regards to the moral relations between humans and our social environment.

Thus, there cannot be civil rights without civil duties (as a balance of opposites), and no personal duties without personal rights. This is the dialectical unity of opposites, a natural balance between contradictions. In nature, this works just as well, probably even better, between members of different species when it is to their mutual benefit. The ancient hunter, for example, needed a spear to hunt, and the weapons maker needed meat. So both the hunter and the spear maker traded in order to support their opposite needs. In nature, the honeybee needs nectar to survive and the flower needs pollinating to also survive. The unity of opposites is evident. The flower cannot fly so it supports the bee's survival needs by providing nectar. In turn, the flower needs the bee's legs and wings to carry on the pollination. Both species benefit from the balanced unity of opposite transactions.

Natural and human social environments are both rich in examples of unity of opposite relationships: hummingbirds and tubular flowers; water-buffaloes and ox-peckers; a carpenter contracted for a fee which results in you having new windows in your home etc. Furthermore, there is an altruistic morality between individuals who have a closely connected genetic kinship of maintaining the exchange of favours given the anticipation of returning the favour, if and when needed. This moral reciprocated act, however, is not absolute or fixed, for at times we may also act morally without potential reciprocation, as is the case of helping someone who has an accident, or helping a homeless person who is unable to reciprocate. In this sense, human moral acts are not religious-based. This can be confirmed by the fact that morality is both learned and instinctual, as natural opposites which are built into our brains. The spontaneous way in which humans respond to moral acts are something natural and this confirms the fact that morality is largely independent of people's religious beliefs or lack of them.

One of the most important of human moral obligations concerns environmental responsibility towards our natural world, including all animal and plants that inhabit the natural ecosystem of our planet. Some wild ecosystems in both water and land environments have been internationally protected by laws and any sort of commercial activities are prohibited. Certainly some human activities on our planet have turned the wild biotic environment into a vast exploitation of natural resources, not only on the surface of the Earth, but also in the oceans, lakes, rivers and atmosphere itself.

In reference to the domain of human morality and nature, the content of valid humanist moral rules has to do with humans as members of a social group. From this dialectical perspective our social outlook on nature must include our human activities upon it, as an integral part of the natural order on Earth's biosphere. Dialectically, we thus place human acts within the system of nature, in the same way we place activities of other species in the respective environments. Therefore, in Earth's support of life there is a common relationship of all species in their biological and botanical environments. We share this with wild animals and plants. In short, humans, as members of the earth's community of life, see the differences between our species and other species, but we put aside these differences and we view ourselves as but one species-population among many. Our common origin is one of evolutionary process—not creation—and the common environmental material circumstances that surround us all is fully acknowledged.

The question for humans is this: are we ready to affirm our commonality with other species as being equal members of the whole Biological Community of Life? To honestly recognize this would reject the biblical moral fallacy for humans "to dominate the earth and all the animals," for under the materialist principle of First Things First, humans are a recent arrival on Earth, a relative newcomer to an older forms of life that has been in existence for hundreds of millions of years before us.

Scientific materialist knowledge of environmental problems caused by human destructive activities would be empty if it were not motivated by concern. Care, responsibility, respect and morality are mutually earned and interdependent. These are instinctual practices and attitudes which are to be found in an environmentally mature person, that is, in the community of persons who have developed a productive power which only genuine social productivity is able to give—consumerism's greed is not included.

What moral significance the natural environment has upon us does not depend on our point of view of the whole biological system of our world. Our role in it cannot be based on a system of belief which would idealise the whole or only a sector of our environment. For this is the case now, and atheists and dialectical humanist may risk an "ideal" which would underline and support an attitude that "the earth shall be dominated with all the animals."

Loving and respecting nature is not enough, for these are sentiments that must be materialized with their external opposite as physical activities that would prevent environmental destruction. The natural environmental order is the point of First Things First, thus carrying us into moral responsibility in accordance with that order. Otherwise, each one of us may follow a belief to protect the animal we prefer or like—most likely the domesticated ones—thus choosing an attitude/belief "clothed" with explanations and justification as to why "we" should protect "little Bambi" and not the "bad" sharks.

External reality requirements for survival are imposed on all living things. The constant motions to adjust to environmental changes, the activities of other organisms in the area, all are in the natural order to preserve their existence with members of other species. To enhance the well-being of living things, which is essential to both human and animals, we must have the capacity to relate to other organisms in ways which allow successful ecological co-existence with other species. Awareness of reality moral reasoning leads to this conclusion, and it is an appropriate moral attitude to take toward the natural world.

This balance of opposites has extended itself throughout the natural world, but humans have purposes in life other than simple biological survival and physical well-being. In short, unlike the rest of earth's animal kingdoms, humans have the moral responsibility to choose their continuing activities and how they affect or harm the entire earth's biological and botanical environment.

Do not forget that the social stage for environmental neglect was set by the biblical messages that humans have been following for hundreds of years. This has also set people's belief system that human beings are superior to all other living things. This is a religious perversion of responsibility. The majority of people in Western civilization for the last twenty centuries were indoctrinated by a delusional idealist belief system that God has given humans a kind of superiority not present in other "low forms of life."

The politico-economic system established in the last 500 years, reinforced this destructive attitude–which our natural environment was there for the taking. Religion and concentrated wealth have been the artificial unity of opposites. Their survival and continuity depends victimization and the regeneration of repetition (re-occurrences). The hidden religiosity of such a belief system is so deeply and pervasively embedded in our economic, social and cultural customs and practices that it has brought about the destructive environmental consequences we are facing today.

The moral question is this: just because humans are indeed different from the rest of the animals, are those differences a sign of superiority? The fact that humans have the destructive power and capacity to kill the rest of the animal kingdom, and the capacity to pollute the environment, is this destructive power a sign of superiority?

Dialectical materialists regard as a human imperative the moral responsibility for the preservation and enrichment of human civilization. Clearly, it is from this humanist standpoint that we recognize human activities—not ideological theories—as desirable and good. Religious institutions and idealist believe in human superiority over animals from an ideological point of view, that is, a point of view which takes as a moral standard the one set by the biblical God, to "dominate the earth and all the animals."

In this brief analysis, I have tried to show that scientific materialism and its ethics are based on the external reality of social and environmental situations that must not be in conflict when deciding what to do. When there are some environmental and social opposites between materialism and perceived human benefits, the dialectical principle of First Things First will give us a clear indication of what priorities we assign. We cannot adopt randomly chosen resolutions. The external reality of humanist social and environmental normative moral principles must be unified and acted upon in a dialectical balance of opposites for materialist resolutions to such conflicts.

No system of human morality of rules and standards must be fixed as a world order. We cannot treat our social and natural environment as a system of beliefs, or as philosophical or ideological ethics, for only human decisions that tend to reinforce the external reality of humanist aspirations can be pronounced as truly worthwhile.

15

HUMANIST ART OF LOVING

"In a non-theistic system…The realm of love, reason and justice exists as a reality only because…man has been able to develop these powers in himself throughout the process of his evolution."

Erich Fromm

"It is an illusion to assume that one can separate life in isolated compartments: in love from life's other spheres. The capacity to love demands awakens and vitality, which can only be the result of one's humanist orientation in other spheres of life."

Unknown

This book's overall message is to show that ideals, emotions, sentiments, love, humility, courage and mental discipline all must be interconnected with their material opposite in order for a person to achieve a natural balance. One thing I can claim to be true is that the sentiment of love must not be separated from external realism, and that it must be both active and receptive at the same time. Thus, I would exclude idealism's distortion of the sentiment of "love" that one witnesses in movies, and in women's and men's magazines.

I wish to caution the reader who might be disappointed should you expect an instruction on "how-to" love or be loved. Rather, this brief analysis is on the dialectical concept of love.

Let's begin by stating that the dialectical description of love demonstrates how a man and a woman form a natural opposite. This balance of opposites is interconnected and interdependent in our human culture. A man and a woman create a unity of balance in support of each other. In the center of the sentiment of love lies its various branches–fatherly love, motherly love, brotherly and sisterly love, erotic love–which follow the patterns of many natural occurring opposites (balances): male and female, day and night, love and hate etc.

Based on the natural laws of nature, complementary opposites are also embedded within the greater humanistic whole. They constantly interact, as a natural balance of opposites, and never exist in a fixed or one-sided state. One essence of opposite is **receptive**, the other essence is **active,** and both are **inter-active** in an equilibrium state. This interaction of the two opposites provides "matter-in-motion" and change in dynamic equilibrium that applies to social structure, family values, judgment, morality, ethics, love, good and evil etc.

A one-sided extreme or fixed state will negate the natural balance of opposites. One-sided love can turn into hate; extreme good can be transformed into evil, etc. The natural balance of **receptive** is yielding, negative and nurturing. The qualitative balance of **active** is initiating, positive and creative.

These characteristics have a broad application in the natural and social world including love, the arts, natural science, and philosophy and life in general. In all, one can see the unity and interaction of natural opposites, such as order vs. freedom, reason vs. passion, strength vs. grace, gradual vs. sudden change etc.

There is permanence to the unity of opposites in the physical realm, as well as in story writing, which is both logical and passionate, or in a song which represents the **social** and **natural** structure of the real world. The sentiment of love is thus embedded in these essential receptive and active natural and social structures.

The first thing that comes to mind is the song *What a Wonderful World* by Louis Armstrong. Can you identify the active and receptive characteristics of the social and of the natural world?

> *I see trees of green...red roses too*
> *I see them bloom...for me and you*
> *and I think to myself...what a wonderful world*
>
> *I see skies of blue...clouds of white*
> *bright blessed days...dark sacred nights*
> *and I think to myself...what a wonderful world*
>
> *The colors of the rainbow...so pretty...in the sky*
> *are also on the faces...of people...going by*
> *I see friends shaking hands...saying...how do you do*
> *They're really saying...I love you*
>
> *I hear babies cry...I watch them grow*
> *They'll learn much more...than I'll ever know*
> *and I think to myself...what a wonderful world.*

As a cultural interactor, this song describes a social and natural environment where human relations are the gravitational primacy of the genuine natural sentiment of love. It also describes a sensual blooming and flowering of roses, whose natural quality of beauty gives great pleasure to the human senses. The song implies that human friendship really exists and bonds it to the materialist environment where babies, as the next generation, are both the biological (gene) carriers and the next cultural hosts in a wonderful world. This song does not "pollute" the realism of the physical/wonderful world with religious or secular imaginary, a non-existent and unidentifiable "world."

Whatever senses we humans experience, such as seeing, hearing, taste or touch, which derives from our natural world, must be in a dignified relationship of reciprocal mutual care. Our cognitive knowledge confirms that when we hear a song, read a book, visit a museum or attend live theatre, volunteer in a local hospital or library, maintain a clean environment, abstain from consuming pre-fabricated foods or conserve energy, these are cultural practices that promote ideas that should be transmitted to the next human generation.

Thus sentiments, emotions and feelings that are in their essence materialist are all mimetically related to the human race, regardless of cultural differences. This is a materialist sentiment of love that places "matter over mind," and in which perceptual images in our brain connect us to our natural world. This materialist sentiment enables us to witness beauty and sadness, human cultural and social achievements, and acknowledge the child who is growing free from religion in a secure social environment and free from the delusional wishes or phobias of idealism.

The lyrics of John Lennon's song, *Imagine* reflects materialist humanist sentiment:

Imagine there's no heaven
It's easy if you try
No hell below us
Above us only sky
Imagine all the people
Living for today...

Imagine there's no countries
It isn't hard to do
Nothing to kill or die for
And no religion too
Imagine all the people
Living life in peace...

You may say I'm a dreamer
But I'm not the only one
I hope someday you'll join us
And the world will be as one

Imagine no possessions
I wonder if you can
No need for greed or hunger
A brotherhood of man
Imagine all the people
 Sharing all the world

You may say I'm a dreamer
But I'm not the only one
I hope someday you'll join us
And the world will live as one

The lyrics, as language, serve as the product of materialist cultural sentiment that describes and prescribes earthly concepts in real and understandable ways. Materialist based sentiments, emotions, wishes, life's abstractions and hopefulness are all massively profound. These materialist sentiments promote and follow the life's basic clarity of human aspirations.

Materialist/humanist inspired basic activities follow a system of natural selection which is daily scrutinized in every corner of our cultural world, modifying or rejecting that which is harmful to humans, and preserving or increasing that which is harmonious to our social environment, whenever a cultural opportunity arises.

Social evolutionists, humanists and atheists need to devote part of their time and energy to promote the social benefits of the cognitive enhancement of love in its entirety. Love is a social activity and a sentiment (energy consuming and transplanting) which preserves humanist grounded inspirations. Such materialist based culture enhances an atheist and a humanist purpose of life. It actively promotes understandable arts, excellence instead of mediocrity, universality instead of localism, utilitarianism instead of elitism, poetry and books about the natural world, peace instead of war. Love as a social activity will free us from being *prisoners of our ideals*, for "ideals" are no more than wishful thinking which is based on delusions.

As many atheists and humanist social thinkers have said better than I could ever have say, we have an utmost responsibility to promote the concrete fact that we have one earthly home, and one earthly life. This undisputable fact needs to entice us to enhance the sentiment of love, as a social activity, that is based on the affirmation of life. Our social responsibility must include the support of victims of religious delusions, and help them to fill their "mental gap" by becoming materialist social thinkers. They can acquire cognitive knowledge of the social character of love and apply it to the human and natural environment.

Is there such an entity as the humanist art of loving? If there is, then love requires human energy and effort to form a premise that is based on cognitive knowledge. This means that the sentiment of love cannot only be experienced by chance. Love is an **active** and **receptive** inter-activity, for to love and be loved forms a unity of balance of opposites. It is a conscious activity that is shared by two opposites, not something which one metaphorically "falls into it." Should therefore the sentiment of love be based on material reality or on the delusion of idealism?

If love is regarded as art, then such an art should be learned like any other form of art–poetry, music, painting, reading, writing, storytelling, theatre, stage acting or sculpture. These arts require the active and receptive balance of a sentiment and a cognitive knowledge, along with practical skill that makes results possible. In materialist cultural reality, the art of loving is one's reciprocal capacity to create love and be loved. This is not a consumerist exchange value between two lovers. I am sure that I am not the only one who has experienced such an "exchange."

I was once invited to a popular outdoor café in Toronto, Canada, where three female friends and I shared the same table. At some point, their conversation turned to the subject and object of love. I say the "object of love" because they were describing their favourable "man" as one who had "megabucks," who was tall and handsome, successful and with a considerable social status.

Well into the conversation, they noticed that while I was still listening, I was not participating in their lively exchange. The truth is that I was fascinated by listening to what was so common for them. They were describing a "man" as an approved or discarded object before he could love or be loved. Noticing my silence, I was asked for my opinion. After repeating to them what I had understood to be their approved characteristics of an "object of love" I asked for their "exchange value" for having that "object of love." I simply asked them only two questions: *"In exchange for what?"* and *"What do you offer in return?"*

The silence that followed was deafening. They all looked at me as if I were from another planet. Some of them suggested that the exchange was being a "wife," while others pointed out the "virginal" exchange-value and that of being a "wife-mother." To be fair, this attitude is also common amongst some men in our society who are also looking for their own "market" exchange-value of their "object of love."

The humanist emotion of love, however, lies within the social functioning of the active and receptive equilibrium of the sentiment and its praxis. To practice this, one must be aware that the art of loving, as human life itself, is a cognitive activity. As a cultural and social activity, love has a dialectical relationship that reciprocates sentiment with humanist practice, for without this natural balance of opposites, the sentiment of love becomes a problem of faculty. I will explain:

We need to accept the scientific fact that men and women are products of their social and cultural environment. Delusional idealization of both sexes contrasts with their material reality, because an idealization is contrary to real cultural relations. Material reality of social or humanist relations always wins over any idealization or virtual reality. Placing any ideals, feelings or emotions alone **as a directional force** to find love conflicts with the external reality of the person who is about to reciprocate love and be loved.

For a man and a woman who are seeking to learn how to sustain a loving union is to understand and acknowledge the extent to which both idealize the other. Both man and woman must also cognitively accept that one's ideals or emotions–used as directional guidance–will not be able to live up to **that** idealization of love union. Attaining a love-union lies in the balance of the **active** and the **receptive** opposite to become a potential unity.

Love as a creative social activity unites one with another person who exists outside the idealization of him or herself.

Hence, the full sentiment of love lies in the propagation of interactive relationship, a fusion with another person, in love. What matters is that both men and women know what kind of interactive love-union they are referring to when they speak of love. Love is both a fundamental human passion and an interactive social relation. It is the kind of life-force that bonds human active and receptive opposites together, as the foundation of society. It is love which makes humanity capable of social and cultural functioning.

With a love relationship as an optional choice rather than as a necessity for survival, both men and women place love higher up in their personal as well as their cultural hierarchies of needs. Both sexes have come a long way to confirm that sexual and romantic unions, marriage and socio-financial needs can only be met when both do not project their idealization on the other. In the elegance of the reality of human love, mature romantic love is a union under the realization of preserving one's personal integrity, respect, and individuality, through which the sexes unite with each other, yet each retain their own characteristics with their interdependency of their love-union.

Love is an human artistically creative activity, an act of human capacity which can only be put into praxis when there is freedom from compulsion and delusion. As a social and cultural activity, the interactive character of romantic love can be described as an act of giving and receiving, as active and receptive natural opposites.

We must be careful here, for the term giving is not synonymous to giving up, being deprived of, sacrificing, or giving in exchange for receiving an "object-love" The social and romantic giving I refer to lies within the human expression of being fully alive, in the natural and complementary balance of unity of opposites.

The most important characteristic in the act of "giving-love," is not the necessity of giving goods and gifts, for love lies in the human realm, not in the realm of the "object-love." A loving person gives that which is alive in her person: in his joy, in her interest, in his understanding and dialectical cognitive knowledge, in her sense of humour or sense of sadness. These sentiments are all expressions which must be alive in one's person.

It is during the active giving of love that the opposite's receptive sense of being fully alive is enhanced. This implies that the giver of love is also the receiver of love, and both share the love-joy which brought them together. The reciprocity is based on the sentiment of trust for trust, love for love, confidence for confidence, joy for joy, honesty for honesty, dignity for dignity, respect for respect, integrity for integrity, care for care, and knowledge for knowledge. Such a romantic reciprocated giving/receiving love is also common to all other forms of care-love for lovers, for children, for neighbours, for grandparents and for the world's cultural and natural environment.

No one who seriously regards the materialist reality of love can offer a trivial recipe of "how-to" love. The praxis of love-giving is not a trivial prescription of "how-to do it yourself," whether the sentiment exists or not or whether it is shared or not by the other person. The praxis of the art of romantic love-giving should only be directed to another's existing sentiment of receptive love. Women's magazines and Internet sites provide trivial metaphorical recipes for instant love, attraction, the spark of magic-love, "chemistry," and ways to get men to "talk about their feelings." Those are ideals which magazines advise their readers to accept and in turn, try to impose upon the humanist realm of love.

Idealizing the humanist sentiment of love is not a realistic expectation that one should follow as a pre-condition to be imposed upon the other person. Ideals of "love" are delusional desires which disregard the natural unity of opposites, each with its own biological, social and cultural characteristics. To do otherwise is to have contempt for the social and cultural world, an unseeing desire to live in a mental delusion.

Reality demonstrates that all social relations are directly or indirectly attached to the persons who are an integral part of such a cultural process. In other words, no person or relationship exists in a void. The sentiment of love and caring relationships are also an integral part of a cultural and social life which involves two people, their families, their friends and associates etc. Within this social circle meaningful relationships begin with honest conversations leading to productive and genuine praxis within a family environment, business, friendships etc.

Conversations and activity should and must be relevant, provided that the persons experience what they are talking about, and do not treat love in a trivialized or idealized way. Avoiding trivial conversations is as important as avoiding trivial activities. Keeping relations with meaningless persons makes a clear statement about one's own person. The saying, *"Tell me whom you associate with, and I'll tell you who you are,"* holds true. Of course, it is not always easy to avoid a trivial person. However, responding directly and humanely will either change his/her behaviour or this person will leave you alone.

To be able to give and receive love requires courage, the ability to take risks, and the readiness to accept sadness. Anyone who is not willing to take a chance or who insists on safety and security as primary social conditions of life cannot give or receive love. Thus, whoever loves in an idealized system of thought, remains *a prisoner* of his/her ideals. To love and to be loved, to care and be cared for, to love more than your lover, to love life, the environment and all productive cultural expressions, requires courage. It is your kind of courage that judges certain human values as being of ultimate concern and takes the chance to stake everything you have on these human values.

The interactivity of love-giving begins with the small details of daily social and cultural life. It may begin with the love and care of an elderly person, a child, with love as a human trust, love of a poem, love of a meaningful activity, awareness and an alertness of the sentiment of love and the praxis of it. Lovers must link themselves beyond the candlelight dinner or a walk in the park to fulfil their sentiment of love-giving.

If all two lovers wish or want is to receive love, if each expect only to be loved, if each is waiting to be loved by the other, who then will know how to actively or receptively practice and give love? In other words, when lovers-to-be know the art of loving, then both will receive love from the other, rather than remain passive expecting to be loved. Indispensable for the sentiment of the art of loving is for a person not to be in doubt that he/she will be loved by someone. It is also imperative for a person to overcome the doubt of loving another, for to love another means that the sentiment of love must be realized in the active/receptive praxis of the other person's giving love. If the sentiment of love remains as an ideal-in-the-mind, then the fear or doubt of loving will dominate one's life, and thus one will remain of prisoner of his/her ideal. On the other hand, the active-praxis of the art of loving does not mean "doing something" regardless of whether the sentiment of love is not receptive, not reciprocated or is inactive.

It is also imperative that one's capacity to love be beyond his/her love, for the sentiment of love demands a state of energy, awareness, vitality, and an active involvement in various areas of cultural and social life. The humanist art of loving cannot be restricted to one's romantic realm. It must be interactive with social relations, as a loving and caring attitude towards friends, family and associates, within business ethics, and wherever the natural world needs one's care.

Cynical persons may regard these as being incompatible to the sentiment of love. In this idealistically driven world, the marketing of "ideals" is much more profitable when preaching that "true love" is the "inner-love," "inner-passion", "inner-consciousness," "inner sub-consciousness" or "inner-self" etc. All this promotes mental laziness because this axis of "inner-love" lacks its fundamental natural balance, the love activity that goes beyond one's mental ideals.

True enough, men and women capable of practicing the humanist art of loving, under our society's idealist system of thought, are necessarily a distinct minority. Not so much because others do not respond to their loving attitude, but because of the consumerist-driven social market exchange structure of "object-love." It is a recurring theme in the idealization of love, both sexual and romantic. In spite of all corporate marketing/advertising, women's "equality" is structured within the realm of **sameness** with men, although both sexes are different from one another. You may accuse me of being politically incorrect, and I am prepared to accept your criticism. But I also want to make it clear that I am a proponent of political, social and economic equality amongst men and women, within their unequal needs and their respective sphere of balanced unity of opposites.

The idealist desire for instant results is such that only a non-conformist humanist can reject it. Those who seriously advocate a dialectical system of thought as the rational balance of active and receptive love-giving need a good deal of personal latitude. Our social and cultural reality demonstrates that the humanist art of love-giving must be practiced beyond the individual lover. The art of loving must be promoted into the socio-cultural realm, where the sentiment of love will be activated by a wide expression of dialectical mimesis, beyond one's unity of the balance of opposites.

With both sexes, the idealization of love is restricted or confined within the mental faculty of the sentiment. Women tend to spend a lot of time idealizing romance and wondering *"What could he be thinking?"* which puts them on a mental roller-coaster. In return, men tend to sexually idealize women in body, dress, and body movement and in the "image" of sexual encounter. Both modes of idealized thinking are used as directional forces, and are imposed upon the physical reality of the opposite sex. Thus, our idealization of potential romantic alliances is occurring more and more rapidly. By the time of the "walk in the park" or "candlelight dinner," both potential partners' ideals of sex/romance have being projected on the other.

Let's look at the makeup of both sexes as complementary natural opposites characteristics:

A woman is biologically:

- **Receptive** - as an interactive natural opposite;
- **Negative** - meaning refusal or denial
- **Yielding** - give cause to happen
- **Nurturing** - the act of bringing up

A man is biologically:

- **Active** - as an interactive natural opposite
- **Positive** - meaning presence of particular qualities
- **Initiating** - introducing something new
- **Creative** - inventive and risk taking

Metaphorically speaking, a woman represents the essence of life. Man represents the force of life. Both carry a reciprocal quality of the other's essential qualities. One must note that those qualities are not fixed or exclusively one-sided, but are interconnected and interrelated dialectically to the other.

The degree of quantity/quality in each opposite would depend on input by the social/cultural conditions in which both the man and the woman live. A woman who seeks to learn about love actively must take on the principle of *"first thing first"* as a priority, in that she must truly understand the quality/quantity of the *essence of her receptiveness*. Based on the characteristics of her receptiveness, she must also understand and acknowledge the degree to which she may idealize a man.

The biological and social reality of men confirms the fact that **most** men cannot deal with the "task" of "talking about their feelings." This is a receptive ability, mostly a woman's characteristic, in which they are able to express their most intimate feelings. Women's projection of or insistence on **sameness** in men is to ignore men's *essence of activeness*. While men may take the "task" of talking about their feelings, it is nevertheless not essential, other than as a task. With that in mind, we must now answer the question: *"Can men talk about their feelings?"* The answer is a qualified "Yes," because it is for them a task, a project, something to be done when it is **required** of them. But the fact that men are not receptive to easily expressing their feelings at will is not a shortcoming, or a default of men's biological make-up. The overwhelming pressure from female romantic-idealization of men only increases the friction between them, in the balance of natural opposites.

Men and women need to recognize two fundamental characteristics in both sexes: men are visually-responsive and women are acoustically-responsive towards their natural opposites. The visual vs. acoustical characteristics are complementary opposites. When a woman and a man are united in a romantic union, the **visual** and the **acoustical** natural opposites form a **unity** of opposites. Thus, they also form the desired balance between these opposites. They depend on the active and receptive balanced interaction between these two essences.

Women need to realize that men may not talk about their feelings at the same level women can do, but this does not mean that men do not care. The man a woman loves is the same man not just as a lover, but he is also a leader, a provider, a teacher and a protector of his family's safety. At the same time, a woman is the same woman even though her romantic expectations do change as she adopts the role of mother or as she gets older. These changes are naturally occurring because both men and women are an integral part of natural change (matter-in-motion), as active/receptive partners within the sentiment of love.

The dialectical analysis of romance and sex provides both men and women with an opportunity to balance the opposites of activity and receptiveness in love. This opportunity can provide a better understanding by not idealizing who we are and who our partner is. Now both man and woman can recognize that each alone cannot ensure the success of a love relationship or marriage without the effort of adjusting their individual idealization and personal expectations of the other. Both need to recognize that the idealization of any concept or situation is simply a distortion of reality. By idealizing "something," it does not make "it" better or worse.

As a woman adjusts her own idealized expectations during and through the initial period of love-relationship, it does not diminish her sentiment of love. On the contrary, it helps to solidify the sentiment of her love into the external reality of her natural opposite. It makes communication easier by relating to what a man and a woman need from each other. Both need to know that a romance between a man and a woman does not have to include "love of suffering," pain or torment to make the love affair as exciting as "love" is projected in Hollywood movies and in women's magazines.

Instead, romance between two natural opposites must place its emphasis on change, not on static or fixed stereotypes. That is what the sentiment of love is not. It is not a mere mental image which can be "packaged" as a "love-object" and "labelled" into something fixed, immutable and inactive. Instead, the multifaceted sentiment of love must be appreciated as how it changes as activity and as sentiment—as unity of opposites.

This also means that this unity of opposites in love situations is the main directional force to what is going on now and what is likely to change.

It starts by recognizing how the existence of natural opposites–whether man/woman or in nature—depend on one another. In our natural world, this means that each person of a polar opposite seems to need the other to make it what it is. It would make no sense to talk about woman's love if it does not relate to man's love in that interaction. One-sided gravitational leaning would form a counter-balance that would really start to show that love is related to hate, for there is some hate in every love, and some love in every hate. This natural principle is evident in the natural world as there is light in every darkness, and darkness in every light, as day follows night, and as night follows day. To recognize such a balance of natural opposites frees both lovers from the "either-or" which can be fixed, short and oppressive.

An active-receptive love relationship is a natural balance, but now we need to talk about the potential extremes, the one-sided leaning in some love situations. To take an opposite to its ultimate extreme is to make it absolute, fixed, and sterile, for it would actually turn it into its opposites love turns into hate. Thus, if a loved-one makes his/her love absolute, it turns to hate-love (fatal attraction), which cannot interconnect with the reality of the other person. If both take love in its one-sided absolute, they are equally blinded, for they are unable to enjoy what they have.

This is an ever-present situation where both man and woman idealize love to its extreme and turn it into hate (its opposite). So, if both lovers take the sentiment of love to its extreme, by idealizing it, the whole love relationship depends completely on one or the other person. In turn, if one lover takes hate to its extreme, and thus idealizes it, one lover becomes morbidly dependent on the other lover. In both cases, their whole existence of love-giving is negated.

A good metaphorical symbolism of the unity and balance of natural opposites is the Chinese philosophy of Yin-Yang, the symbol of Taoism. Within the round symbol, each half shows the interdependence of opposites, and each half is defined by the contours of the other half. Thus, the unity of opposites is shown by the circular line surrounding the symbol, which in itself symbolizes the achievement of total unity, the serenity in and through all of life's opposites. Of course, after all, this Yin-Yang symbol is just that, a symbol, not a comprehensive dialectical analysis.

The lessons of dialectical opposites in love-giving need to be studied and taken into consideration for the moral, social and cultural values we practice. They too, if held to their extremes (one-sided), will become delusions. If one takes a "side" and excludes its opposite, the external social and cultural reality will forcefully include it. This means that personal and family relationships, social and cultural relationships, sentiments, ideals, emotions, delusions and illusions, expectations and desires, are realistically doomed to failure, if held to their absolute extreme. One must remember that the only emotional or sentimental values which are truly harmonious, stable—but not fixed—and coherent are those that include/recognize their opposite, rather than excluding.

How then can we actually use dialectical thinking in dealing with or as the natural balance of opposites in love, family and in other aspects of our daily life? *"First Thing First."* One must recognize that dialectical thinking is close to everyday life. True enough, dialectics is not as simplistic as idealism is, nor does it invent concepts that are limited to delusional thoughts. Dialectics is evident and ever-present when dealing with the everyday social, cultural and personal external reality of life. Humanist inclusion of love, personal and social relations shows that we all can use dialectical thinking in community and voluntary activities, social functions, cooking or eating, studying, reading or writing. However, our daily life is guided by "gate-posts" of activity-thoughts processed for best outcome. These are:

- **Do not take your pre-conceived ideas as a directional force:** Do not trust what you believe, for beliefs may be ingrained categories of fixation, rigid "ought to be" or "should-be's" that distorts and conceals reality and stop you from seeing the world as it actually is. In fact, our beliefs are the greatest obstacles to clear perception. The further you can focus away from your pre-conceived beliefs (perfect-love, ideal-man, and ideal-woman), the more dialectical external conclusions you can let in.

- **Change in the unity of opposites can be harmonious:** It is up to you to set your life's priority or direction on the basis of *First Things First*. Spontaneity is a paradox which may or may not be conclusive, but one can let it go when it is required.

- **Qualitative and quantitative changes of opposites:** This dialectical process states that when you add things or ideas on side of one of the opposite, this addition eventually arrives at something quite different, thus quantity (additions) changes the quality (original state of an opposite). Whether this change from quantity to quality is positive or negative it often brings more pronounced concepts or events into the other opposite. Adding more onto one side can transform an idea into a concept or a simple circumstance into a set of complex circumstances. As such, new vision may appear that must be tested with external reality.

- **Avoid pre-conceived ideas, beliefs and routine behaviour:** Breaking the pattern of fixation is not an easy task. We are daily bombarded by this or that idealized propagation in a mimetic transmission of fixed patterns of thought and behaviour. Women's and men's magazines, Internet sites, advertising of all sorts push the belief of consumption of unnecessary wants etc. These entice us to adopt a routine in eating time, driving in the same routes, repeated patterns of dressing, sitting in the same seat on the train or bus, getting up or going to bed at the same time, job routine, monotonous love behaviour or having an "order-in-life."

In addition, if is a one-sided extreme opposite, with no change, unity or balance of its other opposite. It is a slow "sterilization" of personal behaviour that is not related to external reality as matter-in-motion. Avoiding changes (matter-in-motion) in these cases decreases choices in our lives. Being both responsible and spontaneous, a balance of opposites, at the same time is the main practical application of dialectics in your aim to break the fixation or routine of your personal behaviour. This means that taking responsibility for your actions is choosing a healthy direction for your life.

- ❖ **Avoiding stereotypes:** Equally damaging in human relations is the perpetuation of stereotypes, whether a stereotype is of racial or ethnic profiling, traditional masculine or feminine roles, or new trends in social culture. Closely related to this factor is the transformation of human behaviour into *consumerist* behaviour based on the idea of love-relation as a mutually favourable "object-love" exchange. In this case, men and women look at each other as the prize-package they are after. Thus "attractive" becomes a nice package of attractiveness which is popular and sought after on the "personality" market. For a woman, a "tall man" is someone that is over 6' feet tall, yet statistics show that in the US only 14% of men are over 6' tall. In turn, for a man, the attractiveness of a woman depend on the fashion of the time, physically as well as mentally.

MEN AND WOMEN AS COMPLEMENTARY NATURAL OPPOSITES

In the biological sexual and romantic relationship between women and men, women hold a greater selective power in choosing a sexual partner and when sex should take place. Having said that, in our western culture sex takes place very rapidly between potential couples. From school age to adulthood, men spend less time performing their "love-song" or "love-dance" and competing with other men for women's attention. Our cultural trend has made women more sexually available to men, which is part of their sexual liberation.

In turn, a woman also spends less time evaluating the personal traits and potential compatibility of a man before engaging in sex with him. Our cultural trend has separated the act of sexual selection from the act of active and receptive love. Both men and women have adopted this new cultural trend as a way of evaluating each other's worth after sex. For a woman, if the man calls the next day, this is an act upon which a woman's hope may be based for potential receptive love selection. This is where a woman's base of female power lies. Therefore, sex is used as a means of making a potential love selection rather than the object of conquest.

Due to cultural differences, this new innovation is less observable in the Latin American and Asian cultures where the emphasis on "love-dance" is promoted through love songs, extensive TV soap-operas, distinct cultural roles for women and men, and man's romantic role as *conquistador*. This is a continuation of the biological power inherent in the nature of woman's sexual selection. It permits a woman to delay sexual favours in order to evaluate the man's worth, something that in western cultures women have relinquished in recent decades.

Humanist values maintain that it is up to the women to consider whether they have surrendered this natural power lightly. It requires a balance in the dialectical unity of natural opposites—sexual selection vs. love selection—in order to arrive into a positive conclusion i.e., natural balance.

In order to achieve this natural balance, both sexes can evaluate their biological opposites, which may assist them to unite, and thus, not end up lonely. What then will work? In purely biological terms, both sexes can let nature speak to them loudly here, rather than pseudo-moralizing the value of sexual behaviour. It is important for both to remember that during this stage of love, the primary objective is to select a partner, not a "one night stand."

For a man this means doing whatever it takes to attract the woman's attention and trigger her receptive-love and hormonal inclination. It is not unusual that during this initial stage, the man will do his best to make the woman happy (within reason). At this stage, a woman will try to get the man to perform his "song and dance" without sex as an object of seduction. If and when this stage is encouraged by both sexes, a unity of opposites will emerge without balance. This means that during the initial stage of a relationship, the balance is less solidified if this first emotion of sexual selection is not utilized by the woman.

Love selection and sexual selection must form the unity of opposites, so that a natural balance between sex/romance will gradually emerge. Extreme one-sided balance on one opposite—far too long of a "song and dance" period without sexual intercourse, or far too long purely sexual encounter without the sentiment of love–will negate the natural balance between its two natural opposites. For example, if a woman exceeds the romance time but withholds sexual intercourse, even though she may enjoy oral sex and other fun games, this would lean the balance of opposites to its one-sided extreme.

I am not saying that a female who does not engage in sexual intercourse during the romance stage will necessarily be emotionally hurt by the man. I am stating honestly about the cultural trends of our western world. *An exception to the rule is always present.* Countless well-adjusted women experience personal hurt in their short sexual encounters with men. This emotional hurt can be somewhat reduced and self-confidence restored if the man's "song and dance" during sexual and love encounters is controlled by the woman rather than by the man.

The withholding, however, may have something to do with the woman's self-image of her body or self-esteem, which prevents her from reaching her potential sexual maturity. When the balance of the unity of opposites is achieved, a consenting man and a woman may engage in oral sex, and other sexual options which are useful for the female during the romance stage of the relationship. Adults who engage in consenting sexual experimentations enrich their relationship by avoiding monotonous sexual behaviour. Both are behaving in a responsible and playful way at the same time, thus forming a new dialectical balance of unity of spontaneity and responsibility.

Now I can speak to my female readers, not as an intellectual, but as a biological male who is sexually healthy. If and when you fall in love with a man, do create a sense of mystery. Listen to him and watch him and see what kind of a man he is. Learn to like him, not instantaneously, but gradually. Learn to like him for his short comings, so long as those short comings are not directed against you personally. Above all, remain aware of your romantic "ideal" of him. At the time of your choosing, if you are still in love with him, and you feel a controlled anticipation, give him **nearly** all, but **not** all, and still retain some for yourself (as a balance of opposites). Tilt the balance at will–sometimes towards him…other times towards yourself.

As most men, I am not shy or submissive. It is because of my natural aggression that I need to unite and balance it with my natural opposite, a non-aggressive female. For example, the "bitch" is not my natural opposite. A man of my natural make-up would want to love my natural opposite rather than an image of her that is contrary to the unity of complementary opposites. If I wanted to create a sexual idealization of her, the principle of balance of opposites would be distorted and negated.

Like most western-oriented educated men, I am a supporter of women's equal power in the work place, in education, in the media, in romance and sexual pleasure, and everywhere women seek to apply their intelligence and skills without having to give up their equal intimate status at home. I do not want to maintain just an intimate separation of sameness. Having said that, I would find it very difficult to romance and love a highly aggressive female who has, in essence, the same natural aggressiveness as me, and simply "put-up" with an intimate separation of sameness.

For a non-aggressive man who prefers a sedentary life, an aggressive woman would provide a better chance for him to enter into a romance and sex. Since both are two natural opposites—aggressive vs. non-aggressive—they form a unity of opposites.

It is imperative to remember that a man or a woman's natural aggressiveness is not a controlling, dominating or oppressive characteristic, for those are the natural opposites of **submissive vs. dominance**. Only a weak person needs to be controlled or dominated and a dominant person to be oppressive and dominant upon another, in order to bypass his/her own weakness. These are the people who call their partners insulting names, full of sexual ostracisms and mockery. Only a dominant "bitch" will go out and conquer the submissive man who prefers a sedentary life, a life of nurture, children and emotional domestication. I also want to make it clear, that it is common today to see dominant women doing "their thing" and by no means am I moralising the "good" or "bad" of natural opposites in men or women. My aim is not to teach the reader about love, for this is beyond the scope of this brief presentation.

My aim is to demonstrate the validity of the dialectical concept of the natural unity of opposites that, is present in the natural environment, in social, cultural and personal settings, and in the biological and botanical world. Luckily, I understand and acknowledge the usefulness and social practicality of dialectical-materialism. Both men and women have the ability to take charge of our lives and learn how not to become *"prisoners of our ideals."*

Both men and women can also discover the value of non-aggressiveness when it is needed, as is also advocated by the Chinese philosophy of the Yin-Yang symbol. It advocates that not every biological condition is so ingrained in our natural make-up that we cannot act to the contrary. Both men and women can be happier and have a greater understanding of their biological traits, and still turn these traits into romantic partnerships. We can be in charge of our emotions, commitments and passions with dialectical reason and in balance with our natural opposites.

In the 1993 novel *Correlli's Mandolin,* by Louis de Bernieres, one of the main characters, Dr. Iannis, speaks to his daughter Pegalia who is madly in love with Captain Antonio Corelli:

"Love is a temporary madness, it erupts and then subsides. When it subsides you have to make a decision. You have to work out whether your roots have grown so intertwined that it is inconceivable that you should ever part. Love is not breathlessness; it is not the promulgation of promises of eternal passion. It is not the desire to mate every second minute of the day, it is not lying awake at night imagining that he is kissing every cranny of your body, that is being [idealized] in

love, which any fool can do. Love itself is what is left over when being in love has burned away...[lovers] who had roots that grew towards each other underground, and when all the blossoms had fallen from [their] branches [they] found that [they] were one tree [unity of opposites], not two."

We all have to recognize that the sentiment of love is related to our biological traits, and that understanding the relationship between our sentiments and traits is the key to finding and promoting the balance of the dialectical unity of opposites. We no longer need to be *"prisoners of our ideals."*

16

A DIALECTICALLY SECULAR SOCIETY

"First they came for the drug addicts, and I did not speak out–because I was not a drug addict;
They came for the working poor, and I did not speak out–because I was not a working poor;
They came for the non-conformists, and I did not speak out–because I was not a non-conformist;
Then they came for the illegal immigrants, and I did not speak out–because I was not an illegal immigrant;
Then they came for me, and there was no one left to speak out for me."

Unknown

"A man's ethical behaviour should be based effectively on sympathy, education and social ties; no religious basis is necessary. Man would indeed be in a poor way, if he had to be restrained by fear of punishment and hope of reward after death."

Albert Einstein

I am convinced that any social theory that is separated from the reality of a layperson's daily life is restricted to the intellectual elites or it is meaningless. Secularism is the topic to which I turn in this final section. However, I want to avoid staying within the common definition of secularism, which simply mean that religion be kept out of politics and affairs of state.

Dialectical secular thinking means to shake off the fears of delusional servile beliefs and attitudes, under which most of us today function. For instance, while our society has advanced technological process that has improved our daily lives–at least in the western world–our intellectual cognitive knowledge has not advanced to the extent. True enough, our scientific discoveries have increased many-fold. But we still spin-off countless elaborate philosophical ideologies to entice us to follow delusional beliefs of primitive cults set five thousands years ago. It is a testimony to our continue limitation as social beings. Also, we still talk about invisible entities and use them as a directional force and thinking tool in our lives. More than two hundred years ago, one of the Founding Fathers of America, Thomas Jefferson stated:

"To talk of immaterial existences is to talk of nothings. To say that the human soul, angels, god, are immaterial, is to say they are nothings, or that there is no god, no angels, no soul. I cannot reason otherwise...without plunging into the fathomless abyss of [delusions], dreams and phantasms. I am satisfied, and sufficiently occupied with the things which are, without tormenting or troubling myself [with existence of entities]... of which I have no evidence."

How is it then that the richest and most technologically advanced country in the world, which was by and large founded by secular leaders, is now the most fanatically Christian religious country? Is it because Americans are less intelligently educated than the British people who are the least religious? Americans of the Right are not secularist. They are not different than any other Christian believer living in Christendom. They hold a political position as fixed as their religious beliefs. They hold onto an invisible and powerful entity called God or Christ, and use this like a powerful weapon. God's or Christ's name is used to instill fear of "others" who are guided by reason, wisdom and rationality. They form a social body which is guided **not** by a set of political solutions of the day, but by a slew of the *apolitical riff-raff* gathered from marginal groups.

If one is racist, anti-abortionist, anti-gay, anti-immigrant, anti-labour unionist, anti-secularist, anti-"big" government, survivalist, morally righteous, creationist, and so on, this person has limited choices of support other than joining a marginal group forming the Right. As such, they try to force local, state/federal government leaders into following their religious or moral convictions. They become angry when a legislator refuses to endure their threats by withholding money or votes. The name *conservatism* has become meaningless because it is an all inclusive term that embodies anything that is reactionary or "anti."

Precisely because American institutions are legally secular, religion has all the characteristics of free market enterprise, no different than the ancient Greek or Egyptian Temples. In the Middle Ages, the Catholic Church was also noted for selling "forgiveness" papers called *indulgences*. The argument was based on the notion that if a believer did a good work, or suffered a sudden death, or forgot to confess a crime or sin, he/she could be sold "confession insurance" against eternal damnation. Priests argued that they had inherited an unlimited amount of pending good works. They needed money towards them and credit for these good works could be sold to the believers in the form of indulgences. Later, the sale of indulgences spread to include sins of believers who were already dead.

Today, rival churches compete for affluent congregations and fat donations with the aggressive hard-sell methods prevalent in the "anything-goes" marketplace. The hard-sell techniques of the televangelists–selling a made-to-order miracle or a salvation–resemble the delusion of, *"The more you spend the more you save,"* or *"the more money you give to the church, the closer you are to God."*

What works in the advertising industry also works for God, and this has resulted in the mass deception of the vulnerable, the insecure, the less-educated working persons and inner-city inhabitants. These people embrace anything that makes them feel more secure and offer an avenue to express their anger.

Religious leaders have **no** scruples about abusing people, corrupting and exploiting them, spreading fear among them, all in the name of wealth accumulation, power and control. They sell God as a product similar to companies selling detergent or second-hand cars. The good works they perform refer to their own schools that indoctrinate the next generation of devoted believers, their selected "spiritual" TV shows and movies, talk shows and the selling of religious products. If the story of merchants in the King Solomon Temple is true, the religious marketers have a long established method of selling religious products. Today, they simply have developed new market avenues.

How then can both humanists and atheists lay the foundations to a genuinely social rather than a theistic social structure? Let me first elaborate this point by stating in clear terms to my readers that any atheist worldview cannot justify restrictions on our freedom of speech! We cannot restrict social, cultural and literary traditional expression in our educational system. Nor can we restrict *naive* religious rituals such as baptisms, funerals, marriages or other *harmless* traditions, historically related to theistic beliefs. A humanist atheist society cannot function under a fixed secular ideological blueprint that causes the limitation or elimination of humanity's inheritance. These points are just social "goal posts" upon which my focus would be concentrated.

Let's briefly note some of the difficulties present day atheists face regarding their socio-political position. To begin with, most atheists publicly declare themselves as agnostics. This is their "comfort-zone" social area, avoiding family shunning and discomfort among close neighbors. I personally have encountered these difficulties in my own life with family members and people who were friendly to me, when I declared myself an atheist. In the work place, openly declared atheists may face social isolation or lack of promotion if they are employed by a right-wing religious employer, or if their co-workers are devout Christians.

When one is visiting some of the North American "Bible-Belt" areas, one can witness that God is ever-present in a whole host of social and cultural practices–not just in the political level of these communities. Indeed, it is virtually impossible for a socially-conscious atheist to win a public election in North America. Under these circumstances most atheists running for public office are forced to conceal their true atheist identity in order to get elected. No one should blame them, for given the mentality of the electorate they have to convince, what choice do atheists have? It is widely accepted that a public admission of being an atheist would bring about instant political downfall for any political candidate. I remember when political candidate Barak Obama, running for President in 2008, referred to some "gun-toting" people as "holding on to their religion and guns" as a way of living. I am not sure of what to make of this statement, for I have no additional evidence to support any assumption, that he is a "closeted-atheist."

My point is what kind of world atheists might achieve if they too organized themselves properly?

- ❖ They could use similar strategy and tactics as other minorities who have achieved near parity of their social goals. Today, discrimination against sexual orientation in hiring, promotion, housing, etc., can now be legally challenged.

- ❖ The same civil laws must apply to the atheist minority.
- ❖ Atheist legal experts should be sought out to volunteer their services.
- ❖ Legal challenges would be advanced on the basis of the atheist's freedom of speech, guaranteed by most western societies.
- ❖ Strategies could be set to promote *agnosticism* in public education starting at the elementary level.
- ❖ Children's picture-books promoting *agnosticism* could be widely available in public libraries.
- ❖ Socially conscious psychologists should advocate the prevention of mental-illness caused by religion on children and adults.
- ❖ Atheists should seek the elections or appointments of local school-board trustees to advocate agnosticism as part of the educational curriculum.
- ❖ Privately-funded atheist schools of high scientific educational quality should be established and supported by local humanist and atheist associations in large and mid-size cities. Their members should be contacted for monthly financial support and their own children should they sent to these schools.
- ❖ Financial contributions could be sought-out through known atheist entertainers and other public figures.
- ❖ Public or privately funded non-commercial TV stations could hold interviews with scientists, biologists and atheist social thinkers to promote *agnosticism*. Fund-raising could

be promoted through such establishments to cover various agnostic public educational programs.

I want to turn our brief attention to the issue of publicly-funded schools. Catholic religious schools, for instance, are funded through federal and local educational budgets. Other religious schools are run by Protestant, Hindu, and Muslim in which children are educated from a very early age. They are probably privately funded as a way to preserve their cultural and linguistic diversity.

My objection to religious-run schools is in the *labeling* of children, **not** in their cultural diversity. Children are described as "Catholic," "Protestant," "Muslim," or "Hindu," from an early age, before they are able to make up their own minds on what they think about religion. My objection is in defense of children, not for setting up a cultural censorship on parents. Yet, the contradiction between parent's freedom of speech and the prevention of children's indoctrination needs to be addressed.

My dialectical principle of First Things First sets a priority in defense of children. *Nothing is absolutely absolute and parent's freedom of speech is not an absolute right!* While parents have the right to determine for their children their moral education of what is true or false, or right or wrong, they do not have the right to cripple their children's minds with the falsehoods of religion.

Genuine civic rights, like freedom of speech, have always been rooted in the humanist value system. It is not a "divinely-given" right to limit children's cognitive knowledge in a cloud of dogma and superstition.

Choosing children's rights over parent's rights regarding freedom of speech is not an exception to the rule. Parents are not as vulnerable as children are, for the gravitational balance between them is in favor of the adults. In short, the dialectical balance of opposites must lean towards the children's rights, balanced by parent's rights to their cultural identity–not in favor of the narrow paths of their own religious faith. This leads to children's indoctrination of *what to believe and* **not** *how to think!* Religious parents have the right to take their Qur'an, Torah or Bible literally, not metaphorically. That is their privilege. But do they have the right to withhold their children's exposure to all scientific evidence–even though such evidence may contradict their own beliefs?

Dialectical education should be seen as a way of understanding the world, not seeing it as a collection of things but as naturally (matter) evolving process. Nature cannot be understood as fixed and isolated collections of things, without seeing that the planted seed is a transitory stage of an ongoing process which turns it into a cedar tree, or observing the caterpillar turning into a butterfly. In the dialectics of nature, such processes are opposing forces in reality–which is internal and inherent– whose unity of opposites produces a synthesis or a metamorphosis.

On the social and cultural level, it is important:

❖ to start children's education in a positive way so they can recognize and learn about their own connections with the real external world.

❖ to use the *literal* rather than the *metaphorical* meaning of words.

I have probably said enough in this book to convince the reader of the value of critical dialectical thinking in analyzing nature and social reality.

A secularist society is not a utopian society where everyone can live happily ever after! It is not built on the ideals of metaphorical wonders–that is, a secular egalitarian society. It is based on the *humanist pedagogy of social praxis*. This cannot be mere academics, for humanists, secularists and atheists actually practice the dialectical theory of praxis.

For instance, we cannot theorize about the perils of our biological and botanical life on earth without taking action on the level taken by Greenpeace organizers and other environmental groups. In other words, we could not merely write or talk about the *theory* of secularism or social pedagogy without dialectically balancing it to its natural opposite, *social praxis*.

- ❖ It is with the latter conception that we atheists must align ourselves and from which point we must begin to contribute to the realm of social education translated into social praxis.

- ❖ This must include feminist, race and ethnic contributions.

- ❖ This should be revealed with modest language that expresses truths that cannot be too certain–otherwise "truths" would turn into dogma.

- ❖ Atheists, secularists and humanists must take a social stand–without displaying social arrogance–and must openly declare that we do not hold a monopoly on wisdom, and that our position is **not** the only position with no other possible recourse. Unity of dialectical opposites of Social Praxis with Social Theory means *Matter over Mind*.

It now seems appropriate that we should also deal with the concept known as *The Gap*. What does it mean that secularists, and in particular atheists, need to fill a much referred to "Gap"?

Does it refer to a God-meme in the brain which needs to be filled after it has been replaced? But what is this new "something" that would replace the God-meme which has been embedded in the human brain for thousands of years? Does this "something" have to be a singular or variable meme? Evidence suggests that throughout human history, religious metaphorical beliefs, in one form or another, have fulfilled basic human needs. For the purpose of clarity the concept of "Gap" will here be divided into two opposites: that of the religious-seeking Gap against science and the need for atheists fill that Gap.

The religious concept of the Gap is an unscientific term which advocators use; that is, their premise is based on ignorance. They seek to find any gap existing in present-day sciences, personal knowledge or understanding, in order to fill it with God's divine mind or power. It is a theological strategy that turns an apparent gap into a sense of doubting in the mind of anyone seeking a scientific explanation.

It begins in a normal conversation with people of opposite views by introducing the question *"How do you know that God did not create man."* This is obviously a "dead-end" question because one cannot prove or disprove something that does not exist. But what is apparent is that the Gap between faulty religious claims and scientific explanation shrinks at the advance of scientific knowledge. This will hold true regardless of scientific evidence yet to be discovered. It is also true that theologians fear that as the sciences advance, they threaten not only God's hiding place, but also the whole set of religious fallacies that have been promoted by exulting in ignorance and primitive superstition.

What can secularists and atheists do to contravene the bad effects religion has when teaching that it is a virtue to satisfy one's beliefs with something that one does not understand? How can we contravene and unite against the populist religious ignorance of "Gap-theology?" An ongoing debate between evolutionary scientists and creationists might be useful, but I personally think that atheists should explore another level: the pedagogy of social praxis.

Let me sidetrack for a moment before I expand further on the pedagogy of social praxis. In 2007 and again in 2008, I stood at the mountain top of the Inca capital of Machu Picchu. A week before my first visit, I happened to spend some time at the natural wonder on the Canadian side of Niagara Falls. In both places the emotions I felt were focused on life, human culture and the geo-botanical processes. Being a perpetual thinker, I discovered that the object of my reflections and my innate tendency to focus on the reality of things distinguished the *literal* from the *metaphorical* explanations of such awesome places.

My literal definition of such awesome places can be summarized by a single word: geo-philia (Greek for the "Love of the Earth"). The geo-cultural structure of the city of Machu Picchu and the physical evidence left behind by the Incas, generated *a real sentiment of reflection* about the diversity of their cultural geo-philia. I say diversity, because the culture of the Incas was both positive and negative, religious human-sacrifices committed there. On the positive side, their pedagogy of *literal* social praxis educated them to be successful in performing brain surgeries, as well as the construction of irrigation systems used to meet both domestic and agricultural needs.

On the other hand, the *literal* reality of the awesomeness of Niagara Falls can be easily distinguished from any *metaphorical* conception of it, which is mere illusion. That much was clear to me. However, a great deal more needs to be added. My human existence is fulfilled by the literally physical sentiment of geo-philia.

Modern science has produced a genuine new way of looking at the wonders of the physical world. Observing what was before me, my human sentiment was aligned with dialectical reasoning. The conclusion I draw from the above is positive, to the degree that I came to understand my human bond with other species and with my own species, and to place a greater value on it. In this sense, there is no room for metaphorical illusion, for such an attempt would most definitely distort the literal sentiment of geo-philia.

As stated above, atheists need to fill the Gap by first and foremost educating our species on the literal value of the sentiment of geo-philia. This is the core essence of the pedagogy of social praxis. We must be careful here, for the pedagogy of social praxis is not a metaphysical or philosophical theory. It does not scholastically reinvent the sentiment of geo-philia, for the rich geo-environment of the natural world has existed long before humans appeared in it. Nor do we need to "beautify" our world in metaphorical terms, for our natural world is *literally beautiful*. Atheists, secularists and humanists comprise a pedagogical body of social praxis that the rest of the population can benefit from it.

We must speak, write and present our social programs in as *literal* terms as possible. We can express our most sincere sentiments using literal terms as much as possible, as I have tried using them in the above brief description of Niagara Falls and Machu Picchu. In fact, I am certain that I have avoided using the term "I believe" in this book in order to maintain clarity of statements: that "I believe" is not a literal or factual substitute for the term "I think."

If literal terms do not pervade language, and the literal use of language does not pervade our thinking processes, then we are led into illusions. Metaphorical or figurative terms lead to "remarkable ideals" that have distorted implications of how we literally or factually view the world.

Pedagogy of social praxis *explains* in literal terms our existence in the natural world. In explaining this relationship to our children–with literal terms supporting geo-philia–their knowledge of the natural world becomes positive. It is the Darwinian deep understanding of geo-philia which teaches us and our children that the natural world is the original territory of biology and botanical life. This would intrigue them as well as raise their understanding, and give them something with which to surprise their parents. This is one of the greatest gifts we atheists, secularists and humanists can bestow on the next generation of children. It is freedom *from* religion. It is this Gap that needs to be dialectically filled, by explaining natural selection in simple literal terms.

Pedagogy of social praxis focuses on geo-philia which includes the straightforward explanation of moral social behavior. Again, humanist social behaviour is not a metaphysical, philosophical or metaphorical ideal. Moral social behaviour is a literal, not a figurative, concept. Above all, it is **not** a metaphorical instruction of how one "ought" to behave because, as a literal rule, we *instinctively know how to morally behave.*

What gives us the powerful sentiment of compassion to contribute to a food-bank, help earthquake or tsunami victims, donate money or clothes, help a car accident victim, and give blood to a blood bank? Are these social practices humanist? Can a secularist or an atheist be a morally social person? Pedagogy of moral social praxis draws its inspiration from our natural animal ecosystem, of which humans are an integral part.

Survival of the species is an instinct and an altruistic sentiment directing us to help our own kind. There are indeed circumstances in which a soldier would endanger his/her own life to save another's or throw a lifeline to save someone from drowning. In nature we see elephants forming a protective perimeter around a newborn, regardless of who are the real parents.

We need to demonstrate to our children that morality and love are literal reciprocal altruisms. They work because we share a mutuality of relationships with the essence of the natural animal world.

It should also be pointed out that there are always exceptions to the rule, for there are those who take but do not give when their turn comes. Other cynics may say that at times, "no good deed shall go unpunished." The first thing to say in response to this cynical statement should need no saying. Religion threatens its own believers with God's divine punishment. Anyone, even those who do good deeds, or give large amounts of money, still fear they are far from divine immunity. Atheists, humanists and secularists need to teach children that morality is instinctual to humans. This is a literal fact, not a metaphorical hypothesis.

This, then, leads us to the extension of the theme of geo-philia which regards our natural world as our all-inclusive life support base. Geo-philia boldly asserts the existence of a biologically based pedagogy of social praxis. Learning is an inherent human need to affiliate social changes with life processes. This premise suggests that human progress and personal fulfillment both depend on their relationship with our sustainable natural and social environment.

This need is also linked not just to prevention of excessive natural exploitation of nature, but to the influence such excessiveness may on have our cognitive, aesthetic, emotional and rational thinking processes. The present tendency to continue the over-exploitation of natural resources can be viewed as an extension of past Biblical propagation of the last twenty centuries. All biblical influence was a basic phobia or *geo-phobia,* an out-and-out hatred for our physical world. It is related deeply to religious irrationality, and the consequences are evident in the vast spectrum of biological and social life about us. There is more to it!

Dialectical materialists of the pedagogy of social praxis and genuine environmentalists should create "goal-post" structures and evaluate our present evolutionary struggle to adapt, persist, and thrive as social species and as individuals. Conversely, this geo-philia notion powerfully asserts the need for humans to search for a *coherent social environment* which would relate to, not just depend upon, our relationship with the natural world.

Secularists and humanists need to convince our friends and our children that the best of childhood is when geo-philia is supported and adopted. In turn, we should convince ourselves to enter into deeper layers of dialectical understanding of our natural and social environment that will permit life to flourish on a personal scale. Pedagogy of social praxis includes contributions to real health and ecological stability, not to destroy the forest, soils, natural landscape and wildlife in the name of corporate greed.

We socially-inclined secularists must draw our moral and social standards not from some biblical geo-phobia, but from the dialectics of nature. With humility, we must forever propagate the natural and social pedagogy of praxis by recognizing the wise governance of the natural world. We atheists must introduce a New Covenant for religious believers to believe in our natural world as the only real one we have inherited. Hatred for our natural would is not a rational substitute for "loving" the invisible place called Heaven.

We need to *pro actively propagate* the secularism of social praxis. Our social human environment needs a unified front, a true frontier for all humanity to regard *human life on earth* as the only means to transmit knowledge, science, culture, love, emotions, art, and coherent socio-economic affairs. Life around us dialectically exceeds in complexity anything else humanity is ever likely to encounter. There is a wealth of scientific and aesthetic possibilities yet to be discovered.

Within the secular pedagogy of social praxis, dialectical materialists need to fully focus on the propagation of *Matter over Mind*. Materialist [as in *behaviorist*] psychologist B.F. Skinner, at the age of 83, addressed the American Psychological Association in *literal terms* on the metaphorical concept of the mind. An overview of Dr. Skinner's focal points confirms that many of the words we use to describe the mind's functions are simply metaphors whose origins reveal they really refer to physical, not mental phenomena. Although I have dealt with this issue in other parts of the book, I think that it is worthwhile to read an expert analysis from a materialist psychologist as well. Here are excerpts from the speech:

"Extraordinary things have certainly been said about the mind. The finest achievements of the species have been attributed to it...But what it is and what it does are still far from clear...To understand what "mind" means we must first look up "perception," "idea," "feeling"...and we shall find each of them defined with the help of others. Perhaps it is of the very essence of mind that it cannot be defined. Nevertheless, we can look at how the word is used and what people seem to be saying when they use it...

The evidence is to be found in the history of the language–in the analogy of the words that refer to feelings. Etymology is, in a sense, the archaeology of thought....The words we use to refer...began as references....And only very slowly have they become the vocabulary of something called the mind...

...Take any sentence in which "the mind" is said to do something and see if the meaning is substantially changed if you substitute "person"...

There is nothing inside the...organism but the organism itself. It is the whole organism that behaves."

Dialectical materialists should hold pro-active public forums advocating:

- ❖ That there are really no transformations of matter into spirit, mind or soul as idealists mistakenly believe

- ❖ That matter has energy [matter in motion] but that energy is not a divine spirit

- ❖ That advanced biological and botanical chemistry has **no** knowledge and **no** literal terminology to describe it. In other words, *there is a visible matter and measurable energy.*

We need to persuade the layperson to be content in accepting the brain and its energy as coexistent, but **not** independent of each other. We should feel duty-bound to answer questions such as whether "mind" gives rise to brain [matter]. Yet, merely asking this question begs it, for by literally and dialectically analyzing *perception,* we will **not** speculate that there is, in reality, any two such entities to reconcile.

It is time to face up to our collective responsibility to promote the pedagogy of social praxis. The groundwork has already been laid by biological scientists, secular social thinkers, public educators and progressive political leaders. It is a humanitarian challenge. We need to fill the Gap of people's emotional needs to feel protected by some entity. We must show people that such an entity is an emotional "just in case" trump card. What we have to offer are humanist-based sentiments such as friendship, community, love and comforting support to those who need it. We have to demonstrate that religious dependency is a false "well-being," a superficial belief, for in the final analysis, our positive sense of humanity for our fellow human beings is the only conclusive truth. We must recognize that people's desire to believe does not make the belief true.

The religious repetitive propagation for believers to profess their belief in God follows a marketing technique: if you repeat something often enough, you will succeed in convincing consumers of your "product's" benefits. Most religious believers, however, will buy the "product" out of long established habit, rather than out of conviction of the product's benefits. Both may be noticeable but they are not the same thing. Or, maybe they do not really fall within the rational human feelings.

I do not want to downplay human feelings, although I consider them secondary, as a supportive rather than as a directive element. I do not have statistical evidence showing a balance between human happiness and religious beliefs. Nor do I have any evidence showing a relationship between happiness and secular idealism. Of course, I do not think that atheist or secularists are happier than religious believers.

What I have witnessed, however, is that the *burden* of religious delusions about life are misinterpreted as personal failures. You are poor or sick because God is punishing you; you can earn your subsistence by toiling hard, as God has willed. I have seen this tendency in Greek villagers, as well as in Central and South American under-developed countries. There is a permanent social melancholy in the personal lives of devoted religious believers. In the small town of Chaclacayo, Peru, I witnessed Belgian nuns offering theology classes to villagers who were depressed. The villagers had an immediate "feeling good" relief; this feeling did not last more than a few hours.

I shall end this book by arguing that the pedagogy of social praxis of atheists and secularists must be fulfilled by introducing humanist sentiments to replace any Gap that may be created by the renunciation of religious delusions. Building a secular society is, thus, a practical affair.

REFERENCE

"Knowledge is of no value unless you put it into practice."

Anton Chekhov

"Happiness is not achieved by the conscious pursuit of happiness; it is generally the by-product of other activities."

Unknown

17

YOU ARE NOT ALONE

A BRIEF WEB SITE LIST FOR PERSONS SEEKING SUPPORT IN ESCAPING FROM RELIGION!

Australia

- Atheist Foundation of Australia Inc: www.atheistfoundation.org.au

- Council of Australian Humanist Societies: http://home.vicnet.net.au/-humanist/resources/cahs.html

- Australia Skeptics : www.skeptics.com.au www.atheistfoundation.org.au

- Humanist Society of South Australia; www.users.on.net/-rnc/hsofsa.htm

Austria

- Freidenkrbund: www.freidenker-oesterreich.at

Belgium

- Centre d' Action Laique: www.ulb.ac.be

- Humanistisch-Vrijzinnige Vereniging: www.h-vv.be

- Ribz : www.ribz.be

- Vrijzinning studie: www.vsad.be

Britain

- British Humanist Association: www.humanism.org.uk
- Counsil of Ex-Muslims: www.ex-muslims.org.uk
- One Law for all Campaign against Sharia Law in Britain: www.onelawforall.org.uk
- Freedom from Religion Foundation: www.ffrf.org
- International Humanist and Ethical Union-UK: www.iheu.org
- National Secular Society: www.secularism.org.uk
- New Humanist: www.newhumanist.org.uk
- Rationalist Press Association: www.rationalist.org.uk
- South Place Ethical Society: www.ethicalsic.org.uk
- Humanist Society: www.humanist.eusa.ed.ac.uk
- UK Armed Forces Humanist Association: www.armedforceshumanists.org.uk
- Cumbia Humanist Group: www.cumbia-humanists.org.uk
- Gay and Lesbian Humanist Association: www.galha.org

Canada

- Humanist Canada: www.humanistcanada.com
- Humanist Association of Canada: http://hac.humanists.net
- Society for Secular Humanist in Calgary: http://calgaryhumanist.ca
- Central Ontario Humanist: www.cohumanists.ca
- Humanist Association of Manitoba: http://nb.humanists.ca

- Humanist Association of Toronto: www.humanist.toronto.on.ca
- Victoria Secular Humanist Association: www.vsha.ca

Denmark

- Humanistisk Debat: www.humanistiskdebat.dk
- Humanistisk: www.humanistisksamfund.dk

Europe

- European Humanist Federation: www.humanistfederation.eu
- European Humanist Professionals: www.humanistprofessionals.org

Finland

- Vapaa-ajattelijain Liitto ry: www.vapaa-ajattelijat.fi

France

- Cercle gaston-Cremieux: www.cercle-gaston-cremieux.org
- Mouvement Europe at Laicite: www.europe-et-laicite.org
- Union des families laiques: www.ufal.org
- Union Rationaliste: www.union-rationaliste.org

Germany

- Counsil of Ex-Muslimes: www.ex-muslime.de
- International League of Non-Religious and Atheists: www.ibka.org

Greece

- Delphi Society: www.delphisociety.org

Hong Kong
- Humanize Hong Kong: www.tonyhen@org.hk

India
- Atheist Centre: www.atheistcentre.in
- Rationalist International: www.rationalistinternational.net

Italy
- Comitato Torinese Per La Laicita Della Scuola: www.arpnet.it/laisc/
- Unione degli Aleie degli a gnostici Razionalsti: www.uaar.it/

Iran
- Iranian Secular Society: www.iransecularsociety.com
- IslamicFaithFreedom.org: www.faithfreedom.org/index.htm
- Institute for the Secularization of Islamic Society: www.secularislam.org/default.htm
- Apostates of Islam: www.apostatesofislam.com/index.htm

Iceland
- Siomennt: http://sidmennt.is

Ireland
- Atheist Ireland: www.atheist.ie

New Zealand
- New Zealand Skeptics: http://skeptics.org.nz
- Humanist Society of New Zealand: www.humanist.org.nz

Netherlands

- HVO: www.hvo.nl/hvo
- HSHB: www.hshb.nl
- Humanistisch Verbond: www.humanistischverbond.nl

Norway

- Human-Etisk Forbund: www.human.no

Northern Ireland

- Belfast Humanist Group: www.belfast.humanists.net

Poland

- Polish Humanist Association: http://humanizm.free.ngo.p

Romania

- Asociata Umanista Romana: www.secularhumanism.ro

Scandinavia

- Scandinavian Counsils of Ex-Muslims: www.exmuslim.net

Scotland

- Humanist Society of Scotland: www.absoluteastronomy.com
- www.humanism-scotland.org.uk

Slovakia

- Prometheus Society of Slovakia: http://slovakia.humanists.net

Spain

- Europa Laica: www.europalaica.com

Sweden

- Humanisterna: www.humanistena.org
- Trinidad and Tabago Humanist Association: http://humanist.org.tt

Uganda

- Humanist Schools Trust: www.ugandahumanistsschoolstrust.org

USA

- International Humanist and Ethical Union: www.iheu.org
- American Alliance International: www.atheistalliance.org
- American Atheist: www.atheists.org
- American Humanist Association: www.americanhumanist.org
- Atheist Alliance International: www.atheistalliance.org
- African American for Humanism:
  www.centerforinquiry.net
  www.secularhumanism.org
  www.campusfreethought.org
- The Corliss Lamond Chapter of the American Humanist Association: www.corliss-lamont.org
- Freedom From Religion Foundation; www.ffrf.org
- Freethought Society of Greater Philadelphia: www.fsgp.org
- Internet Infidels: www.infidels.org
- Great Lakes Humanist Society: www.glhumanist.org
- New Humanist: www.newhumanist.us

- Secular Coalition for America: www.secular.org
- Secular Student Alliance: www.secularstudents.org
- Society for Humanist Judaism: www.shj.org

18

BIBLIOGRAPHY

"There are two motives for reading a book, one, that you enjoy it; the other, that you can boast about it."

Bertrand Russell

"A book is not only a friend, it makes friends for you. When you have possessed a book with mind/spirit, you are enriched. But when you pass it on you are enriched threefold."

Henry Miller

Alexander, R.D. and Tinkle, D.W. eds *Natural Selection and Social behaviour* (1981), New York

Dawkins, Richard, *The God Delusion* (2006) New York: Houghton Miffin

Dawkins, Richard, *The Selfish Gene* (1976) Oxford: Oxford University Press

Dawkins, Richard, *The Blind Watchmaker* (1986) Harlow: Longman.

Dennett, D. *Dawkin's Dangerous Idea* (1995) New York: Simon & Schuster

Godotti, Moacir, *Pedagogy of Praxis* (1996) New York: State University of New York Press, Albany

Guest, D. *Dialectical Materialism* (1939) Lawrence and Wishart, UK

Huxtley, T.H. *Lectures and Essays* (1931) London: Watts

Kishore Kumar, Theckedath, *Dialectics, Relativity and Quantum* (1998) National Book Agency Private. UK

Lefebvre, H. *Dialectical Materialism* (2009) University of Minnesota Press

Pinker, S. *How the Mind Works* (1997) London: Allen Lane.

Russel, B. *Why I Am Not Christian* (1957) London: Routledge.

Russel, B. *Religion and Science* (1997) Oxford: Oxford University Press.

Shermer, M. *Why People Believe Weird Things: Pseudoscience, Superstition and Other Confusions of Our Time* (1997) New York: W. H. Freeman

Strachey, J. *Literature and Dialectical Materialism* (1934) Covici: Friede Publishers, UK

Warraq Ibn, *What The Koran Really Says* (2002) New York, Amherst, Prometheus Books

Warraq Ibn, *Leaving Islam: Apostates Speak Out* (2003) New York, Amherst, Prometheus Books

Warraq Ibn, *Defending the West: A Critique of Edward Said's Orientalism* (2007) Prometheus Books

ZA, Jordan, *The Evolution of Dialectical Materialism: A Philosophical and Sociological Analysis* (1967) Macmillan: London UK

19

INDEX

"There's probably NO GOD, now stop worrying and enjoy your life."

Atheist Bus Campaign

"Wisdom lies neither in fixity nor in change, but in the dialectics between the two."

Octavio Paz

Abortion 56
Abraham 66, 86, 106, 124
Absolute 124
Adolf Hitler 47, 140
Advertising 2, 195
Afghanistan 26, 58, 77, 94, 102, 137
Allah 18, 27, 109
Astrology 46
Astronomers 46
Atheism 33, 71, 96, 97, 145
Beliefs 2, 15, 17, 29, 35, 53, 57, 101, 107, 124
  false 15
  Idealist 16, 202
  Secular-idealist 16, 202
  Bible 56, 67, 81, 225
  New Testament 65, 75, 81, 87, 98, 123, 147, 150, 225
  Old Testament 65, 81, 87, 88, 123, 147, 189, 225
  Environment 112, 131, 214
Brain 2, 11, 242
  Parts 245
Bridge-link 2, 33, 221, 223, 232, 236

Catholic Church 79
  Inquisition 83
Children 102, 121, 153
  Education 102
  Imaginary friends 39, 41-42, 62

Christianity 40, 64, 79, 97, 227
  Televangelists 103
Crusades 22
Darwin, Charles 9
Delusions 2, 16, 54, 101, 124
Destructive-idealism 39, 41-42, 47, 62, 71, 125, 255
Dialectical 27, 207
  Materialism 8
  System of thought 60
Dreams 131
Dogma 22

Evolution 218, 319

Faith 207, 211

Gravitational primacy of ideas 443

Hell 61
Hinduism 48
Homosexuality 94
  Humanism 12, 20, 97, 145

Idealist system of thought 4, 9, 14, 131, 232
Ideals 13
Ignorance 26, 28, 96, 130, 222, 256
Illusions 22
Imaginary friend 43
Imitation 4

Intelligence 24, 41
Iran 80, 94, 113, 152
Iraq 26, 58, 137, 163
Islam 32, 42, 64, 73, 227
   Slavery 152
   Status of women 152
Israel 222
Jesus 49, 72, 79, 104, 121
Jews 47, 73, 95, 97, 132, 147
   Anti-Semitism 47, 139
Judaism 64, 227

Language 36, 218, 241
   Literal 61, 216-241
   Metaphorical 33, 218-241
Lennon, John 376
Love 373-398
Love of suffering 127-146
Luther, Martin 48
   "Jews and their lies" 48, 139
   Kristal Night 49, 140

Magic, 41, 125, 172
   Trickery 172, 181
Matter Over Mind 53, 235, 258, 327, 497
Matter in motion 27, 53, 61
Memes 5, 44, 115
Mind 5, 26, 61, 242
   God's 17, 54
   Metaphorical 30, 31, 208, 214, 232, 240
Mental health 12, 101, 120
Mimesis 5

Mind over matter 19, 28, 40, 43, 46, 49, 56, 197, 203, 206, 214, 239, 249
Miracles 21, 84, 104, 189
Monotheism 18, 155
Morality 47, 66, 148
   religious 66
Moses 106
Muhammad 81, 88, 106

Nature 53
Naïve-idealism 39, 41-42, 62, 255
Natural selection 255

Paedophilia 49, 80, 107, 115, 164, 170
Pantheism 2
Patriotism 42, 128
Pedagogy of praxis 73, 101, 222, 225
Polytheism 155, 173, 182, 294
Psychology 15, 25, 101
Purgatory 83

Qur'an: 66, 67, 88
   Hadith 88, 102, 152
   Suras 65, 88, 152
   Verses 88, 95, 112, 153

Race 47, 223
Reality 5, 52
Religiosity 17
Rituals 34, 105, 189, 226, 223

Satan 61, 83
Saudi Arabia 94, 113
Scientific Materialism 11, 26, 27, 33
Secularism 6, 18
Secular-idealism 6, 35, 40, 70, 214
Sharia Law 94
Slavery 75, 147-171
Skinner, B.F. 413
Socialism 77
Spiritualism 6, 12, 41, 61
Suffering 127-146

Taboos 30
   Ritual 30
Thomas, Jefferson 400
Twain, Mark 254

Unity of opposites 60, 350-353

Virtual reality 31, 41, 50, 57

Warraq, Ibn 157
Women 56, 74, 77, 79
Witches 25, 29, 41, 81, 130

www.ingramcontent.com/pod-product-compliance
Lightning Source LLC
Chambersburg PA
CBHW030238170426
43202CB00007B/37